The Exceptionalist State and the State of Exception

RETHINKING THEORY

Stephen G. Nichols and Victor E. Taylor, *Series Editors*

The Exceptionalist State and the State of Exception

Herman Melville's *Billy Budd, Sailor*

WILLIAM V. SPANOS

The Johns Hopkins University Press

Baltimore

© 2011 The Johns Hopkins University Press
All rights reserved. Published 2011
Printed in the United States of America on acid-free paper
9 8 7 6 5 4 3 2 1

The Johns Hopkins University Press
2715 North Charles Street
Baltimore, Maryland 21218-4363
www.press.jhu.edu

Library of Congress Cataloging-in-Publication Data
Spanos, William V.
    The exceptionalist state and the state of exception : Herman Melville's Billy Budd, sailor /
William V. Spanos.
        p. cm.
    Includes bibliographical references and index.
    ISBN-13: 978-0-8018-9849-5 (hardcover : alk. paper)
    ISBN-10: 0-8018-9849-8 (hardcover : alk. paper)
    1. Melville, Herman, 1819–1891. Billy Budd. 2. Melville, Herman, 1819–1891 —
Political and social views. 3. Melville, Herman, 1819–1891 — Knowledge — History.
4. Melville, Herman, 1819–1891 — Knowledge — United States. 5. Imperialism in literature.
6. National characteristics, American, in literature. 7. Exceptionalism — United States.
8. Literature and history — United States — History — 19th century. I. Title.
PS2384.B7S55 2011
813'.3 — dc22   2010019682

A catalog record for this book is available from the British Library.

*Special discounts are available for bulk purchases of this book. For more information,
please contact Special Sales at 410-516-6936 or specialsales@press.jhu.edu.*

The Johns Hopkins University Press uses environmentally friendly book materials,
including recycled text paper that is composed of at least 30 percent post-consumer waste,
whenever possible. All of our book papers are acid-free, and our jackets and covers are
printed on paper with recycled content.

To my beloved Assimina Karavanta
this testament of fidelity
from our crippled
zone

Yet in the light of recent events it is possible to say that even slaves still belonged to some sort of human community; their labor was needed, used, and exploited, and this kept them within the pale of humanity. To be a slave was after all to have a distinctive character, a place in society — more than the abstract nakedness of being human and nothing but human. Not the loss of specific rights, then, but the loss of a community willing and able to guarantee any rights whatsoever, has been the calamity which has befallen ever-increasing numbers of people. Man, it turns out, can lose all so-called Rights of Man without losing his essential quality as man, his human dignity. Only the loss of a polity itself expels him from humanity.

— HANNAH ARENDT, *The Origins of Totalitarianism*

[T]he reign of ethics is one symptom of a universe ruled by a distinctive [*singulière*] combination of resignation in the face of necessity together with a purely negative, if not destructive, will. It is this combination that should be designated as nihilism. — ALAIN BADIOU, *Ethics*

The fact that must constitute the point of departure for any discourse on ethics is that there is no essence, no historical or spiritual vocation, no biological destiny that humans must enact or realize. This is the only reason why something like an ethics can exist, because it is clear that if humans were or had to be this or that substance, this or that destiny, no ethical experience would be possible — there would be only tasks to be done. — GIORGIO AGAMBEN, *The Coming Community*

CONTENTS

ACKNOWLEDGMENTS

This is the third and last volume in a trilogy whose essential aim is to retrieve Herman Melville's subversion of the myth of American exceptionalism, which all too much criticism has censored in the name of or by accommodation to that myth. The book had its immediate origins a few years ago, when I received reports from the readers of my earlier book *Herman Melville and the American Calling: The Fiction After* Moby-Dick, *1851–1857*. Both reports were quite positive, but one of the unknown readers wondered why I had not included a discussion of *Billy Budd*. I had, in fact, thought of doing so, but I finally decided against it because it would have deflected attention from the focus of that book: those works of Melville's post–*Moby-Dick* period whose heretical nature led his contemporary critics to "freeze him into silence." In my revisions, however, I did add a brief conclusion invoking the Melville of *Billy Budd* as a specter — a revenant — returned from the oblivion to which he had been relegated to haunt the exceptionalist ethos of the custodians of American national memory who had buried him. Shortly before my book came out — it was at a *boundary 2* editorial meeting at the University of Pittsburgh — I mentioned the favorable readers' reports, and the qualification about *Billy Budd* expressed in one of them, to Jonathan Arac, who told me that he had in fact written it himself. He added that he had made the observation because there was something about *Billy Budd* that seemed to him to run counter to the gist of my reading of Melville's earlier work. This qualification of Jonathan's praise for my manuscript inspired me to undertake a reading of this last work of Melville's life after the publication of *Herman Melville and the American Calling*. I am, therefore, grateful to Jonathan Arac, not only for instigating my project but also for providing me with the inaugural challenge. I hope my reading will convince him of the essential continuity of the early Melville of *Moby-Dick*, *Pierre*, *Israel Potter*, "Bartleby," "Benito Cereno," and *The Confidence-Man* with the late Melville of *Billy Budd*, though I shall be pleased if it persuades him that my interpretation of this powerful but, in so many uncanny ways, bewildering and finally ineffable book is a viable one.

I also wish to thank my friend and *boundary* 2 editorial colleague Donald Pease not only for his pioneering work as a New Americanist but also for his general sympathy for my controversial reading of *Billy Budd*. His inaugural deterritorializing and reenvisioning of the Americanist field imaginary, which estranged the terrain of American literature, enabled me to see things in that hitherto territorialized landscape, especially in Melville's writing, that were rich and strange — and creatively dislocating. And his positive response to my first tentative articulation of my unconventional argument about *Billy Budd* at a *boundary* 2 conference he hosted at Dartmouth College in the summer of 2008 encouraged me to pursue the project beyond the essay I originally intended it to be into the book it has become.

In the process of writing this book, I have incurred deep and abiding debts to a number of people who read or listened to and commented on parts of it. Among these are my *boundary* 2 colleagues Donald Pease and Daniel O'Hara; my former student Assimina Karavanta, now of the National and Kapodistrian University of Athens in Greece; my colleagues David Bartine and Susan Strehle; and, not least, my son Adam Spanos, a graduate student in the Anthropology Department at Columbia University, all of whom, wittingly or not, contributed significantly to my effort to bring the meaning of *Billy Budd* to its hauntingly absent presence by way of the agonic dialogues they engaged me in. I also want to express my gratitude to a number of my former students who have, in one way or another, become abiding presences in my life — Susan Winnett, Aliki Bakopoulou Halls, Paul Bové, Joseph Buttigieg, Rajiopalan Radhakrishnan, Giovanna Cove, Jan McVicker, David Randall, Michael Clark, Robert Marzec, and Asye Temiz. More immediately I want to thank the graduate students who participated in my Fall 2008 and Spring 2009 courses on Herman Melville, Thomas Pynchon, and Toni Morrison and modern and postmodern American poetry, respectively, while I was immersed in the process of writing this book. Above all, Robert Wilson, Uberaj Katawal, Guy Risko, Sarah Bull, José Rodrigues, and Ji Hye Ahn were insightful commentators on my key words — "grace" (*charis*), "occasion," "profane," "event," "bare life," "counterpoint," "exception," "vocation," "measure," and so on.

Not least, I want, as always, to express my gratitude to Paul A. Bové, this time, however, for his exemplary — and moving, if sometimes baffling — book *Poetry and Torture*, which I was reading as I was writing about Melville's anticipation, by way of his interrogation of Captain Vere's "measured forms," of the George W. Bush administration's obscene resort to torture in the name of the American exceptionalist "errand" in the global "wilderness." Some of the affiliations in the network of affiliations I develop in this book will, no doubt, raise Paul's hackles, but I trust that he will perceive below the surface of these disagreements the fundamental and abiding solidarity between his work and mine.

Finally, I take great pleasure in thanking the editors and staff of the Johns Hopkins University Press, not least Matt McAdam and the series editor Steve Nichols, for their support of my project and the generosity, goodwill, care, and efficiency with which they carried it through to its completion.

ABBREVIATIONS

AE	William V. Spanos, *American Exceptionalism in the Age of Globalization: The Specter of Vietnam* (Albany: State University of New York Press, 2008)
AR	F. O. Matthiessen, "*Billy Budd*, Foretopman," in id., *American Renaissance: Art and Expression in the Age of Emerson and Whitman* (New York: Oxford University Press, 1941)
BB	Herman Melville, *Billy Budd, Sailor (An Inside Narrative)*, ed. Harrison Hayford and Merton M. Sealts Jr. (Chicago: University of Chicago Press, 1962)
CE	*Critical Essays on Melville's* Billy Budd, Sailor, ed. Robert Milder (Boston: G. K. Hall, 1989)
C-M	Herman Melville, *The Confidence-Man: His Masquerade*, ed. Harrison Hayford, Hershel Parker, and G. Thomas Tanselle (Evanston, IL: Northwestern University Press; Chicago: Newberry Library, 1984)
E	Alain Badiou, *L'éthique: Essai sur la conscience du mal* (Paris: Hatier, 1993), trans. Peter Hallward as *Ethics: An Essay on the Understanding of Evil* (London: Verso, 2001)
EA	William V. Spanos, *The Errant Art of* Moby-Dick: *The Canon, the Cold War, and the Struggle for American Studies* (Durham, NC: Duke University Press, 1995)
EM	Warner Berthoff, *The Example of Melville* (Princeton, NJ: Princeton University Press, 1962)
HM	Newton Arvin, *Herman Melville* (New York: William Sloane Associates, 1950)
HMAC	William V. Spanos, *Herman Melville and the American Calling: The Fiction after* Moby-Dick, *1851–1857* (Albany: State University of New York Press, 2008)

HMS   John Middleton Murry, "Herman Melville's Silence," *Times Literary Supplement*, no. 1173 (July 1924), reprinted in CE

HS   Giorgio Agamben, *Homo Sacer: Sovereign Power and Bare Life*, trans. Daniel Heller-Roazen (Stanford, CA: Stanford University Press, 1998)

IA   Alan Trachtenberg, *The Incorporation of America: Culture and Society in the Gilded Age* (New York: Hill & Wang, 1982)

ISP   Alfred Thayer Mahan, *The Influence of Sea Power upon History, 1660–1783* (Boston: Little, Brown, 1890; reprint, Gloucester, U.K.: Dodo Press, 2008)

M-D   Herman Melville, *Moby-Dick or The Whale*, ed. Harrison Hayford, Hershel Parker, and G. Thomas Tanselle (Evanston, IL: Northwestern University Press; Chicago: Newberry Library, 1988)

MF   Barbara Johnson, "Melville's Fist: The Execution of *Billy Budd*," in id., *The Critical Difference: Essays in the Contemporary Rhetoric of Reading* (Baltimore: Johns Hopkins University Press, 1980)

RBB   Hershel Parker, *Reading* Billy Budd (Evanston, IL: Northwestern University Press, 1990)

SE   Giorgio Agamben, *State of Exception*, trans. Kevin Attell (Chicago: University of Chicago Press, 2005)

TA   E. L. Grant Watson, "Melville's Testament of Acceptance," *New England Quarterly* 6 (1933): 319–327, reprinted in CE

WAW   Samuel P. Huntington, *Who Are We? Challenges to America's National Identity* (New York: Simon & Schuster, 2004)

WI   Raymond Weaver, "Introduction," in *The Shorter Novels of Herman Melville* (New York: Liveright, 1928, xlx–li), reprinted in CE

YI   Donald Yannella, "Introduction," in *New Essays on* Billy Budd, ed. id. (Cambridge: Cambridge University Press, 2002)

The Exceptionalist State and the State of Exception

CHAPTER ONE

Late Melville and His Historical Occasion
Prolegomenon to a Rereading of *Billy Budd, Sailor*

In all four [Giuseppe di Lampedusa and Luchino Visconti, on the one hand, and Richard Strauss and Theodor Adorno, on the other] . . . one has a sense not just of a certain profligacy, a desire to go the whole way toward extravagance, and an arrogant negation of what is acceptable or easy but also of a very risky yet adversarial pact with authoritarian systems, not least of which is the authority of the imperious author, whose innermost characteristic seems to be to elude system entirely. Each of the figures I have discussed here makes of lateness or untimeliness, and a vulnerable maturity, a platform for alternative and unregimented modes of subjectivity, at the same time that each — like the late Beethoven — has a lifetime of technical effort and preparation. [They] play off the great totalizing codes of twentieth-century Western culture and cultural diffusion. . . . The one thing that is difficult to find in their work is embarrassment, even though they are egregiously self-conscious and supreme technicians. It is as if having achieved age, they want none of its supposed serenity or maturity, or any of its amiability or official ingratiation. Yet in none of them is mortality denied or evaded, but keeps coming back as the theme of death which undermines, and strangely elevates their uses of language and the aesthetic.

— EDWARD W. SAID, *On Late Style:*
Music and Literature Against the Grain

The intellectual's role is to present alternative narratives and other perspectives on history than those provided by combatants in behalf of official memory and national identity and mission.

— EDWARD SAID, *Humanism and Democratic Criticism*

The "Worldliness" of *Billy Budd*

As I have observed in my books *The Errant Art of* Moby-Dick (1996) and *Herman Melville and the American Calling* (2008), Melville, more than any other American writer, constellated the local (America) into the global context, a fictional strategy epitomized by rendering the site of the immediate event into a ship of state, literally in *Moby-Dick*, "Benito Cereno," and *The Confidence-Man*, and symbolically in "Bartleby, the Scrivener." And this constellation of the micrological and the macrological worlds enabled him to anticipate America's future — the weaknesses, if not exactly the self-destruction of its exceptionalist strengths — in a way uncannily proleptic of poststructuralist theory. *Moby-Dick*, for example, discloses the vulnerability of the forwarding American war machine in the Vietnam War; *Pierre* and *Israel Potter*, the amnesia incumbent on the perennial American obsession to monumentalize its history; "Bartleby, the Scrivener," the subjection of the subject inhering in the celebration of the democratic capitalist individual; "Benito Cereno," the life-destroying blindness of the American exceptionalist "vision"; and *The Confidence-Man*, the lunatic violence of American optimism.[1] Though written thirty or so years after his last published prose fiction, *Billy Budd*, contrary to the great majority of opinion about it, is no exception to this unruly rule of Melville's post–*Moby-Dick* writing. In fact, in this late novella, I argue, Melville brings this proleptic fictional strategy to its culmination. I stress this point because, despite the obviousness of the indissoluble relationship between the global historical "background" and the immediate event, the various gazes of the immense, mostly American, archive of scholarship, commentary, and criticism on Melville's elusive novella have, following the misleading interpretive imperatives incumbent on his thirty-year "silence," discounted it.[2] To be more specific, in reading Melville's long silence as symptomatic of his renunciation, in one form or another, of the (political) world, this archive has either willfully disregarded the resonant and patently inextricable relationship between the post–French Revolutionary war being fought by England and France over imperial command of the global seaways and the alleged mutiny on board the fictional British warship HMS *Bellipotent*, or, what is even more telling, has labored to render the macrological dimension marginal, mere background, an afterthought as it were, to the events on board the *Bellipotent* culminating in the hanging of an ordinary seaman, Billy Budd.[3]

As all too often in the history of American Melville criticism, Melville's radically historical/secular emphasis, in other words, has, in one way or another, been universalized — reduced to allegory — and his cultural and sociopolitical subversions have been accommodated to the very discourse he is subverting. In what follows, I intend, against the grain of this neutralizing marginalization or erasure, to put the macrological context (which, to anticipate, includes the America of Melville's contemporary occasion) back into play with the micrological. Such a reconstellation of this marginalized history in *Billy Budd* to the abyssal center of the narrative will instigate an estrangement of the world of the *Bellipotent* domesticated not only by traditional Americanists but also, as I shall show, by avant garde (deconstructionist) critics. In a way reminiscent of "Benito Cereno," it will, in Louis Althusser's Marxian phrase, instigate a "change of terrain"[4] that will *force* us to see what the "uniformed gaze" of most Old Americanist criticism is, willfully or not, blind to: a ship of state that has been transformed into a permanent state of exception, that is, a polity saturated by and inextricably bound to a historical global world in crisis, in which the laws pertaining to the well-being of political man (human rights, etc.) have been abrogated in the name of preserving them. In so doing, furthermore, this reconstellation will enable us also to perceive Melville's *Billy Budd* as uncannily proleptic of the national security state the United States has increasingly become under the aegis of the myth of American exceptionalism, especially during the George W. Bush administration, and, not least, of the state-of-exception theory that has emerged to explain this ominous contemporary global condition.

Billy Budd: A Cautionary Tale about America in Late Melville

Before undertaking a reintegration and recentralization of this disintegrated and marginalized history (and its relation to the America of Melville's occasion), however, it will be necessary to address the question likely to be posed by the Americanists who have taken their bearings on *Billy Budd* from the "definitive edition" established by Harrison Hayford and

Merton Sealts in 1962:[5] why the American writer Herman Melville set his meditation on the meaning of the state of exception as it pertains to America aboard a British man-of-war. After all, the state of exception, as Giorgio Agamben has made clear, becomes a matter of crucial concern only within the context of the rule of constitutional or parliamentary law in democratic societies, since absolutist regimes are by definition permanently governed by arbitrary fiat.[6] My answer to this admittedly difficult but, as far as I can tell, *hitherto strangely unasked* question, will take its point of departure from Melville's fiction from *Moby-Dick* to *The Confidence-Man* (1850–57): the heretical fiction, that, as I have argued elsewhere, compelled the American critics of his generation to "freeze him into silence,"[7] and later, when the irresistible force of his work reasserted itself (in England), to accommodate his subversions to the hegemonic truths of exceptionalist America.[8] I am referring to his deeply backgrounded ironic insight into the arrogant, optimistic, and, to use one of his favorite words to characterize the forwarding linearity of its practical imperatives, unerring — and eventually self-destructive — exceptionalist ethos of the American national identity, and, therefore, to his acutely proleptic awareness that criticism of such a monogrammatic America must be undertaken indirectly or, more specifically, as we shall see, in the genealogical mode (as Nietzsche and Foucault would later understand it). To be more precise, Melville, I contend, invokes the terrible events on board the *Bellipotent*, the British ship of state — the Father/Old World state from which the young America freed itself and against which it defined its New World exceptionalism — not to verify America's superior uniqueness for his American public, but, on the contrary, to suggest the ultimate continuity between the youthful "democratic" American state and the degenerate, tyrannical — counterrevolutionary and imperial — British state.

The apparent "inside narrative" of Melville's novella is about the arbitrary hanging of an innocent ordinary seaman, Billy Budd, whom the officers of the *Bellipotent*, authorized by the declared state of emergency, have impressed into the British Navy from a merchantmen pointedly named by its owner the *Rights-of-Man* after the pamphlet written as a "rejoinder" to the arch-conservative Edmund Burke's *Reflections on the Revolution in France* by the English radical Thomas Paine in 1791.[9] Celebrated in the United States, and often read as a defense of the French Revolution, this document affirmed the equality of all humanity against the then prevailing idea that human rights originated in a charter, an origin, in other words, that, in assuming the exceptional sovereign authority of the king to establish a charter (the law) of rights, also assumed his exceptionalist authority to rescind it, that is, the permanence of the state of exception. "It is a perversion of terms to say that a charter gives rights," Paine wrote. "It operates by a contrary effect — that of taking rights away. Rights are inherently in all the inhabitants; but charters, by annulling those rights in the majority, leave the right, by exclusion, in the hands of a few. . . . Those whose rights are guaranteed, by not being taken away, exercise no other rights than as members of the community they are entitled to without a charter; and, therefore, all charters have no other than an indirect negative operation. They do not give rights to A, but they make a difference in favour of A by taking away the right of B, and consequently are instruments of injustice."[10]

And Billy's arbitrary execution is ordained by the captain, Edward Fairfax Vere, the commanding officer of the man-of-war, which in telling contrast with the Billy's civilian ship, is named HMS *Bellipotent* (a Latin compound, "warpower," that identifies the ship [of state] with the state of exception), despite his intuitive certainty that the accusation of inciting mutiny against the sailor made by the master-at-arms, John Claggart, is false. It is no accident, therefore, that this apparent "inside narrative" is introduced, that is, encompassed, by, a past- and future-oriented reference to the highly charged, indeed, epochal, historical situation — global in scope and depth — that impacts in an insistently fundamental way on a particular British man-of-war, the *Bellipotent*.

In the earlier published versions of *Billy Budd*, those of Raymond Weaver (1924), and F. Barron Freeman (1948, 1953), this resonant global historical reference — the epitome of an apparent "outside narrative" — is printed as the "Preface" of Melville's novella, apparently on the basis of a note in pencil on a leaf of his unfinished manuscript, which, the early editors surmised, was the title of the story:

Billy Budd
Foretopman
What befell him
in the year of the
Great Mutiny
&c

According to Harrison Hayford and Merton Sealts, the editors of the "definitive" text (and to Hershel Parker, who, three decades later, in his book *Reading* Billy Budd, came to their "defense" in the context of the emergence of the New Historicism and other anti-biographical heresies), however, this evidence for justifying the placement of the historical reference at the beginning of the novella is erroneous, since the handwriting, they claim, is not Melville's but that of his wife, Elizabeth (see BB, pp. 279–280). They argue that Melville had, in fact, discarded it from a much later chapter of the novella at a late stage of composition, and that, to invoke an earlier defining moment in Melville's fiction commenting ironically on the question of a text's authenticity, the "Preface" is thus "apocryphal":[11]

> The mislabeled "Preface" that opens every published text of *Billy Budd* before the present edition is a conspicuous example of such change [in violation of Melville's intention], and an important one. A number of recent critical essays are grounded squarely on the assumption that in this "Preface" Melville intended to establish a basic tone and point of reference for the entire novel; as we have shown, however, *Billy Budd* under its author's hand never began with a preface, and the passage so labeled is actually a discarded fragment of what is now Ch. 19. A reader who in good faith interprets the novel in terms of the "Preface" will scarcely be honoring Melville's intention, nor will he be in a position to write definitive criticism.[12]

On the basis of the resonant symbolic prominence of the *Rights of Man* (both the ship and the idea) in the text at large — when, for example, in chapter 1, Billy has been forcibly transferred to the *Bellipotent*, he bids his former comrades a "genial goodbye. Then, making a salutation as to the ship herself, 'And good-bye to you too, old *Rights-of-Man*' " (BB, p. 49) — and a certain laboring of the editors' "genetic reading" of Melville's unfinished manuscript, I am not convinced of their implicit conclusion: that Melville deleted the passage forming the conjectured "Preface" to minimize the historical context and thus definitively to foreclose a political reading of the novella. Melville, after all, *wrote* that powerfully political, history-orienting passage. And the rest of the text, as I shall show in chapter 3, is saturated by both direct references to the fraught history of which it speaks (the historical matter of chapter 3, for example, more or less repeats that of the earlier "Preface") and indirect (dramatic) references (in the drumhead court scene, for example). Given this ubiquitous presence, then, to refer to the historical matter of the "Preface" categorically as having been discarded takes on the aura of an anxiously willful burial of a disconcerting — I am tempted to say spectral — "reality" that threatens a certain preestablished reading of the story. Despite their obviously authentic effort at objectivity, Hayford and Sealts's argument, however scholarly its foundation, suggests that their careful "genetic reading" of Melville's unfinished manuscript, that is, their representation of its interpretive frame of reference, is symptomatically ideological: no less "political" than those they are attempting to delegitimize. To put it broadly, this interpretive perspective or, as I prefer, following Althusser, this problematic,[13] seems in the end, like that of the official historians that "abridged" the actualities of the "Great Mutiny," to be intended to confirm their (and the post–Cold War academic establishment's) image of Melville as *the* canonical American writer and proleptically to defend it against those emergent politically or, rather, worldly Left-oriented critics of America's global Cold War interventions in the Third World. I mean by this last those critics who, following the critical genealogical directives of Melville's fiction of the period between *Moby-Dick* and *The Confidence-Man*, would read the late work *Billy Budd* — its "errancy" — as highly critical, if not subversive, of the American national identity by way of ironically disclosing the reactionary violence latent in the forwarding "Ahabian" logic of its exceptionalist ethos. In short, Hayford and Sealts's "Editors' Introduction" and the detailed "Notes & Commentary" summarizing their "genetic reading" of Melville's manuscript convey the impression, at least to one conversant with contemporary poststructuralist theories of "discourse," that their real purpose is to inter by indirection the recalcitrant specter of Melville's eccentric subversive imagination, the specter that has haunted the triumphalist discourse of the custodians of the American exceptionalist cultural memory from the time of the publication of *Moby-Dick* through the so-called Melville revival in the 1920s and the Cold War era to the present post–9/11 occasion, in which the state of exception tacitly reigns.

This symptomatic damage control becomes manifest in the conclusion of Hayford and Sealts's "Editors' Introduction," when, identifying themselves with Melville against "the critical experts" and assuming that he and the narrator are the same, these meticulous academic scholars assert that the drive behind the various stages of Melville's composition of *Billy*

Budd was insistently away from any form of political positionality toward "dramatization" (BB, p. 38),[14] that is, to the achievement of deliberate "ambiguity":

> The disagreements and prolonged contention among what Melville might have called "the critical experts" are but the proper issue of his requiring every reader to "determine for himself." But the rhetorical question "Who in the rainbow can draw the line . . . ?" should be a warning to critics who find the lines of demarcation in the story easy to determine and who suppose Melville's own attitude was altogether clear cut. To Melville's mind, after all, the question was not simply the rightness or wrongness, sanity or insanity, of the captain's action, but also the very existence of a problematic world in which such a story as he had been so long developing and brooding upon was (in his guarded phrase) "not unwarranted." His story was an epitome, in art, of such a world. (BB, pp. 38–39)

Reverting to the unfinished status of the manuscript, the editors go on to invoke the narrator's terminal comment about authorship in *Billy Budd*: "Truth uncompromisingly told will always have its ragged edges; hence the conclusion of such a narration is apt to be less finished than an architectural finial" (BB, p. 128), an interpretive gesture they reinforce by quoting (BB, p. 39) the famous passage from *Moby-Dick* where Ishmael observes "This whole book is but a draught — nay, but the draught of a draught" (M-D, p. 145). Despite this apparent qualification of the dramatic form (I say "apparent" because their implied interpretation of this passage as well as the similar one they quote from *Moby-Dick* is misleading)[15] and their implicit resistance to the New Critics' dogma of the autotelic text, the development of the authorial stance they attribute to the stages of Melville's revisions is remarkably reminiscent of (the New Critics' reading of) Stephen Dedalus's history of the development of art in *A Portrait of the Artist as a Young Man*:

> The personality of the artist, at first a cry or a cadence or a mood and then a fluid [lyric] and lambent narrative [epic], finally refines itself out of existence, impersonalizes itself so to speak. *The esthetic image in the dramatic form is life purified in and reprojected from the human imagination.* The mystery of esthetic like that of material creation is accom-

plished, the artist, like the God of the creation, remains within or behind or beyond or above his handiwork, invisible, refined out of existence, indifferent, paring his fingernails.[16]

Though they acknowledge its unfinished status, that is, the editors of the "definitive" text of *Billy Budd* come perilously close to identifying its "dramatic" art with the kind of "inclusive" and "stable" (i.e., "autonomous") art, that, unlike the "unstable" didactic art organized by "exclusion," according to I. A. Richards and the American New Critics, was invulnerable to irony, which is to say, to criticism:

> The structures of these two kinds of experiences are different, and the difference is not one of subject but of the relations *inter se* of the several impulses active in the experience. A poem of the first group is built out of sets of impulses which run parallel, which have the same direction. In a poem of the second group the most obvious feature is the extraordinarily [*sic*] heterogeneity of the distinguishable impulses. But they are more than heterogeneous, they are opposed. They are such that in ordinary, non-poetic, non-imaginative experience, one or the other set would be suppressed to give as it might appear freer development to the others.
>
> The difference comes out clearly if we consider how comparatively unstable poems of the first kind are. They will not bear an ironic contemplation. . . . Irony in this sense consists in the bringing in of the opposite, the complementary impulses; that is why poetry which is exposed to it is not of the highest order, and why irony itself is so constantly a characteristic of poetry which is.[17]

Despite Hershel Parker's assertion to the contrary in 1990, the "authoritative" conclusion about the text of *Billy Budd* that the editors draw from their "genetic" examination of Melville manuscript has (as we shall see) contributed significantly to the tendency of later criticism, both sympathetic with and resistant to these editors' conclusion, to marginalize, if not to efface, the global historical matter *in which* the crisis on board the *Bellipotent* involving Billy Budd, Claggart, and Captain Vere is embedded. By this marginalization, I do not simply mean marginalization of the imperial war between Britain and postrevolutionary France, but also, it is important to emphasize, marginalization of the mutinies that the depredations of this ferocious global war were instigating in the British Navy, as in the texts of the British naval historians who, as the narrator pointedly notes, "naturally abridged" the episode of the Great Mutiny at Nore (BB, p. 55). Their conclusion has, thus, not only obscured the *radical imbalance, indeed, the absolute one-sidedness, of power* on board this ship of state,[18] or, to anticipate, the state of exception, that, under the aegis of the sovereign's biopolitical decision, reduces the humanity of the likes of Billy Budd to disposable "bare life." In so doing, it also contributed decisively to the pacification of the subversive force of Melville's posthumously published narrative, the process begun by the British critics (John Middleton Murry, H. M. Tomlinson, John Freeman, E. M. Forster, and E. L. Grant Watson) who inaugurated the Melville revival.[19] For this reason and those articulated above, I shall, despite the accusation of flaunting objective scholarship, retrieve and put back into play the "discarded" "Preface" in its entirety, while reminding the reader of the presence of its historical matter in chapter 3 of the "definitive" text, albeit in a more complex form:

> The year 1797, the year of this narrative, belongs to a period which, as every thinker now feels, *involved a crisis for Christendom not exceeded in its undetermined momentousness at the time by any other era wherof there is record.* The opening proposition made by the Spirit of the Age involved rectification of the Old World's hereditary wrongs. In France, to some extent, this was bloodily effected. But what then? Straightway the Revolution itself became a wrongdoer, one more oppressive than the kings. Under Napoleon it enthroned upstart kings, and initiated that prolonged agony of continual war whose final throe was Waterloo. During those years not the wisest could have foreseen that the outcome of all would be what to some thinkers apparently it has since turned out to be—a political advance along nearly the whole line for Europeans.
>
> *Now, as elsewhere hinted, it was something caught from the Revolutionary Spirit that at Spithead emboldened the man-of-war's men to rise against real abuses, long-standing ones, and afterwards at the Nore to make inordinate and aggressive demands — successful resistance to which was confirmed only when the ringleaders were hung for an admonitory spectacle to the anchored fleet.* Yet, in a way analogous to the operations of the Revolution at large, the Great Mutiny, though by Englishmen naturally deemed monstrous at the time, doubtless gave the first latent prompting to most important reforms in the British navy.[20]

Let me make it clear at the outset that this "Preface" (and chapter 3, which rehearses the historical matter it contains) is neither Melville's encomium to the French Revolution and its aftermath nor, more emphatically, a political conversative's revulsion against the irrational violence precipitated by the rebellion of the French people against the tyrannical French monarchy.[21] It is, rather, a symptomatic expression of the betrayal of an epochal possibility, not simply for human emancipation, but also for an entirely different way of thinking emancipation. For the contemporary *American narrator* (and Melville) — this crucial narratological fact has been overlooked by virtually all the commentaries[22] — attuned to the exceptionalism of the New World/Old World distinction (as his reference to the "Old World" makes clear) and to the past and future in which the year 1797 is embedded, the local and global history of that moment was something like an "event" in Alain Badiou's sense of the word:

> [S]ince a situation is composed by the knowledge circulating within it, the event names the void inasmuch as it names the not-known of this situation.
>
> To take a well-known example: Marx is an event for political thought because he designates, under the name "proletariat," the central void of early bourgeois societies. For the proletariat — being entirely dispossessed, and absent from the political stage — is that around which is organized the complacent plenitude established by the rule of those who possess capital.
>
> To sum up: the fundamental ontological characteristic of an event is to inscribe, to name, the situated void of that for which it is an event.[23]

By "event," then, I mean a historical rupture incumbent on the self-destruction of the logic of a regime of truth that *dis-closes* the void at its origin for positive thought or, to put it alternatively, a concatenation of events (a "situation") the singularity of which calls the global world structured in domination (in this case of the long tyranny of monarchical government sanctioned by Christianity) into question, and, by way of the self-destruction of this determinative foundational structure and the disclosure of that which did not count in the old dispensation, opens up space — signaling a radically new beginning — for the emergence of the possibility of radically new anti-identitarian subjectivities and a radically new anti-foundational polity.[24]

It is not simply that, to the American narrator, this resonant singular event — and the betrayal of its emancipatory imperatives — rendered the local world Americans inhabited global in scope; it also enabled him, as I shall show, to know this local American world for the first time. In other words, by tethering the events on board the *Bellipotent* to the "evental" (*événémentiel*) year 1797, Melville's intention, through his narrator's errant meditations on it, is to compel in his American readers a dislocating estrangement — a "change of terrain" — of the local exceptionalist "New World" they inhabited, to make them acutely aware that what happened in Old Europe or on the distant oceans it commanded at the end of the eighteenth century profoundly affected their lives as New Americans a century later. More specifically, his purpose in embedding the events on board the British man-of-war beginning with the impressment of a civilian from a noncombatant vessel pointedly called *Rights-of-Man* in the year 1797 is to evoke in the minds of his recalcitrant provincial American readers the disconcerting analogy between their contemporary American state and the British ship of state — also, as we shall see, representing itself as "chosen" and exceptionalist — a century before, and to render that globally fraught event symbolic of both the paradoxical promise — the avocational vocation, as it were — opened up by the French Revolution and the betrayal of that promise.

In these prefatorial paragraphs, the narrator epitomizes this global event that will invade and determine the fate of the world of the *Bellipotent* by representing it (1) as "a crisis of Christendom," that is, of Western power relations, precipitated by the disintegration of the traditional structures of domination — monarchical tyranny justified by Christianity — under the assault of the awakened oppressed populace[25] — followed by (2) the inevitable reactionary effort by the traditional rulers of the ancien régime to reorganize the old structures of domination under the more complex aegis of imperialism — the global control of the high seas in the ("exceptionalist") name of domestic prosperity and the white man's burden. Understood in the light of this resonant historical setting, we are justified, not simply in wondering what it was about the contemporary American occasion that compelled Melville, after long silence, to write such a story, but also to ask why most Melville scholars and critics of the novella have not addressed (shrunk back from?) this conspicuously manifest question.

One significant exception to this apparent scholarly indifference to the issue of Melville's sense of his immediate American world is Alan Trachtenberg's provocative (but contradictory) discussion of *Billy Budd* in the chapter on "Fiction of the Real" in his *The Incorporation of America* (1982). There, Trachtenberg observes that "the story of the 'fated' Billy, a common sailor consigned to death by a possibly deranged captain during the naval war between revolutionary France and counterrevolutionary England, also reflects the turbulence of Melville's own times."[26] By the latter, he means primarily the domestic turbulence precipitated by the relentlessly acquisitive capitalist juggernaut's "incorporation of America" in the second half of the nineteenth century, "the period that came to be called the Gilded Age":

> Just months before the events [on board the *Bellipotent*], British sailors had rebelled at Spithead and Nore, signaling their mutiny by running up the royal flag "with the union and cross wiped out [by which I take Trachtenberg to mean the constitutional monarchy of Britain and Christianity], thus "transmuting the flag of founded law and freedom defined, into the enemy's red meteor of unbridled and unbounded revolt." Growing out of "reasonable discontent" over "glaring abuses," the revolt flamed into an "irrational combustion," a "distempering irruption of contagious fever." It was a time, like the days and months following the summer of 1877 [the ruthlessly repressed nationwide workers' strike against capitalist exploitation at the beginning of President Rutherford B. Hays's presidency (IA, p. 40)], or Haymarket in 1886 [the bloody riot in Chicago precipitated by the state's brutal suppression of a planned nationwide strike in behalf of an eight-hour workday (IA, p. 90)], when the red banner terrified established authority, portending even further unbounded revolt. Officers at sea felt compelled [like the public and private police in the cities of the United State as Melville was writing] "to stand with drawn swords behind the men working the guns." (IA, pp. 202–203)[27]

Having arrived at this resonant historico-political insight, however, Trachtenberg goes on to marginalize it by reverting to (a more sophisticated version of) the old motif of resignation:

> History discloses itself as the realm of power, the laws and iron weapons of the state set against the receding utopia of the "rights of man."

Not in nature but in the King's yarn lay the hidden meaning of the law. . . . But so much, in treating of narratives inside larger events, remains unclear. Melville's message thus includes a severe commentary on interpretation itself, on the ways of knowing and judging behavior. Melville's message, translated freely, argues not only that the state must be seen as distinct from "nature," grounded in power and social interest, but also that the process of seeing and knowing must be freed from "fable," from utopian wish. To perceive their new world, Melville implies, Americans must reckon with ragged edges, the cunning currents and deceits of history. (IA, p. 206)

Given Melville's distinctive worldly penchant to think/imagine the American occasion in historical terms, a characteristic of mind that is manifest everywhere in his writing, Trachtenberg's inaugural interpretive gesture, his juxtaposition of the "Great Mutiny" with the domestic social turmoil in the United States in the volatile 1880s — should not be taken lightly, especially in its evocation of a "national emergency" that "justified" the use of executive force to suppress domestic rebellion. But the historical sense he attributes to Melville, as his reference to the fading agrarian utopian America suggests, remains, however vestigial, predictably exceptionalist, like that attributed to the United States by most of the Old Americanists — Frederick Jackson Turner, Leo Marx, Henry Nash Smith, and John Kasson, for example — who have studied this crucial period in the development of America: its national identity, its culture, and politics.[28]

Without denying the viability of this connection between the Great Mutiny within the British fleet during the Napoleonic wars and the ominous social volatility of America in the 1880s, I want to suggest that it is likely that, in *Billy Budd*, Melville had in mind a historical reality that was indissolubly related to but deeper and broader than the rapacious and brutally exploitative forwarding momentum of American techno-capitalism under the aegis of the robber-baron mentality to which Trachtenberg restricts it, a reality, in other words, that, given the status of America's domestic development in the 1880s, was global in scope. In thinking the American occasion at the time when Melville was writing *Billy Budd,* it should not be forgotten, as it too often has, that the rapid, indeed, revolutionary and virtually unrestrained rise of capitalism, epitomized by the inexorable development of the transcontinental railroad system in the United States (which precipitated the nationwide workers' strikes in the 1880s), was not an isolated phenomenon. It was not only indissolubly related to the westward expansionist momentum, which bore witness to the removal and eventual decimation of the Native American peoples and an imperialist war with Mexico, which resulted in the latter's cession of all its land north of the Rio Grande to the United States. This expansionist and incorporative momentum — this relentless "march" of "democracy" across the continent — was also instrumental in the closing of the American frontier, an event that was both a matter of geography and, far more important for the American future, an epochal matter of the American national psyche, as the historian Frederick Jackson Turner anxiously put it to his audience in the precincts of the "White City" — the ideal model of the American capitalist worldview — at the Chicago Exhibition of 1893,[29] a mere two years after Melville's death, in his famous essay "The Significance of the Frontier in American History":

> In a recent bulletin of the Superintendent of the Census for 1890 appear these significant words: "Up to and including 1880 the country had a frontier of settlement, but at present the unsettled area has been so broken into by isolated bodies of settlement that there can hardly be said to be a frontier line. In the discussion of its extent, its westward movement, etc., it can not, therefore, any longer have a place in the census reports." This brief official statement marks the closing of a great historical movement. Up to our own day American history has been in a large degree the history of the colonization of the Great West. The existence of an area of free land, its continuous recession, and the advance of American settlement westward, explain American development.[30]

This relay of historical events epitomized by Turner — techno-capitalist hegemony, westward expansion, and the closing of the frontier — that is to say, spoke not only of the practical fulfillment of the American exceptionalist ethos that had been established two centuries before with the founding of the Massachusetts Bay Colony. Far more important, the completion of this "march of American civilization" — this closing of the frontier — precipitated a disintegrative national anxiety. It annulled, that is, the immensely productive anxiety endemic to the American jeremiad, that paradoxical cultural instrument of American exceptionalism that posited the *insecurity* of the frontier — a perpetual crisis situation or enemy — as the means of always already reuniting the American people, rejuvenating their covenantal energies, and re-calling them to their exceptionalist vocation: their "messianic" errand in the world's wilderness.[31]

I shall return to the crucial relationship between the practico-symbolic frontier, crisis or emergency, national rejuvenation, and global mission later in this book (chapters 3 and 4). Here, it suffices to underscore two aspects of the cultural histories of the United States that Trachenberg and the Americanists of his generation leave unsaid: (1) The closing of the frontier by way of the forwarding dynamics of capitalist and westward expansion — and the consequent incitement of the anxiety that exceptionalist America would revert to the overcivilized decadence, division, and tyranny of the Old World — induced the dominant culture to extend the always rejuvenating frontier of the United States beyond its continental borders into the Caribbean and the Pacific Ocean; and (2) this relentless global imperial momentum, which culminated in the United States's annexation of Hawaii, and, following its imperialist war against Spain in 1898, its establishment of colonies in Cuba and the Philippines, had its immediate origins in the mid-1880s. This, not incidentally, was the very time when Melville, who was deeply conscious of American history, not least the filibustering initiatives in the Caribbean area,[32] was writing *Billy Budd*, a historical fiction about a vessel whose entire community is affected down to its capillaries, as I have been suggesting, by the epochal global struggle beyond its periphery between England and France over the control of the world's seaways, following the *event* of the French Revolution.

One of the most vocal spokespersons of this American imperialist momentum was Alfred Thayer Mahan (1840–1914), a flag officer in the U.S. Navy and lecturer in naval history and theory at the Naval War College (1885–1889, 1892–1893).[33] Mahan's first book, *The Influence of Sea Power Upon History, 1660–1783*, was not simply a history arguing the importance of the rise of military and economic sea power in the making of modern global history, but also — and primarily — a calculated ideological effort to persuade the U.S. government — a government without a substantial merchant and military navy at this crucial historical conjuncture — to build military and commercial fleets capable of competing with the European nations that, suddenly and decisively, in the latter half of the nineteenth century, had fulfilled the globalizing imperial momentum inaugurated by England and France during the Napoleonic wars. This book, which consisted of the lectures Mahan had been delivering since 1885, was published in 1890, about five years after Melville began writing *Billy Budd* and one year before he died. Given the anxious American state of mind precipitated by the closing of the frontier — and the author's friendship with the then assistant secretary of the Navy, Theodore Roosevelt, who, epitomizing the American exceptionalist ethos and its emphasis on the importance of national rejuvenation by violence, was an ardent advocate of a war against Spain — it is no accident that this foreign policy expert's book gained immediate widespread popular attention and became inordinately influential in governmental and corporate circles.

I have found no evidence indicating that Melville was aware of Alfred Thayer Mahan's existence, his lectures, his book, and his influence on American maritime and foreign policy at the end of the nineteenth century. As I have noted, there are only three rather brief and oblique references to America in the main narrative of *Billy Budd*. The first occurs in chapter 3, where, in representing the global context of the events on board the *Bellipotent*, the narrator, in a gesture he will repeat at the end of his story, pointedly and ironically alludes to Britain's official historians' will to obliterate the Great Mutiny from the cultural national memory:

> Such an episode in the Island's [i.e., Britain's] grand naval story her
> naval historians naturally abridge, one of whom (William James) can-
> didly acknowledges that fain would he pass it over did not "impartiality
> forbid fastidiousness." And yet his mention is less a narration than a ref-
> erence, having to do hardly at all with details. Nor are these readily to
> be found in the libraries. Like some other events in every age befalling
> states everywhere, *including America*, the Great Mutiny was of such a
> character that national pride along with views of policy would fain
> shade it off into the historical background. (BB, p. 55; my emphasis)

The second reference to America occurs in chapter 8, where, generalizing about the rumor that Claggart's presence on the *Bellipotent* was the result of the British policy that — given the urgent necessity of "keeping up the muster rolls," and in the context of the national sense of insecurity and the hysteria unleashed by the outbreak of the French Revolution — resorted to the impressment and enlistment of vagabonds, derelicts, and criminals, the narrator distinguishes between his chronologically distanced historical perspective and that of those who immediately experienced the crisis precipitated by the events about which he is writing:

> But to the grandfathers of us graybeards, the more thoughtful of them, the genius of it presented an aspect like that of Camoëns' Spirit of the Cape [of Good Hope], an eclipsing menace mysterious and prodigious. *Not America was exempt from apprehension.* At the height of Napoleon's unexampled conquests, *there were Americans who had fought at Bunker Hill* who looked forward to the possibility that the Atlantic might prove no barrier against the ultimate schemes of this French portentous upstart from the revolutionary chaos who seemed in act of fulfilling judgment prefigured in the Apocalypse. (BB, p. 66; my emphasis)[34]

The third, and most telling, reference occurs in chapter 21, where the narrator, commenting on the effect on the "drumhead court" of Captain Vere's invocation of the "outbreak at the Nore" (BB, p. 112) in his unerring argument in behalf of the execution of Billy Budd, invokes the future analogy of the frame of mind of those officers of the USS *Somers*, who, in 1842, not long before the Mexican-American War and on the way to the West Indies, ruled to hang three alleged mutineers without public trial, an event that some commentators claim constituted the origin of Melville's story:

> Not unlikely they [the members of court] were brought to something more or less akin to that harassed frame of mind which in the year 1842 actuated the commander of the U.S. brig-of-war *Somers* to resolve, under the so-called Articles of War, Articles modeled upon the English Mutiny Act, to resolve upon the execution at sea of a midshipman and two sailors as mutineers designing the seizure of the brig. Which resolution was carried out though in a time of peace and within not many days' sail of home. An act vindicated by a naval court of inquiry subsequently convened ashore. History, and here cited without comment. *True, the circumstances on board the* Somers *were different from those on board the* Bellipotent. *But the urgency felt, well-warranted or otherwise, was much the same.* (BB, pp. 113–114; my emphasis)[35]

Brief and oblique as these allusions to America are, however, they are quite provocative, especially when it is noted that they occur — strategically? — near the beginning, middle, and end of the inner story and that, in each case, they implicate America not only in the larger global history involving the struggle between Britain and France for control of the world's oceans in general and, more particularly, Britain's counterrevolutionary effort to contain the global violence unleashed by the French Revolution, particularly by Napoleon, "this French portentous upstart from the revolutionary chaos," but also in the local issue of the suspension of the law in the context of the state of emergency on board the *Bellipotent.*

I shall return later to the implications for the "law" — more specifically, for human rights — of these telling allusions comparing young America to the powers of the Old World. Here, I want to focus on Melville's calling attention, however tentatively, to the relationship between a marginal America and the wider, global events, especially to the human consequences of the proclamation of a planetary state of exception incumbent on Europe's globalization of war — and the crisis of national security it reflects and produces — in which the inner story is embedded. In so doing, I suggest, Melville could also be alluding negatively to his contemporary Alfred Mahan's sustained and enormously influential effort, by way of his history of European sea power between 1660 to 1783 (i.e., the period culminating in Admiral Horatio Nelson's decisive victory over the combined French and Spanish fleets at Trafalgar in 1805) to persuade the U.S. government (and the corporate world) that America should become an imperial sea power capable of competing with the European powers in the struggle for supremacy over the global seaways and the scramble to colonize the rest of the world.

Given Melville's and Mahan's contemporaneity and the convergence of their domestic and global interests, not least, of their mutual, if antithetical, obsession with American exceptionalism, the providentially ordained errand of the United States in the (global) wilderness, and its imperial expansionism, and their similar consciousness of the global importance of the seas in the making of American history (particularly the Caribbean and the Pacific in the case of the United States), the possibility that Melville is alluding to Mahan's expansionist imperial project is greatly enhanced by a closer examination of the latter's text. As I have noted, the historical analysis Mahan undertakes in *The Influence of Sea Power* is fundamentally ideological and is informed by two related intentions. The first is to show that the history of the world, especially modern history —

the imperial history inaugurated by European powers in the so-called age of exploration — has been determined, not so much by nations warring over control of continental land masses, but by those aggressively enterprising mercantile and colonialist nations that sought control of the seas' highways and the scattered network of ports of call that dotted them. The second is to show that this history — although not fully conscious of its call, most American leaders were highly receptive of it, thanks to their exceptionalist ethos — had produced conditions that, given the United States's favorable geopolitical situation, could, if acknowledged and acted on, make the country a powerful global colonial power. With this ideological scenario constantly in mind — and, I would add, Mahan's acute, if internalized, awareness of the anxiety over the enervation of the collective national psyche produced by the closing of the American frontier, an anxiety implicit in his insistently repeated reference to the strategic military and economic value of the Gulf of Mexico, the Isthmus of Panama, and, not least, the Pacific Ocean — Mahan undertook a meticulous globally oriented history of European sea power between 1660 and 1783, the period of fierce planetary struggle between Portugal, Spain, the Dutch United Provinces, France (in the reign of Louis XIV), and Britain for supremacy of the oceans, which culminated in the defeat of the comte de Grasse by Admiral George Rodney in the Battle of the Saintes (April 9–12, 1782) in the West Indies. And in the process, he "finds" that this epochal history, which set the stage for Nelson's conclusive defeat of the French at Trafalgar, not only rendered the British Navy a renewed threat to the newly formed United States, but also, in Mahan's mind, precipitated the United States as Britain's new global competitor at sea.

My intention in invoking Mahan's book has not been to rehearse the complex history he invokes as model and lesson for deputies of the dominant culture in America such as Theodore Roosevelt. It has been, rather, following the genealogical directives suggested by the official marginalization or pacification of the historical context of *Billy Budd*, to show what it is about Mahan's peculiar historiography that might have attracted the attention of Melville at that late moment in his life to the ideological argument of the naval historian and theorist. And for this purpose what comes immediately and tellingly to hand is Mahan's pointed account at the end of the introductory chapter of his book (and again at the conclusion of chapter 1, "Discussion of the Elements of Sea Power," where he sets out his theoretical position on Napoleon's plan to invade Britain) of the events that culminated in Nelson's victory at Trafalgar. It is an account, not incidentally, that attributes this victory, by which "England was saved" (ISP, n.p.), not simply to the strategic genius of Nelson, but also and, even more emphatically, to Napoleon's (Old World–oriented) overdetermination of land strategy and his relative indifference to sea power.

> Within ten years of the peace of 1788 came the French Revolution; but that great upheaval which shook the foundations of States, loosed the ties of social order, and drove out of the navy all the trained officers of the monarchy who were attached to the old state of things, did not free the French navy from a false system. It was easier to overturn the form of government than to uproot a deep-seated tradition . . . . Of the inaction of Villeneuve, the admiral who commanded the French rear at the battle of the Nile, and who did not leave his anchors while the head of the column was being destroyed [a high-ranking French naval officer writes]: —
>
> "A day was to come [Trafalgar] in which Villeneuve in his turn, like De Grasse before him . . . would complain of being abandoned by part of his fleet. We have come to suspect some secret reason for this fatal coincidence. It is not natural that among so many honorable men there should so often be found admirals and captains incurring such a reproach. If the name of some of them is to this very day sadly associated with the memory of our disasters, we may be sure the fault is not wholly their own. We must rather blame the nature of the operations in which they were engaged, and that system of defensive war prescribed by the French government, which as Pitt, in the English Parliament, proclaimed [sic] to be the forerunner of certain ruin. That system, when we wished to renounce it, had already penetrated our habits; it had, so to say, weakened our arms and paralyzed our self-reliance." (ISP, pp. 46–47)[36]

Following this all too brief summary analysis of the disastrous failure of French maritime strategy in the Napoleonic wars, culminating at Trafalgar, Mahan goes on to conclude this first, theoretical, chapter by turning to its lessons for contemporary governments and their peoples, inasmuch as the question of sea power pertains to both peace and war. Mahan generalizes here, but, as his insistent references to the paucity and weakness of the U.S. Navy — and the United States's lack of colonies — suggest, he is actually referring to the U.S. government, the American corporate world, and the American people. In the context of peace, the government's sponsorship of "a strong navy" and an expansive maritime strategy will favor "the natural growth of a people's industries and its tendencies to seek adventure and gain by way of the sea," a familiar locution that resonates with the exceptionalist ethos (in its late filibustering mode) in the form of the rejuvenating pioneer spirit. In the context of war, a modern government attuned to the benefits of sea power would be able to create institutions "favoring a healthful spirit and activity, and providing for rapid development in time of war by an adequate reserve of men and of ships and by measures for drawing out that general reserve power which has before been pointed to, when considering the character and pursuits of the people" (ISP, p. 48). With this institutional inscription of what, without violating Mahan's intention, could be called a rejuvenated wartime national mentality, the mind-set of a people that has willingly become a standing or disposable reserve, comes its natural corollary: not simply the conquest and establishment of far-flung colonies, as the text states, but also, as the omission of any reference to the condition of the colonized in his global history suggests, colonies in which the natives do not exist or, rather, may exist but do not count. In Giorgio Agamben's term, to anticipate, they exist only as "bare lives."[37] In a rhetoric that is remarkably proleptic of the global reach of contemporary America's naval and military facilities, Mahan wrote in the 1880s:

> Undoubtedly under this second head of warlike preparation must come the maintenance of suitable naval stations, in those distant parts of the world to which the armed shipping must follow the peaceful vessels of commerce. The protection of such stations must depend either upon direct military force, as do Gibraltar and Malta, or upon a surrounding friendly population, such as the American colonists once were to England. . . . Such friendly surroundings and backing, joined to a reasonable military provision, are the best defences, and when combined with decided preponderance at sea, make a scattered and extensive empire, like that of England, secure; for while it is true that an unexpected attack may cause disaster in some one quarter, the actual superiority of naval power prevents such disaster from being general or irremediable.

History has sufficiently proved this. England's naval bases have been in all parts of the world; and her fleets have at once protected them, kept open the communications between them, and relied upon them for shelter. (ISP, pp. 48–49)

Despite the theoretical "realism" of his geopolitical discourse, it could be said, in short, that Mahan's history of the influence of sea power on history — the global history that culminates with Nelson's epochal victory at Trafalgar and the precipitation of Britain as imperial master of the global maritime highways and as a threat — and model — for the United States — is one that (re)calls the jading America of the 1880s. I mean, specifically, the America whose closed frontier Frederick Jackson Turner, as we have seen, was not simply to lament a mere two years later, but also to transform into a national anxiety that would refuel its exceptionalist "errand in the wilderness," now, however, as Mahan's insistence on the geopolitical importance of the Isthmus of Panama makes manifest, on the Pacific frontier. Equally important, it could also be said that, in thus calling for such a re-"awakening" — a remembering of the original conditions of the American "errand" — he was also (re)calling for the institutional (i.e., state) imposition of a new psychological frontier, a new enemy, a new crisis of national security   that is, a state of emergency, now on a global scale and, given his emphasis on the *condition* of global crisis rather than on an identifiable enemy, on a relatively permanent basis, that would always renew and rejuvenate the American (covenantal) people.

In sum, Alfred Mahan's history of the influence of Western sea power on history represents its mise-en-scènes — the local (Nelson's victory over Villeneuve at Trafalgar) and the global (the decisive triumph of the British Navy over the French in the Napoleonic wars that enabled Britain to become the imperial master of the global oceans), and the lessons this history (or, rather, History) is intended to convey (the crucial importance of sea power for exceptionalist America's future in the age of globalization) — in a way that remarkably coincides with and is opposed by the fictional history Melville represents in *Billy Budd*. If, moreover, one remembers Melville's lifelong interrogations of (providential) History, of the myth of American exceptionalism, of the American jeremiad, of the American frontier, of the American pioneer spirit, of the philosophy of optimism, of the unerring march of progress, and of American imperialist capitalism, one is enabled to perceive another uncanny parallel with Mahan. In recalling Melville's insistent critique of the "American calling," that is, one also sees that Mahan's vision of America's global future incumbent on the lessons of Trafalgar — an implicit exceptionalist America always already renewed by the recurring insecurity of the frontier condition and thus immune to the decline that, as Mahan's history shows and, in the case of Britain, implies, is the inevitable fate of Old World polities — coincides with and is opposed by Melville's implicit vision of America's global future in the wake of the events on board the *Bellipotent*.[38]

In implying that Melville's attitude to Nelson in *Billy Budd* is antithetical to Mahan's, I shall, no doubt, be accused of not taking account of, or willfully misreading, the narrator's "err[ing] into . . . a bypath" (BB, p. 56) by way of the brief chapter (4) he devotes to the British naval "hero." More specifically, I shall be accused of reading the narrator's reference to Trafalgar in that chapter, not as the heroically enacted triumph of British (civilizational) order over the bestial anarchy precipitated by the French Revolution (as virtually every commentator on *Billy Budd* has claimed),[39] but as the reactionary triumph of the counterrevolution over the revolutionary force of freedom. This, however, is not what I am suggesting. Melville, as virtually everything he wrote testifies, abhorred binaries, the unerring linear logic that subsumes them, and the unerring narratives and reductive closures they produce. But this did not mean undecidability. In the historical world (as opposed to the worldless world of liberal debate), to repeat, conflicting forces are rarely, if not never, equal. My point, rather, is that, for Melville, the combination of Britain's reactionary policies (represented as exceptionalist, as we shall see) and Napoleon's betrayal of the French Revolution constituted not only a shoring up of the collapsing structures of power of the old European world, a world structured in domination, but also an expansion of these predatory structures of power to include imperial domination of the world. As such this combination resulted in the betrayal of what Badiou would call the "evental" *(événémentiel)* potential of the event of the French Revolution[40] — the globalization of the emancipatory impulse[41] — in favor of the production of a permanent global state of emergency in which the multitude — the likes of Billy Budd — do not stand a chance.

Virtually all the critics, both before and after the establishment of the "definitive" text of *Billy Budd,* have assumed the narrator's "digression" on Nelson in chapter 4 to be a straightforward encomium to the "hero" of Trafalgar, despite the various interpretations of its role in the narrative as a whole. This assumption, as it pertains to previous commentary, which is also that of the editors, is conveniently summarized by Hayford and Sealts's note on leaf 58 of Melville's manuscript (BB, p. 56):

The significance of Melville's treatment of Nelson has been variously assessed, particularly in relation to the ensuing characterization of Captain Vere in Ch. 6 and 7. [Wendell] Glick (1953) holds that "the digression on Nelson, though it intrudes upon the plot, is central to an understanding of Melville's final resolution" of his old problem, "the eternal conflict between absolute morality and social expedience" (p. 103): Nelson, by transcending the merely expedient, provided an immortal example of "supreme heroism, conformable to the highest ideals governing human behavior" (p. 109). [Laurence] Barrett (1955), pp. 622–23, takes the chapter as "really a statement of the theme of the whole story, . . . that measured form . . . makes it possible for man to live" with such "ambiguities"; Nelson, in exposing himself to danger and death at Trafalgar, "is both captain and condemned man, both Vere and Billy Budd, and his act is an assertion of form." But [John B.] Noone (1957), p. 261, argues conversely that "whereas Vere equates successful leadership with complete submission to form, Nelson is noted for his daring departures from forms. . . . As against Vere's belief in force as the best preventive of mutiny," Nelson possessed "that feeling for primitive instincts which . . . led him . . . to expose himself in battle." Barrett and Noone agree, however, in seeing Nelson as an ideal figure in whom head and heart, reason and instinct, are fused.

[Milton] Stern (1957), pp. 206–10, similarly finds Melville's "by-path" a "direct road into the center of this 'inside narrative,'" leading to "a statement of the kind of heroism that . . . may lead to salvation" — for Stern, the heroism of "the Governor." Nelson is "a political and moral administrator" who offers "the sacrifice of self to the possible victory that the combined head and heart may achieve." But where Stern sees a "perfectly complete parallel between Nelson and Vere" (p. 209), [Merlin] Bowen (1960), p. 229, thinks the virtues here attributed to Nelson "bring the lesser man's own qualities, by the force of contrasts, unavoidably to mind."[42]

There is, admittedly, some justification for assuming that the narrator's invocation of Nelson is intended by Melville as an idealization of the heroic military commander who sacrifices himself for the cause of civilizational order against barbarism, especially if the nostalgia he expresses in introducing Nelson to the reader for the "glorious" past when "sea warfare" involved "sailing ships" rather than prosaic ironclads, as in the present, is taken straightforwardly. I quote this familiar passage at length to recall its (unstable) rhetoric:

> Very likely it is no new remark that the inventions of our time have at last brought about a change in sea warfare in degree corresponding to the revolution in all warfare effected by the original introduction from China into Europe of gunpowder. The first European firearm, a clumsy contrivance, was, as is well known, scouted by no few of the knights as a base implement, good enough peradventure for weavers too craven to stand up crossing steel with steel in frank fight. But as ashore knightly valor, though shorn of its blazonry, did not cease with the knights, neither on the seas — though nowadays in encounters there a certain kind of displayed gallantry be fallen out of date as hardly applicable under changed circumstances — did the nobler qualities of such naval magnates as Don John of Austria, Doria, Van Tromp, Jean Bart, the long line of British admirals, and the American Decaturs of 1812 become obsolete with their wooden walls.
>
> Nevertheless, to anybody who can hold the Present at its worth without being inappreciative of the Past, I may be forgiven, if to such an one the solitary old hulk at Portsmouth, Nelson's *Victory,* seems to float there, not alone as the decaying monument of a fame incorruptible, but also as a poetic reproach, softened by its picturesqueness, to the *Monitors* and yet mightier hulls of the European ironclads. And this not altogether because such craft are unsightly, unavoidably lacking the symmetry and grand lines of the old battleships, but equally for other reasons. (BB, pp. 56–57)

As Melville in *White-Jacket,* however, the narrator reiteratively, if only symptomatically, observes that the romantic "knightly valor" that was endemic to the "poetry" and "blazonry" of these "picturesque" wooden men-of-war of old, including Nelson's *Victory,* was won at the horrific cost of the very real blood of the common sailors, or, as Melville in *White-*

Jacket and the narrator in *Billy Budd* repeatedly and pointedly stress, "the people" (in the sense of "the multitude")[43] on board their decks.[44] If this qualification signaling the radical difference between romance and reality — "measured forms" and "jagged edges," in the narrator's language — is remembered, it will also be seen that this introductory passage celebrating "the old battleships" — their "symmetry and grand lines" — at the expense of the unsightliness and asymmetry of the modern "*Monitors* and yet mightier hulls of the European ironclads" is, in fact, fraught with an irony that will carry over into the following "celebratory" portrait of Nelson:

> *There are some, perhaps*, who while not altogether inaccessible to that poetic reproach just alluded to, may yet on behalf of the new order be disposed to parry it; and this to the extent of iconoclasm, if need be. For example, prompted by the sight of the star inserted in the *Victory*'s quarter-deck designating the spot where the Great Sailor fell, these martial utilitarians may suggest considerations implying that Nelson's *ornate publication of his person in battle* [the reference is to the admiral's conspicuous dress on the day of the battle, which rendered him an easy target for enemy sharpshooters] was not only unnecessary, but not military, nay, savored of foolhardiness and vanity. (BB, p. 57; my emphasis)

The narrator, it is true, reiteratively identifies the naysayers to the "romance" of the old sail-propelled battleships and the heroic greatness of Nelson as modern "utilitarians" and "Benthamites of war" (BB, p. 57). But this identification, insofar far as the Benthamite utilitarians, like the seafaring knights long before them, are utterly indifferent to the slaughter of the ordinary sailor (the "people"), is intended by Melville to demonstrate the complicity of the former with the latter. It does not soften the parodic indictment of Nelson's self-indulgent vanity in the pursuit of "glory" (his tacit projection — dramatization — of himself in the third person) and his callous indifference to the men on his ships:

> At Trafalgar Nelson on the brink of opening the fight sat down and wrote his last brief will and testament. If under the presentiment of the most magnificent of all victories to be crowned by his own glorious death, a sort of priestly motive led him to dress his person in the jewelled vouchers of his own shining deeds; if thus to have adorned himself for the altar and the sacrifice were indeed vainglory, then affectation

and fustian is each more heroic line in the great epics and dramas, since in such lines the poet but embodies in verse those exaltations of sentiment that a nature like Nelson, the opportunity being given, vitalizes into acts. (BB, p. 58)

This inflated rhetorical "defense" of Nelson is exacerbated by the narrator's going on to quote "Alfred" [Tennyson], who, "in his funeral ode to the victor of Waterloo [Wellington]," "invokes Nelson as 'the greatest sailor since our world began' " (BB, p. 58).

In highlighting the absoluteness of the opposition between the old "poetic" mode of naval war and the "prosaic" new, the Old World knightly and the modern utilitarian protagonists, the romantic and the Benthamite, Nelson and the commanders of the ironclads, in this encomium to the hero of Trafalgar, Melville is pointing not only to the narrator's nostalgia at this early point in his narrative, but also to the blindness to the realities — the murderous biopolitical consequences — to the "people," of this romantic nostalgia.

One cannot help, then, but be reminded by the excessiveness of this nostalgic encomium to the admiral — and by its loud silence concerning the horrors of war that mostly the preterite suffer — of another prominent reference in Melville's fiction to Nelson's ornate dress on the day of his unnecessary death, this time in a much earlier devastating satire of American romantic optimism: that lunatic blindness, endemic to the myth of American exceptionalism, in the face of the corrosions precipitated by the incorporation of America that was a central target of Melville's post–*Moby-Dick* fiction, not least in *The Confidence-Man*, particularly in the story of China Aster. I am referring to "Cock-A-Doodle-Do," his tale about an American Job who, despite losing everything to the capitalist system, remains utterly confident that all is well in the best of all possible worlds:

A cock. More like a golden eagle than a cock. A cock, more like a Field-Marshall than a cock. A cock, more like Lord Nelson with all his glittering arms on, standing on the Vanguard's quarter-deck going into battle, than a cock. A cock, more like the Emperor Charlemagne in his robes at Aix la Chapelle, than a cock,
  Such a cock!
  He was of a haughty size, stood haughtily on his haughty legs. His

colors were red, gold, and white. The red was on his crest alone, which was a mighty and symmetric crest, like unto Hector's helmet, as delineated on antique shields. His plumage was snowy, traced with gold. He walked in front of the shanty, like a peer of the realm; his crest lifted, his chest heaved out, his embroidered trappings flashing in the light. His pace was wonderful. He looked like some noble foreigner. He looked like some Oriental king in some magnificent Italian Opera.[45]

Seen in the light of the vast moral distance between Nelson's consciousness of his dramatic heroic identity — the "publication of his person in battle" — and the implicit nonexistence of the sailors under his executive command the narrator's monumentalizing rhetoric cannot but remind us of Michel Foucault's Nietzschean anti-monumentalist definition of genealogical historiography in the parodic mode:

The [traditional] historian offers this [modern] confused and anonymous European, who no longer knows himself or what name he should adopt, the possibility of alternate identities, more individualized and substantial than his own. But the man with historical sense [the genealogist] will see that this substitution is simply a disguise. Historians supplied the Revolution with Roman prototypes, romanticism with knight's armor, and the Wagnerian era was given the sword of a German hero — ephemeral props that point to our unreality. No one kept them from venerating these religions, from going to Bayreuth to commemorate a new afterlife; they were free, as well, to be transformed into street venders of empty identities. The new historian, the genealogist, will know what to make of this masquerade. He will not be too serious to enjoy it; on the contrary, he will push the masquerade to its limit and prepare the great carnival of time where masks are constantly reappearing. No longer the identification of our faint individuality with the solid identities of the past, but our "unrealization" through the excessive choice of identities — Frederick of Hohenstaufen, Caesar, Jesus, Dionysus, and possibly Zarathustra. Taking up these masks, revitalizing the buffoonery of history, we adopt an identity whose unreality surpasses that of God, who started the charade. . . . In this, we recognize the parodic double of what the second of *the Untimely Meditations* called "monumental history": a history given to reestablishing the high points of historical development and their maintenance in a perpetual presence, given to the recovery of works, actions, and creations through the monogram of their personal essence. But in 1874, Nietzsche accused this history, one totally devoted to veneration, *of barring access to the actual intensities and creations of life.*[46]

I shall return to this illuminating genealogical historical perspective in chapter 3, where I undertake a close reading of *Billy Budd*. Here it suffices to say that by monumentalizing its protagonist — by inflating him into another "Frederick of Hohenstaufen, Caesar, Jesus, Dionysus . . . ," this "digressive" chapter on Nelson not only discloses his glorious historical identity to be a masquerade but, in so doing, also retrieves the actual history — the carnage suffered by the preterites as a result of his self-dramatizing vainglory — that the official (monumentalist) historians would discount and forget.

Given the irony of the portrait of the hero of Trafalgar, then, it will be seen, though this goes unobserved by the editors of the "definitive" text and the critics who follow them, that it is not accidental that the next chapter begins abruptly, in a way that deflates what precedes, with a pointed return to the larger, spectral historical context in which Billy Budd's story is embedded (including a reference to the Nelson of that year in the war) — that is, to the very "eventual" matter they would efface as apocryphal: the "contingencies present and to come of the convulsed Continent"; the impressment of civilians on which the British fleet, "insatiate in demand for men," depended; the crisis-provoking mutinies at Spithead and Nore, which, though "put down," "lurkingly survived them" and thus continued to arouse apprehension of "some return of trouble sporadic or general"; and, not least, the vigilant state policing in the name of (national) "security": "So it was that for a time, on more than one quarter-deck, anxiety did exist. At sea, precautionary vigilance was strained against relapse. At short notice an engagement might come on. When it did, the lieutenants assigned to batteries felt it incumbent on them, in some instances, *to stand with drawn swords behind the men working the guns*" (BB, p. 59; my emphasis).

In other words, it is no accident that what follows immediately after the portrait of Nelson is a return to the ultimately irrepressible epochal global situation, which determines life on board the microcosmic HMS *Bellipotent* down to its capillaries: the situation that reduces the humanity of humans to bare life under the aegis of what I have been calling "the permanent state of exception" — and evokes the specter of mutiny.

In the estranging light of the interpretive directives suggested by the retrieval of the historical context that the editors of the "definitive" text of *Billy Budd* have systematically marginalized, the portrait of Nelson thus comes to be seen as neither a digression nor a moral measure against or with which Captain Vere is to be judged. It becomes, rather, a symbol fraught with global historical and political or, in Edward Said's term, "worldly" meaning. More specifically, it becomes, as I have suggested in invoking the ideological use to which Alfred Mahan put his version of Nelson and Trafalgar, as exemplary of America's global future, a warning against America's accommodation to the emergent imperial scramble for colonies and, beyond that, against its participation in the instigation of a global state of exception that threatens to reduce not only American but also global humanity to bare life.

In separating and marginalizing the "outside" history *in which* the "inside story" takes place in favor of foregrounding the "dramatization" of the events in the latter, the editors of the "definitive" text" contributed in a fundamental way to the prevalent tendency (evident in the criticism and in the cinematic, operatic, and dramatic versions *Billy Budd* has inspired) to universalize Melville's novella. More specifically, their edition authorized a general interpretive perspective that "unworlded" the world of Melville's narrative, that is, accommodated its local and global "political" content to an allegorical tragedy epitomized in the struggle within Captain Vere (and Melville) between Billy and Claggart, innocence and experience, good and evil, the claims of the real and the claims of the ideal world (horologicals and chronometricals in the language of Plinlimmon's pamphlet in *Pierre*).[47] In so doing, this "authoritative" perspective not only inadvertently repeated, in its own way, the pacifying gesture of the "official" version of the events on board the *Bellipotent*. It also reaffirmed a dominant earlier tendency to represent the old, forgotten Melville, the Melville in the precincts of his death, as one who, in the authorial tradition of the *apologia pro vita sua*, had made his peace with the world, and *Billy Budd* as "Melville's testament of acceptance."[48] This, for example, is how Newton Arvin (among many others), one of the most influential early Melville critics, put this representation in the final chapter, predictably entitled "Trophies of Peace," in his book on Melville, even as he invokes the *Somers* Affair as the source of

Billy Budd: "There are not many final works that have so much the air as *Billy Budd, Foretopman* has of a Nunc Dimittis. Everyone has felt this benedictory quality in it. Everyone has felt it to be the work of a man on the last verge of mortal existence who wishes to take his departure with a word of acceptance and reconciliation on his lips."[49]

To read this reconciliatory affirmation of resignation — this closure — against the grain, it represents *Billy Budd* as a testament to Melville's final abandonment of his quarrel not only with God but also with exceptionalist America. In thus reading this last work as the final expression of his ontological and sociopolitical quiescence, this reductive perspective and the criticism and commentary it authorized, consciously or not, contributed to that hegemonic interpretation of Melville's writing after *Moby-Dick*. I mean the reading that, as I and other "New Americanists" have shown, has not only domesticated and pacified his unrelenting subversions, usually enacted in the ironic mode, of the myth of American exceptionalism by *accommodating* them to a "higher synthesis" — the exceptionalist–security state discourse of the Cold War era — but, in so doing, also foreclosed the possibility of perceiving the alternative contrapuntal ontological and sociopolitical relationality that these subversions were intended to announce.

Seen in the light of my retrieval of its macrocosmic historical content, however, the microcosmic "world" of *Billy Budd* undergoes a remarkable estrangement. It devolves into a resonant manifestation of what the late Edward Said, following Theodor Adorno's interpretation of Beethoven's last quartets, called provocatively the "late style" (*Spätstil*): "Beethoven's late works remain unreconciled, uncoopted by a higher synthesis; they do not fit any scheme, and they cannot be reconciled or resolved, since their irresolution and unsynthesized fragmentariness are constitutive, neither ornamental nor symbolic of something else. Beethoven's late compositions are in fact about 'lost totality,' and are therefore catastrophic."[50]

Far from being a "testament of acceptance" — a decisively final reconciliation with and acknowledgment of the "way things are" (necessity) that surreptitiously depends on the certitudes of "a higher synthesis," and thus on an irremediable injustice (a radical imbalance of power relations endemic to the state of exception) — *Billy Budd*, on the contrary, bears witness to the dying Melville's radical worldliness. In ontological terms, the novella becomes, like Beethoven's disconcerting last quartets, a decisive secular expression of Melville's fierce allegiance to the "catastrophic" (from the Greek *kata* [down] *strephein* [to turn]), to a profane—or "now time"—time that is always out of joint: that is, to everything in being that refuses to accommodate itself to a higher "totality" or "sacred cause," to everything that contradicts the accepted truth, to everything that resists resolution, in short, to everything that refuses to be answerable to a Calling.[51] And in sociopolitical terms, it becomes a secular manifestation of Melville's fierce commitment to everything in the world that resists confinement and oppression and opposes injustice. To put this refusal positively and in Said's terms, *Billy Budd* becomes a text that "speaks the truth to power," particularly to the disabling power of that aspect of the American exceptionalist ethos that, in always already recuperating the consensus and rejuvenating the collective energies, which is to say, the violent group passions, of the covenantal people against those who are deemed not to count (the passed over in the American Puritan dispensation) must also impose a permanent state of exception that reduces life to bare life: life, that is, that can be killed without it being called homicide.

Let me put what I have said above about Melville's late style alternatively—and in a way that will provide an orienting perspective on my reading of *Billy Budd* in chapter 3. It will be recalled that the penultimate of the three brief (un)concluding chapters appended by the narrator to the story terminating in the hanging of Billy Budd—they are, he tells us pointedly, the "ragged edges" of the "Truth uncompromisingly told" that mar the symmetrical form of "pure fiction" (BB, p. 128)—constitutes an "account of the affair" aboard the *Bellipotent* that "appeared in a naval chronicle of the time, an authorized weekly publication," "doubtless for the most part written in good faith." In this decisively brief linear—straightforward and conclusive—account of the events, the official custodians of British naval history transform, in the name of peace (Pax Britannica)—homeland security, as it were—the criminal offender, Claggart, into the innocent victim and the innocent victim, Billy, into the criminal offender, and conclude with finality: "The criminal paid the penalty of his crime. The promptitude of the punishment has proved salutary. Nothing amiss is now apprehended aboard H.M.S. *Bellipotent*" (BB, p. 130) Despite their, undoubtedly "good faith," the liberal humanist generation of Americanists deriving from the so-called Melville Revival in the 1920s, I suggest, rewrote Melville's *Billy Budd* (indeed, all of his fiction from *Moby-Dick* on) in an analogously pacifying way, if in a different register. In other words, in the very act of "resurrecting" Melville from the grave in which he had been interred in the 1850s by the early, more morally conservative, custodians of the American national identity, this new generation of custodians, paradoxically, however inadvertently, reburied him by reinterpreting his work in such a way as to accommodate its provocative heresies to the myth of American exceptionalism, the very myth that it was Melville's self-appointed calling to delegitimize.

Far from being the epitome of the "magnanimous soul," as so many American humanist critics, especially after Warner Berthoff, have concluded from Billy's cry "God bless Captain Vere!"[52] Melville portrays Billy Budd as a representative of the passive ventriloquized victims of the Western humanist ethical system — the insidious ethics of tolerance that, as Badiou has persuasively shown, in assuming the ontological priority of evil over good, also assumes the subhumanity of those it commands.[53] Billy, Melville's irony implies, has accepted this powerful disabling hegemonic human rights ethics of the dominant Western elect and, in doing so, has forfeited his will to politically resist — to *be* "some-one." In Agamben's resonant term, Billy has accepted the biopolitical status of "bare life" (*vita nuda*):

> Let us now observe the life of *homo sacer*, or of the bandit, the *Friedlos*, the *aquae et igni interdictus*, which are in many ways similar. He has been excluded from the religious community and from all political life: he cannot participate in the rites of his *gens*, nor (if he has been declared *infamis et intestabilis*) can he perform any juridically valid act. *What is more, his entire existence is reduced to a bare life [nuda vita] stripped of every right by virtue of the fact that anyone can kill him without committing homicide*; he can save himself only in perpetual flight or a foreign land. *And yet he is in a continuous relationship with the power that banished him precisely insofar as he is at every instant exposed to an* unconditioned *threat of death*. He is pure *zoē*, but his *zoē* is as such caught in the sovereign ban [excluded yet included] and must reckon with it at every moment, finding the best way to elude or deceive it. In this sense no life, as exiles and bandits know well, is more "political" than his.[54]

And it is this Western (biopolitical) ethics, perfected by America, ironically, that lies behind the peculiar sympathy for Billy Budd expressed by

American humanist commentators: a sympathy that is utter indifference to the outrageous violence of his hanging.

Seen, however, from the perspective — the "informed gaze" — enabled by the retrieval of the marginalized evental history in which the "inside narrative" is embedded, *Billy Budd* — this resonant version of Melville's "late style" — assumes, like the "Nothing" in the last sentence of the official narrative quoted above that menaces its "truth,"[55] the status of a threatening specter, or (in Derrida's term) "revenant,"[56] that returns to haunt the hegemonic interpretive discourse of the old Americanists. It is this menacing, irrepressible, and unaccountable specter of the preterited body that the narrator's final, symmetry-marring addendum evokes. In underscoring the ubiquitous absent *presence* of the "rude utterance" penned "from another foretopman, one of [Billy's] own watch, gifted, as some sailors are, with an artless *poetic* temperament," he intimates, not the apotheosis of Billy's "soul" as it is all too often affirmed, but his spectral return to haunt the American exceptionalist world.

In subtitling Billy Budd "An Inside Narrative," it is not, as the official reading of the novella has it in one way or another, the opposition between the wider history of the Napoleonic wars and the events on board the *Bellipotent* to which Melville would draw our attention. Rather, as I have argued, it is precisely the indissoluble interrelation between — the oneness of — the two that constitutes the "inside narrative." What Melville would have us register is the tension between this macrological-micrological inside narrative and the official narrative: the menacing spectrality that is released in the former by the latter, by, that is, the very act of imposing closure from the outside — a "higher synthesis" and the "peace" it is intended to bring — on its anxiety-inciting heretical provocations. In rejecting the symmetry of narrative closure in the name of truth, Melville, in *Billy Budd*, not only discloses that in *this* world, especially the American democratic world, power, despite the lip service that is paid to equality, is radically uneven, that someone like Billy Budd doesn't stand a chance. In so doing he also points to the need for a revolution in thinking justice. This breaking of the peace — this speaking the truth to power, as I shall show more fully in chapter 3 — is the legacy of Melville's late catastrophic phase.

CHAPTER TWO

Criticism of *Billy Budd, Sailor*
A Counterhistory

In short, with all sorts of cavilers, it was best, both for them and everybody, that whoever had the true light should stick behind the secure Malakoff of confidence, nor be tempted forth to hazardous skirmishes on the open ground of reason. Therefore, he deemed it unadvisable in the good man, even in the privacy of his own mind, or in communion with a congenial one, to indulge in too much latitude of philosophizing, or, indeed, of compassionating, since this might beget an indirect habit of thinking and feeling which might unexpectedly betray him upon unsuitable occasions.

— HERMAN MELVILLE, *The Confidence-Man: His Masquerades*

The Conservative Tenor of the Histories of *Billy Budd* Criticism

The criticism and commentary on Herman Melville's *Billy Budd, Sailor* since its publication in 1924 in England have been massive. As much, if not more, has been published on this short novel written at the end of Melville's life as on *Moby-Dick*. Like *Moby-Dick*, furthermore, it has achieved global visibility. It is not my intention in this chapter to undertake a systematic history of this criticism and commentary. That has already been done on at least three occasions, the first, in 1962 by Harrison Hayford and Merton Sealts Jr. in their introduction to what they have called the definitive reading edition of *Billy Budd*;[1] the second, in 1989 by Robert Milder in the introduction to his edition of *Critical Essays on Melville's* Billy Budd, Sailor;[2] and the third in 1990 by Hershel Parker, in the chapters entitled "The Dynamics of the Canonization of *Billy Budd, Foretopman*," "Close-Reading a Flawed Text," "Textual Curiosity in the New Critical 1950s," and "The Hayford–Sealts Edition (1962)," in his book *Reading* Billy Budd.[3] But since each of these "disinterested" historical inquiries, in fact, begins from the end, that is, with a formulated question that contains its answer, the narrative they have recuperated has obfuscated rather than retrieved this history's singularities. Since 1990, moreover, the emergence of the field imaginary called New Americanist Studies — particularly a number of revisionary essays on *Billy Budd* — has rendered that narrative questionable, if not obsolete, though its influence, I believe, persists among all too many Americanists and Mevillian teachers and scholars. This chapter accordingly offers a counterhistory — or genealogy, in the Foucauldian sense of the word — of this received history, interrogating the more or less systematic conclusions these prestigious Americanist authorities (they call themselves "Melvillians" to distinguish themselves from interlopers) have drawn from their scholarly interpretation of the multitude of essays on *Billy Budd* written from a variety of critical perspectives from the time of its publication to their respective historical moments: historicist, historicist-textualist, Christian humanist, New Critical, psychoanalytic, deconstructionist, New Historicist, Marxist, and so on. More specifically, such a genealogy will disclose that these "authoritative" histories of the reception of *Billy Budd*, undertaken as disinterested inquiries, are, in fact, ideological: they have been prejudiced especially against that minority commentary that interprets the novella *as an act of radical onto-sociopolitical resistance* against an onto-sociopolitically conservative worldview that often masquerades as progressive.

Despite their emphasis on the unfinishedness of his last fictional work, each of these histories represents the *late* Melville, as, in one way or another, anti-political, as one who has "risen above" the "restricted" and partial world of political conflict that in some degree, it is reluctantly admitted, limited his earlier work, but that, each seems to imply, he, as the epitome of the universal humanist artist, was striving all along to transcend. America as a political entity, astonishingly, given the fact that Melville was an American writer who thought and imagined America globally, is rarely mentioned in this universalist commentary on the Melville of *Billy Budd*. Even more particularly, each of these histories represents this late Melville as either giving lie to those politically left-wing critics — they are, it is important to emphasize, far fewer than these historians imply — who have read *Moby-Dick*, *Pierre*, "Bartleby, the Scrivener," *Israel Potter*, "Benito Cereno," and *The Confidence-Man* as the work of a committed (onto)political writer (not to say an "anti-American" American), or as abandoning the last vestiges of any radical resistance to onto-political injustice (not to say to the hegemony of the Puritan-capitalist elect), he had previously expressed in favor of some form or other of ennobling acceptance of necessity. Despite gestures to the contrary (which seem more ethnocentric than substantive), these literary-critical histories collectively reaffirmed the very disabling conclusions about *Billy Budd* (and Melville's earlier fiction) that their (mostly) humanist English forebears had drawn at the time of the Melville revival and the publication of *Billy Budd* in the 1920s, the conclusions that contributed to the canonization of Melville. Equally disabling, in overdetermining the narrator's question vis-à-vis Captain Vere's sanity — "Who in the rainbow can draw the line where the violet tint ends and the orange tint begins? Distinctly we see the difference of the colors, but where exactly does the one first blendingly enter the other?" (BB, p. 102) — as a synedoche of Melville's purpose in the novel as a whole, they also, and despite their assertions to the contrary, established the more or less politically conservative critical orientation towards the novel that has become predominant. And this, unfortunately, as I shall show, applies in some degree as well to a number of prominent anti- or posthumanist deconstructionists, whose theoretical allegiance to undecidability renders them politically complicit with the very conservative and liberal humanist discourse they would delegitimize.

England: The Melville Revival of the 1920s and Its Limits

As many of the New Americanists have pointed out in recent years, Melville's fiction from 1850 to 1857 (particularly *Moby-Dick*, *Pierre*, "Bartleby," "Benito Cereno," *Israel Potter*, and, not least, *The Confidence-Man*) not only rather obviously manifests a deeply structured criticism of modern Western civilization — its coercive and reductive metaphysical interpretation of being, its humanistic notion of the self-present subject, its obsession with narrative closure, its racism, its tyrannical idea of the nation-state, its Eurocentrism, and its imperialism. It also, and not least, insistently discloses the unexceptionalism of American exceptionalism, that is, its continuity with Europe, rather than any radical difference — notwithstanding its appeal to democracy — from what it called "the Old World."[4] Further, as I have argued elsewhere, it was precisely Melville's deeply penetrating ontological, moral, cultural, and political criticism of an America structured in domination that, as one of the intellectual deputies of the dominant culture in America put it in a scathing — and extraordinarily narrow-minded — review of *Pierre*, justified "turn[ing] our critical Aegis upon him" and "freez[ing] him into silence": "But when he dares to outrage every principle of virtue [the reference is in part to the theme of incest]; when he strikes with an impious though, happily weak hand, at the foundations of society, we feel it our duty to tear off the veil with which he has thought to soften the hideous features of the idea, and warn the public against reception of such atrocious doctrines."[5]

Given this patent alternative history of Melville's prime as a writer — and his vulgar dismissal by custodians of American culture such as George Washington Peck — one would expect that any sensitive reader coming upon *Billy Budd* over half a century later would at least entertain the possibility that Melville intended his last novel in one way or another to pursue and extend, rather than renounce the onto-political critique of America that characterized his earlier fiction,[6] if not, as it were, to represent it as the specter — the *revenant* — that returns to haunt the regressive culture that buried him in midlife.[7] It is, then, puzzling, to put it mildly, that the English critics of the 1920s — the period of the revival of interest in Melville more or less inaugurated by the publication, in England, of *Billy Budd* by the American scholar Raymond Weaver — above all, John Middleton Murry, John Freeman, E. M. Forster, and E. L. Grant Watson, said nothing about this prior cultural history. It is also puzzling that they virtually unanimously interpreted this newly discovered late novel as a prose masterpiece by a great American writer who, at the end of a difficult life, had abandoned or abjured or waived whatever anger at injustice, ontological and/or political, he had felt in the prime of his life in favor of closure: the Jobian or Miltonic peace, "all passion spent," of acquiescence to God's mysterious design or the repose of a finally acquired higher — tragic — knowledge. I mean the universal humanist wisdom of necessity, endemic to the modern West, that allegorizes and unworlds the world in which the vast majority of humanity suffers from and struggles against injustice, which is to say, the power of a society structured in domination.[8] Since these humanist critics (Christian or secular) were those who, it should not be forgotten, initiated the process of Melville's "resurrection," which soon culminated in his canonization in and by America, that is, in the representation of *Moby-Dick* and *Billy Budd* (though not *Pierre* and *The Confidence-Man*) as the essence of the American national identity, it behooves anyone engaged in the question of the raison d'être and meaning of Melville's work to reconsider this long history of the reception of *Billy Budd* in the light of this "inaugural" moment.

The first thing that needs to be said about these early, yet authorizing estimates of *Billy Budd,* since the histories I am countering in this chapter tellingly fail to do so, is that they constitute vague, even grossly over-simplified generalizations derived from impressionist responses to the novella. None of their conclusions are the result of a careful reading of the text; nor, by and large, are they read in the context of Melville's earlier fiction. This is not to say that their authors are unintelligent or careless readers. Nor do I wish ungratefully to deny their valuable contribution to the retrieval of Melville's work from oblivion. I want to suggest, rather, that their generally humanistic interpretive frame of reference — their anthropo-logical insight or, more accurately, oversight — renders them blind to what is singular in Melville's text: the *radical worldliness*, to use Edward Said's term, that resists accommodation to (synthesis within) a higher, transcendental cause, in this case, Man: what, following M. H. Abrams but against him, I shall call "the natural supernaturalism" of being.[9]

Inscribed by the age-old humanist notion that the great artist in his (*sic*) old age seeks a grand resolution of the conflicts with which he has strug-gled earlier in life, John Middleton Murry, for example, claims that Mel-ville's "silence" after *Moby-Dick* was "the appropriate epilogue to [his] masterpiece," thus betraying utter indifference to its possible cultural/po-litical cause. After *Moby-Dick*, "there was, in a sense, nothing to be said, just as after *King Lear* there seemed nothing for Shakespeare to say."[10] At the end of his career, however, Shakespeare transcended the "silence" imposed by the tragic in *King Lear* by achieving the "certitude" of *The Tempest*. Analogously, Melville "knew where Shakespeare had been: no doubt he also knew where Shakespeare at last arrived; but he could not communicate those mysterious faint echoes of a certitude — that certitude 'which we seek and shun' — which are gathered together into *The Tem-pest*" (HMS, p. 33). This, according Murry is how we should read Mel-ville's silence: "How much he struggled with his dumbness we cannot say; perhaps during most of those thirty-five years he acquiesced in it. But something was at the back of his mind, haunting him, and this something he could not utter" (HMS, p. 34). Melville tried unsuccessfully to "reveal" this "mystery" in *Pierre* by means of the distinction he makes in that novel between the horologicals and the chronometricals:[11]

> Melville [in *Pierre*] is trying to reveal a mystery; he is trying to show
> that the completely good man is doomed to complete disaster on earth,
> and he is trying to show at the same time that this must be so, and that
> it ought to be so. The necessity of that "ought to be so" can be inter-
> preted in two ways: as Melville calls them, horologically or chronomet-
> rically. Horologically — that is, estimated by our local and earthly time-
> pieces — the disaster of the good ought to be so, because there is no
> room for unearthly perfection on earth; chronometrically — *that is, esti-
> mated by the unvarying recorder of the absolute — it ought to be so, be-
> cause it is a working out, a manifestation, of the absolute, though
> hidden, harmony of the ideal and the real.* (HMS, p. 34; my emphasis)

Following this "failure," Murry goes on, remarkably indifferent to such major worldly works as "Bartleby, the Scrivener," "Benito Cereno," *Israel Potter*, and, not least, *The Confidence-Man*, Melville's "thirty-five years of silence began." Then, "at the extreme end of them, moved perhaps by a premonition of coming death," Melville broke his silence by writing *Billy Budd*: "the last will and spiritual testament of a man of genius" (HMS, p. 34). "[S]tartling like" the hopelessly failed *Pierre*, *Billy Budd* is, accord-ing to Murry, a story "told with a strange combination of naïve and majestic serenity," "of the inevitable and utter disaster of the good and trying to convey to us this must be so and ought to be so — chronologically and horologically. He is trying as it were with his final breath, to reveal the knowledge that has been haunting him — that these things must be so and not otherwise." In short, according to Murry, "Melville was trying to reveal anew the central mystery of the Christian religion" (HMS, pp. 34–35). As my emphasis in the above quoted passage makes clear, what Murry concludes is that, in his final novel Melville rediscovers Leibnitz's philosophy of preestablished harmony, the optimistic ontology that Mel-ville, following Voltaire, relentlessly satirized in *The Confidence-Man* for its lunatic apotheosis of necessity.

With the publication of Murry's piece on *Billy Budd* in 1924, this (Christian) humanistic version of Melville's late style — which effaces

Pierre and *The Confidence-Man* as failed works—was established as a precedent for other early British critics and for most of the early Americans who appropriated it not only for *Billy Budd* but also, retrospectively, for *Moby-Dick*. Thus, for example, the English critic John Freeman, following the conventional structural symbolism of John Milton's itinerary —and the modernist impatience with narrative errancy—represents the *Billy Budd* of Melville's last years as the long-delayed, and hard-earned, triumphal sequel to the "darkness and desolation" of *Moby-Dick*, a *Paradise Regained* to a *Paradise Lost*:

> Finished but a few months before the author's death and only lately
> published, *Billy Budd* shows the imaginative faculty still secure and
> powerful, after nearly forty years' supineness [this would include the
> years in which he wrote *Pierre*, *Israel Potter*, "Bartleby," "Benito Cer-
> eno," and *The Confidence-Man*], and the not less striking security of
> Melville's inner peace. After what storms and secret spiritual turbulence
> we do not know, except by hints which it is easy to exaggerate, in his
> last days he re-enters an Eden-like sweetness and serenity, "with calm of
> mind, all passion spent," and sets his brief, appealing tragedy for wit-
> ness that evil is defeat and natural goodness invincible in the affection of
> man. In this, the simplest of stories, told with but little of the old digres-
> sive vexatiousness, and based upon recorded incidents, Herman Mel-
> ville uttered his everlasting yea, and died before a soul had been allowed
> to hear him.[12]

This (Christian) humanist perspective of the 1920s was crystallized a few years later by the British critic E. L. Grant Watson by way of entitling his piece "Melville's Testament of Acceptance."[13] Blinded by his deeply inscribed (Western) notion that literature in its highest form represents the universal human condition, or, as Grant puts it, "that larger spirit which is man" (TA, p. 44), this famous, though rather pedestrian essay, like its predecessors, eschews reference to the historical context of the story, focusing instead on the differences wrought by age between *Billy Budd* and Melville's earlier texts. "The style of this product of Melville's late years," he writes, "is strikingly different from the exuberant and highly-colored prose of that great period of more ardent creation (1850 to 1852) which produced *Mardi*, *Moby-Dick*, and *Pierre*. The grandiloquence of youth which tempted [Robert Louis] Stevenson's very partial appreciation is here transformed into the dignity of an achieved detachment." For Watson, the Melville of this last work "is no longer a rebel." Despite "the severest provocation," Billy "has not . . . any element of rebellion in him; *he is too free a soul to need a quality which is a virtue only in slaves*. [The contradictory identification of Melville and Billy should not be overlooked.] His nature spontaneously accepts whatever may befall" (TA, pp. 42–43; my emphasis). Similarly, Captain Vere "is marked by this supreme quality of acceptance," though "with full consciousness, and weighted with the responsibility of understanding the natural naturalness of man's volition and the unnatural naturalness of the law" (TA, p. 43). For Watson, that is to say, Vere is Melville's spokesperson. He is, unlike Billy, capable of accommodating in thought and language the killing by hanging of the innocent and utterly defenseless young man to a higher universal necessity: a (naturalized) sacred cause. Watson invokes the figure of Pontius Pilate as an analogy to Captain Vere, but with a significant modification: he does not wash his hands of the "shameful death" to which he condemns Billy. Rather, he "manfully assumes the full responsibility, and in such a way as to take the half, if not more than the half, *of the bitterness of the execution upon himself*" (my emphasis). Read with, say, Israel Potter or Bartleby or China Aster in mind, what this humanist ethic — this typically high-sounding encomium to the grandeur of a few men — really means is that whereas the innocent Billy Budds, the preterite multitude, are destined to suffer violent and degrading physical deaths (there is no political recourse for them), the experienced innocent Veres — those chosen few — who, unlike the preterite, are conscious of the paradoxical harmony inhering in the contradictions of mortal life ("the natural unnaturalness of the law") die, but only vicariously. As Alain Badiou puts this duplicitous Western humanist ethic, in conceiving man as ontological victim (a living animal), it not only denies the multitude a politics; it also feeds its sense of worth on the body of the victim it "sympathizes" with.[14]

In 1928, Raymond Weaver, the American critic who had edited *Billy Budd* for its first publication in Britain in 1924, introduced the novel to the American public in a volume entitled *Shorter Novels of Herman Melville*. In the preface to that edition, Weaver seems to have assimilated the British representation of the novel. Whereas his earlier estimate was negative — "gone . . . the sparkle, the verve. Only the disillusion abided with him to the last" — in the new estimate he reinvokes the ubiquitous Miltonic analogy, including the often repeated sentence from the novel that accompanied this analogy:

> [Melville's] last word upon the strange mystery of himself and of human destiny is *Billy Budd*: "A story," so Melville said in a pencilled note at the end, "not unwarranted by what happens in this incongruous world of ours — innocence and infirmity [*sic*], spiritual depravity and fair respite." It is a brief and appealing narrative, unmatched among Melville's works in lucidity and inward peace. "With calm of mind, all passion spent," Melville turned again to the narrative of one who, like Pierre, reaps death as the wages of virtue.[15]

Like the British critics, furthermore, Weaver also invokes the negative parallel with *Pierre* to suggest the transformation that age induced in Melville's comportment toward being. Invoking the Christian doctrine of the fortunate fall, that is, the Christian humanist version of classical tragedy, he represents the old Melville as writing *Billy Budd* "in witness to his ultimate faith that evil is defeat and natural goodness invincible in the affections of man" (WI, p. 37). Like *Pierre*, *Billy Budd* "ends in disaster and death." But in between Melville's mind undergoes a sea change. Whereas in *Pierre*, "Melville had hurled himself into a fury of vituperation against the world" — a way of putting it that reveals Weaver's humanist bias against the philosophical doubters ("cavilers") that Melville mercilessly satirized in *The Confidence-Man* — in *Billy* Budd, "he would justify the ways of God to man" (WI, p. 38). Weaver goes on to amplify this Miltonic reference by way of identifying *Billy Budd* (as opposed to *Pierre*) with Aristotelian tragedy:

> All of the supremest art is tragic: but the tragedy is, in Aristotle's phrase, "the representation of Eudaimonia," or the highest kind of happiness. . . . Even though in the end the tragic hero finds no friends among the living or dead, no help in God, only a deluge of calamity everywhere, yet in the very intensity of his affliction he may reveal the splendour undiscoverable in any gentler fate. Here he has reached, not the bottom, but the crowning peak of fortune — *something which neither suffering nor misfortune can touch*. Only when worldly disaster has worked its utmost can we realize that there remains something in man's soul which is for ever beyond the grasp *of accidents of existence*,

with power in its own right to make life beautiful. Only through tragedy of this type could Melville affirm his everlasting yea. (WI, p. 38; my
emphasis)[16]

Like his British contemporaries, Weaver invokes Carlyle's optimistic everlasting yea to represent the late Melville as universalizing Man and celebrating the grandness of his soul in *Billy Budd*. And, in the very process of
this apotheosis of the magnanimous being of what can only be called the
elect (the Captain Veres), he passes over, as the absence my italics is intended to suggest, the horrific, unearned misery and suffering of the world's
preterite or, in a more recent vocabulary, the "uncounted," at the hands of
the defining "elect."

The United States: The American Humanists' Interpretation of Melville's Silence after *The Confidence-Man*

Following the publication of *Billy Budd* in the United States, it was generally, but fundamentally, this British tragic humanist interpretation —
Man's transcendence in defeat by the *mere* forces ("the slings and ar-
rows") of contingent being often reduced to "accidents" — of the novella
and (retrospectively) *Moby-Dick* that was appropriated by prestigious
American academics between the 1930s and the 1950s. This, not incidentally was the period during which emergent academic "Americanists"
such as Lewis Mumford, F. O. Matthiessen, Newton Arvin, Warner Berthoff, among others, staged the world as the scene of a global struggle
between American (exceptionalist) democracy and totalitarianism, first
Nazism and Fascism and then Soviet Communism, and canonized *Billy
Budd* and *Moby-Dick* in America and apotheosized the hitherto silenced
and long forgotten Melville as something like the ideal spirit of magnanimous democratic American Man.

In 1941, in a subsection of *American Renaissance*, tellingly entitled
"Reassertion of the Heart" and in keeping with his celebration of the ideal
democracy envisaged by "American renaissance" writers, F. O. Matthiessen invoked *Billy Budd*, despite its setting on a British man-of-war during
the Napoleonic Wars, as a great American tragedy:

> [Melville] stated explicitly once again that his was a democratic stage,
> and affirmed the universality of passion in common men as well as in

kings. Just as, when dealing with Ahab or with Israel Potter, he had re-marked on the outer contrast between his material and Shakespeare's, so now he asserted that "Passion, and passion in its profoundest, is not a thing demanding a palatial stage whereon to play its part. Down among the groundlings, among the beggars and rakers of garbage, pro-found passion is enacted." He chose for his hero a young sailor, im-pressed into the King's service in the latter years of the eighteenth century, shortly after the Great Mutiny at the Nore. By turning to such material Melville made it clear that his thought was not bounded by a narrow nationalism, that the important thing was the inherent tragic quality, no matter where or when it was found. As he said in one of the prefaces to his verse: "It is not the purpose of literature to purvey news. For news consult the *Almanac de Gotha*."[17]

In the main body of his analysis of *Billy Budd*, Matthiessen, following the directives of the American Puritans' representation of their austere and demanding God, subordinates, if he does not entirely bracket the demo-cratic theme in favor of underscoring Melville's de-nationalization, that is, universalization of tragedy, which had hitherto been identified with an Old World structured in aristocratic class dominance. By way of over-determining the final, undisclosed interview between Billy and Vere, or, rather, of the "conjectures" of the narrator about what happened between the two, he seems to arrive at a conclusion about late Melville similar to, if more nuanced than, that of his British predecessors:

Here the search for a father, if latent in all Melville's Ishmaels, and in all the questings of his homeless spirit for authority, is enacted in an ele-mental pattern. Following out the Biblical parallels that have been sug-gested at crucial points throughout the story, if Billy is young Adam before the fall, and Claggart is almost the Devil incarnate, Vere is the wise Father, terribly severe but righteous. No longer does Melville feel the fear and dislike of Jehovah that were oppressing him through *Moby-Dick* and *Pierre*. He is no longer protesting against the determined laws as being savagely inexorable. *He has come to respect necessity.*

He can therefore treat a character like Vere's with full sympathy. As the two emerge from the cabin, the captain's face is a startling revela-tion to the senior lieutenant, since it is transfigured for a moment with "the agony of the strong." In contrast Billy appears serene. He had been shocked to the roots of his being by his first experience of the existence of evil; but the tension has been relaxed by the mutual trust that he found in the captain. [AR, pp. 509–510; my emphasis][18]

In Melville's late phase, Matthiessen goes on to add, as his "steady handling of his old distinctions between earthly truth and heavenly truth, between horologicals and chronometricals," testify, he "has *gained a balance* that was lacking to his angry defiance in *Pierre* and *The Confidence-Man*" (AR, p. 511; my emphasis). Like his British predecessors, Matthiessen not only obliterates the global political context in which the story of Billy Budd is embedded. Like them, he also brings to his reading a metaphysical perspective — implicit in his dubious assumption that "all Melville's Ishmaels" are homeless wanderers desperately in search of an authoritative homeland — that overlooks (blinds him to) the radically uneven power relations that obtain between Billy and Captain Vere, the common sailor and the minister of a higher order, in favor of a politically disabling necessity: an interpretation of being that dialectically reconciles uneven contradictions into a higher synthesis.

Unlike that of his British predecessors, however, Matthiessen's metaphysical perspective, as his inaugural remarks imply, is peculiarly American, that is, exceptionalist. This unspoken ideological perspective enables him, despite the actual historical setting, to read *Billy Budd* as a "tragedy" that is ultimately informed by a logic that perceives democracy in its original, American Puritan-inspired form, the form, that is, that produced the American Renaissance: as radically different from and superior not simply to aristocracy but also to the degenerating American democracy of Melville's "shallow age" (AR, p. 513). Invoking, at the end of an extremely convoluted and labored argument attempting to synthesizes the New England Puritans' biblical depth with the innocence of natural (pre-Gilded-Age) American man, Billy's blessing, which he refers to pointedly as "a common sailor's act of holy forgiveness," Matthiessen's commentary, taking on the lineaments of the American jeremiad (a genre underscored by his appropriation of the first person plural), concludes by returning to his beginning (and title):

Without minimizing the justice of Vere's stern mind, Melville could feel that the deepest need for rapaciously individualistic America was a radical affirmation of the heart. He knew that his conception of the young sailor's "essential innocence" was in accord with no orthodoxy; but he found it "an irruption of heretic thought hard to suppress. . . ."

How important it was to reaffirm the heart in the America in which *Billy Budd* was shaped can be corroborated by the search that was being made for the drift of significance in our eighteen-eighties and nineties by two of our most symptomatic minds. John Jay Chapman was already protesting against the conservative legalistic dryness that characterized our educated class, as fatal to real vitality; while Henry Adams, in assessing his heritage, knew that it tended too much towards the analytic mind, that it lacked juices. Those juices could spring only from the "depth of tenderness," the "boundless sympathy" to which Adams responded in the symbol of the Virgin, but which Melville — for the phrases are his — had found in great tragedy. After all he had suf- fered Melville could endure to the end in the belief that though good goes to defeat and death, its radiance can redeem life. His career did not fall into what has been too often assumed to be the pattern for the lives of our artists: brilliant beginnings without staying power, truncated and broken by our hostile environment, Melville's endurance is a chal- lenge for a later America. (AR, pp. 513–514)

Matthiessen's example, especially his emphasis on the tragedy's precipi- tation of the ideal American values of "boundless sympathy" and "depth of tenderness," set the itinerary for *Billy Budd* criticism in the post–World War II, that is, Cold War, period. In 1950, Newton Arvin, for example, notes the political context of *Billy Budd* — both the *Somers* Affair, involv- ing Melville's cousin Lieutenant Guert Gansevoort, which may have acti- vated his desire to write the story, and the (in)famous Mutiny at the Nore, which constitutes the historical background of the events on board the HMS *Bellipotent*. Like Matthiessen and the great majority of his pre- decessors, however, Arvin dismisses them as "matters of the surface; they have a genuine interest, but . . . say little about the real feeling of *Billy Budd*."[19] Instead he represents the story as a naturalized supernatural, "primordial" event, a "rewriting of the first three chapters of Genesis [the fall of man], this late-nineteenth-century *Paradise Lost*," which, though it alludes to Adam (Billy), Satan (Claggart), and Jehovah (Vere), is devoid of "the unequivocal spiritual and moral simplicity of the Christian legend or of any of its theological formulations" (HM, p. 296). For Arvin, following the often cited deleted sentence, "Here ends a story not unwarranted by what sometimes happens in this incomprehensible world of ours — Innocence and infamy, spiritual depravity and fair repute," "Melville's world is insuperably incomprehensible, and he makes no claim to comprehending it" (HM, pp. 296–297). What Melville does seem to be certain of, however, Arvin appears to claim, is how men comport themselves towards the suffering endemic in this incomprehensible world: the ability to love the good. Though, as the narrator observes, "Claggart could even have loved Billy but for fate and ban," it is, according to Arvin, "his miserable destiny . . . to be incapable of loving the good, indeed to be incapable of love itself, and there is no greater misery. For there is a solid reality in this incomprehensible universe, this universe of equivocations and contrarieties; it is the reality of 'the heart within you'. To mind 'the issues there' is to know that, even in the dark midst of evil and hate, goodness exists, and that its essential reality is that of love" (HM, p. 298).

This ability to love the good is what redeems Billy, and even more so, Captain Vere, since, unlike Billy, Vere's love of the good is "irrevocably at war with the life of the mind," and so he must suffer the pain of choosing:

> Captain Vere is a man with "a marked leaning towards everything intellectual," a passion for books and learning, and a habit of abstracted meditation. Yet he is an image of the high virtue in which the sternest sense of severe and painful duty is united to a capacity for the purest and tenderest love, the love of father for son. And it was in the full imaginative realization of that love, given and received, that Melville brought his work as a writer *to its serene conclusion*. (HM, p. 298; my emphasis)

Like Matthiessen, Arvin predictably ends his commentary by invoking the comment of the narrator (he refers to him as "Melville") about the final interview between Billy and Captain Vere in the stateroom where the former was confined: "What occurred there was never known, says Melville, but he adds that 'the austere devotee of military duty, letting himself melt back into what remains primeval in our formalized humanity, may in the end have caught young Isaac. . . . But there is no telling the sacrament . . . wherever . . . two of great Nature's nobler order embrace' " (HM,

p. 299). About this Arvin concludes: "Whatever took place in the state-room between the ideal father and the ideal son, its effect was indeed sacramental, an effect of the purest unction and the most complete recon-cilement" (HM, p. 299).

In his interpretation Arvin rather definitively displaces the Christian/Miltonic strain of some of the earlier interpretations of *Billy Budd* in favor of a (tragic) humanistic one that, like the myth critics of his day, sees the existential dynamics of lived life as archetypes. But what remains in tact is the certainty that the late Melville brings his life as a writer to its recon-ciled close. Speaking for all his predecessors Arvin writes: "Everyone has felt [*Billy Budd*] to be a work of a man on the last verge of mortal exis-tence who wishes to take his departure with a word of acceptance and reconciliation on his lips" (HM, p. 292). The archetypal humanist ethics Arvin attributes to the late Melville in the process of distinguishing *Billy Budd* from Christian interpretations is nonetheless a secularized transcen-dence that obliterates any semblance of the violent, life-damaging politics in the sociopolitical world the *Bellipotent* symbolizes in the name of an unworldly universal Man.

This curiously quiescent humanist interpretation of Melville's last work of fiction is brought to its apogee of subtlety and eloquence by Warner Berthoff in 1960.[20] Unlike the early British critics, but like F. O. Matthiessen and Newton Arvin, Berthoff refers pointedly to the historical context that constitutes the mise-en-scène of the events on board the *Bell-ipotent*. Indeed, he even goes so far as to allow the possibility (asserted as Melville's perspective by politically conservatives critics such as Milton R. Sterne and Richard Harter Fogle,[21] among others), that in this last work Melville, the ontological, moral, and sociopolitical radical of *Moby-Dick*, *Pierre*, *Israel Potter*, "Bartleby," "Benito Cereno," and *The Confidence-Man*, has come to adhere to "a philosophical anti-Jacobinism":

> So *Billy Budd* opens with several chapters on the historical back-
> ground — the war with revolutionary France, the naval mutinies — and
> repeatedly turns aside to show how this bears upon the action. In fact,
> Melville goes further and introduces or intimates what might seem to
> be even more restrictive considerations, aligning Captain Vere (and
> himself as narrator) with a philosophical anti-Jacobinism, calling one
> ship the *Rights-of-Man* [the slippage here should not go unnoticed] and
> another the *Athéiste*, and so forth. (EM, p. 185)

As the dismissive "and so forth" signals, Berthoff goes on, however, to assert that, despite his implicit conservative politics (curiously, the possibility that Melville's politics are "radical," that is, pro-revolutionary, is outside Berthoff's problematic, that is, beyond the circumference of his vision),[22] Melville does not intend this historical context "to explain the story. The historical circumstances touch on the story at every crisis but do not essentially determine it" (EM, p. 185). For him, it seems, Melville's alleged "allusion" to his anti-Jacobinism should not be taken to imply, as it had been by Norman Holmes Pearson,[23] that "*Billy Budd* is best understood by analogy to Milton's heroic poems," that is, as his politico-religious sympathy with a Christian England against an atheist France. Though he acknowledges the Christian allusions, they nevertheless "prove nothing in themselves about either his intention or his achievement," since these are merely metaphors (among others from different registers) that even in Melville's time, to say nothing about the modern age, had lost their "sacramental" character (EM, p. 186). Besides, such an attempt, "comparable to Milton's, to reanimate the Christian myth of human destiny under divine law is to "claim for Melville the kind of positive testament or settled belief which seems inconsistent with what we know of him" (EM, p. 188). In opposition to the Christian allegorical interpretation of *Billy Budd* (and its politically conservative implications), Berthoff, like Matthiessen and Arvin, reads the novella as Melville's dramatization of the supreme value of human magnanimity in the face of the devastating adversities of mortal existence: "The motions of magnanimity under the most agonizing worldly duress: that is Melville's 'image and his theme'" (EM, p. 200). And its exemplar, predictably, is Nelson at Trafalgar: "Nelson's greatness in command is assumed; what concerned Melville was his personal behavior at Trafalgar and the charge of 'vainglory' and 'affectation' it lay open to. And though Melville was on the defensive here, he unequivocally championed the impulse of the great-hearted hero to display his greatness and love the glory of it" (EM, p. 196).[24]

In a promising gesture, Berthoff rejects the view of the critics who interpreted the martial law by which the innocent young sailor is condemned to death as "symbolic of some universal law or authority, such as divine providence." For him, rather, it is specific to the *Bellipotent's* historical occasion, "War's child." Yet, inexplicably, martial law for Berthoff is also "morally *sui generis*, and in its terms morally unimpeachable" (EM,

p. 189). Berthoff goes on to acknowledge the "rigid contest" in which Melville's story "so easily rides" and that "what it gains from it are absorbing questions," but he adds, astonishingly, that these questions are "beyond the compass of the present essay" (EM, p. 189). On the basis of this fragilely justified dismissal, one can only conclude that Berthoff, like Matthiessen and Arvin, circumvents these burning questions pertaining to the *undiscriminating* violence of martial law in order to impose in the end the anthropological (as opposed to theological) ethical conclusion concerning the events on board the *Bellipotent* that he holds from the beginning, thus contradicting his alleged humanist disinterestedness.

More specifically, Berthoff, like Matthiessen and Arvin, invokes, at the expense of these visible differential contradictions, the narrator's resonant ethical conjectures (for him too they are unquestionably Melville's) on what happened during the undisclosed private interview between Captain Vere and Billy (chapter 23), which he takes to be at the revelatory heart of the story. These speak of the narrator's profound sense that, "*translated out of their customary station*," Billy and Vere come together "as two of great Nature's nobler order" — that is, *as equals* — and in this uncircumstantial or, in Edward Said's word, unworldly, world, this nowhere, as it were, where alone all things are equal, they enact the inexpressible human sacrament of "magnanimity," by which Berthoff means, with Aristotle, "greatness of soul" (EM, p. 193; my emphasis).

> In Vere and Billy, the passage [pertaining to the narrator's conjectures] affirms, we have to do with magnanimity, with greatness of soul, a quality which, though "all but incredible to average minds however much cultivated," is nevertheless according to nature, and is touched with divinity — or whatever in human conduct is suggestive of divinity. . . . As there is a mystery of iniquity in Claggart, there is a mystery of magnanimity in these two. *It is given no power to prevent the now settled outcome of the action. Yet its radiance is beyond catastrophe. It is such as can survive those accidents of individual existence — age, health, station, luck, particular experience — which Melville consistently presented the lives of his characters as being determined by.* Now the narrative has come to its defining climax. Here the tone is set for what remains to be told, and not at the pitch of tragedy — *the tone of exalted acceptance and muted patient joy* which will be heard in the ac-

count of Billy in irons like a "slumbering child," in Billy's "God bless Captain Vere!" in Vere's dying with Billy's name on his lips (not remorse, Melville specifies), and finally, and with what sure art, in the gravely *acquiescent music* of the closing ballad. (EM, pp. 193–194; my emphasis)

In thus overdetermining Melville's (the narrator's) deep attunement to the "unspeakable" mystery — the "radiance" — of human "magnanimity," in other words, Berthoff's immediate intention, like Arvin's (Matthiessen's is unclear on this point), is to displace the Christian/Miltonic interpretation of *Billy Budd* by a humanist/Miltonic reading. But his ultimate purpose, as his repeated references to Aristotle's *Nicomachaean Ethics* imply, is to identify the late Melville with the Western humanist tradition (and its human rights ethic of tolerance). By this he means the tradition that allegedly begins in the "sweetness and light" of classical Greece, is recuperated in the Enlightenment, and, as his location of magnanimity "at the heart of the democratic ethos" and his attribution of greatness of soul to Washington and Lincoln, "whose unique place in the national pantheon is surely something more than the sum of their historical deeds" (EM, p. 194) suggest, culminates in the American Renaissance. As recent scholarship has gone far to prove, however, the humanist tradition that Berthoff invokes in fact was inaugurated in the period of the European Renaissance and the Enlightenment by way of the Romanization of originative Greek thinking and the apotheosis of (imperial) Man.[25]

Read against the grain, that is, according to the directives suggested by my contrapuntal emphases on the slighted terms in the above passages, Berthoff's reading of *Billy Budd* discloses the following related propositions. First, though it undermines the authority of the Christian Miltonic (theo-logical) reading of late Melville in favor of a humanist reading, the latter turns out to be a *secularization* of the Christian *Logos,* a natural supernaturalism or a political theology, as his systematic use of Christian language — "mystery," "sacrament," "sacrifice," "spirit," "divinity" "priestly motive," and so on — as metaphors for the essential qualities of magnanimity suggest.[26] As such this classical brand of humanism is informed by an optimistic anthropological perspective — and a binarist logic that, no less than the providential theological one, is justified in coercing by violence the (lowly) difference into the (higher) Same in the name of peace: in this case,

natural- and man-made violence into the humanistic system at the determinative center of which is "magnanimous Man." Second, despite the
democratic appearance of apotheosizing the lowly seaman, in actuality it
represents him as a member of a deviant multitude that is essentially inferior and threatening to the elect — those who are the intellectual deputies
of the humanistic Word — and the justifiable act of self-protection on the
part of the absolutely powerless against the ubiquity of power as a capital
crime punishable by death. Third, behind its celebration of magnanimity as
the essence of (American) Man and its democratic scope, this optimistic
humanistic ethic conceals its determination by a rigid systemic ontological
and sociopolitical order that, in assuming it possesses the truth, is justified
in instituting a state of exception whenever its peace is threatened by dissent. Which is to say, it obscures the normalization of the state of exception,
the transformation of the exception into a permanent condition.

In putting these disclosures in this way, my intention is to reconstellate
the Melville of *Moby-Dick*, *Pierre*, "Bartleby," "Benito Cereno," and, not
least, *The Confidence-Man* into the context of the late Melville from which
they have been excised. What is revealing about Berthoff's reading of *Billy
Budd* — and all those that approach the novel from this essentially optimist
classical humanist perspective — is the absence of reference to the supreme
theme of the work of Melville's prime: the subversive one that convinced
the custodians of the American national identity that he had to be frozen
into silence. I am referring to his Voltairean parodic genealogical critique of
the American optimism whose origins lay in the myth of American exceptionalism: that paradoxical exceptionalism, that is, which, like the Old
World from which, in assuming its election and its possession of the "true
light," it distinguished itself, monomaniacally subsumed natural and man
made disasters — the catastrophic that Berthoff so easily dismisses — under
a benign higher synthesis: the best of all possible worlds.

I shall return to the indissoluble relationship between these texts of
Melville's prime and his last work, *Billy Budd,* later in this book. Here, in
the context of Berthoff's elegantly articulated (American) humanistic argument, which rests on his translation of Captain Vere and Billy Budd "out of
their customary station," that is, their worldly occasion, it suffices to retrieve and juxtapose against it one of Melville's most resonant articulations
of this subversive critique of American Panglossian optimism, the con men
it enabled, and the disabling humanistic ethics of acceptance it inscribed

hegemonically in the national identity. Early in *The Confidence-Man*, the mise-en-scène of which, not incidentally, is another ship of state, the ironic "man with the travelling cap" (an avatar of the ironic Confidence-Man), having listened to the troubled merchant's tale about the "unfortunate man" whose aptly named wife, Goneril, had transformed her devastating depravity into moral capital by appealing to the prevailing optimistic system, responds:

> Still, he [the man with the traveling cap] was far from the illiberality of denying that philosophy duly bounded was permissible. Only he deemed it at least desirable that, when such a case as that alleged of the unfortunate man was made the subject of philosophic discussion, it should be so philosophized upon, as not to afford handles to those unblessed with the true light. For, but to grant there was so much as a mystery about such a case, might by those persons be held for a tacit surrender of the question. And as for the apparent license temporarily permitted sometimes, to the bad over the good (as was by implication alleged with regard to Goneril and the unfortunate man), it might be injudicious there to lay too much polemic stress upon the doctrine of future retribution as the vindication of present impunity. For though, indeed, to the right-minded that doctrine was true, and of sufficient solace, yet with the perverse the polemic mention of it might but provoke the shallow, though mischievous conceit, that such a doctrine was but tantamount to the one which should affirm that Providence was not now, but was going to be. In short, with all sorts of cavilers, it was best, both for them and for everybody, that whoever had the true light should stick behind the secure Malakoff of confidence, nor be tempted forth to hazardous skirmished on the open ground of reason. Therefore, he deemed it inadvisable in the good man, even in the privacy of his own mind, or in communion with a congenial one, to indulge in too much latitude of philosophizing, or, indeed, of thinking and feeling which might unexpectedly betray him upon unsuitable occasions.[27]

As we have seen, Warner Berthoff's conclusion that the late Melville arrives at an "exalted acceptance and mute patient joy" — which also means a transcendent acquiescence — is based on the scene in which Captain Vere asserts that martial law is "*sui generis*": his execution of a common sailor he knows to be innocent in the name of an absolute "higher truth." On the other hand, virtually all of the fiction of Melville's prime constitute variations of the subversion of a sociopolitical system based on "the true light": a "regime of truth," in Foucault's apt phrase, that is grounded precisely on the kind of philosophy of confidence that, as the passage from *The Confidence-Man* quoted above implies, must necessarily accommodate or, if accommodation is not possible, obliterate, any thought or action that threatens to undermine the august sovereignty of the higher cause. When Melville's ferocious commitment to submitting the "true light" to the jagged edges of history in the heretical work of his prime is remembered, one cannot but conclude that Berthoff's "disinterested" humanist reading is either the consequence of a willful forgetting of this reality or a blindness intrinsic to the "oversight" of his humanist problematic. In other words, it becomes ideologically complicit with the violence endemic to this (American) philosophy of optimism.

In sum, those classical or Christian humanists critics and commentators of the Melville revival period, both English and American, who canonized the author on the basis of the posthumous publication of *Billy Budd* (as well as those who represented the late Melville as a political conservative), not only attributed his thirty-five-year silence after *The Confidence-Man* (1857), when they spoke of it at all, to an enervation of imaginative energy or to dire economic circumstances. They also represented the breaking of his silence at the end of his life as his achievement of "a majestic serenity" (Murry), his "testament of acceptance" (Watson), his utterance of "the everlasting yea" (John Freeman, Weaver), his coming "to respect necessity" (Matthiessen); his departure taking "with a word of acceptance and reconciliation on his lips" (Arvin), his rising into "exalted acceptance and muted patient joy" (Berthoff). These critics could not entertain the manifestly reasonable possibility that Melville's silence after *The Confidence-Man* was induced by the intellectual deputies of the dominant American culture who had found the public (fictional) work of his prime dangerously subversive of the ontological, cultural, and political values endemic to the myth of American exceptionalism. Nor could they see that his breaking of that silence—that is, decision to return to the public sphere—at the end of his damaged life was not a matter of his reconciliation with or acceptance of the contingent conditions, ontological or sociopolitical, of the world he inhabited, but rather a late gesture of subversion, now, however, in the highly nuanced, elusive—or spectral—

exilic idiom he had signaled in Bartleby's silence — his refusal to be answerable to the American calling (his "I prefer not to") — and had begun to develop into the dizzyingly ironic language of directed indirection in *The Confidence-Man.*

The Disabling Influence of Harrison Hayford and Merton Sealts's "Definitive Edition" of *Billy Budd, Sailor* (1962)

In focusing on the early humanist (Christian and classical) commentary and criticism of *Billy Budd*, I do not want to give the impression that there were no opposing views to that which read the novella as, in one form or another, the late Melville's "testament of acceptance." There were, in fact, such opposing views of *Billy Budd* that coalesced around what one of this opposition pointedly called Melville's "testament of resistance."[28] What I am suggesting, rather, is the following: (1) The histories of the criticism of *Billy Budd* to which I have been referring greatly exaggerated the quantity and critical authority of this "resistance" criticism. (2) In so doing, they obscured the fact that the former was dominant in the period between 1920 and the mid-1960s and beyond. (3) They retrospectively affected the reading of the texts of Melville's prime, above all the positive reception of *Moby-Dick* (thus contributing, inadvertently, perhaps, to the harnessing of that novel to the Cold War) and the lukewarm, if not hostile, reception of *Pierre* and *The Confidence-Man.* Above all, in the name of disinterested inquiry, they concealed their ideological bias against a criticism that interpreted the late Melville's work as *continuous with*, rather than as a turning away from, the fiction from *Moby-Dick* to *The Confidence-Man* — the *American* fiction that was intensely critical of the myth of American exceptionalism and the optimistic exceptionalist political praxis it justified. That is to say, these "histories" obscured their complicity with the dominant conservative politic discourse that elided America exceptionalism with the state of exception.

This ideological bias, as I have argued in chapter 1, lies behind Harrison Hayford and Merton Sealts's "disinterested" scholarly preface to their "definitive reading" edition of *Billy Budd*. There, it will be recalled, in arguing from their meticulous analysis of the various incremental stages of Melville's revisions of the manuscript, they not only virtually effaced the politically fraught global historical context — and its implications for a later globally expanding America — which the story of Billy Budd's execution reflects. They also insistently criticized ideological readings primarily for failing to perceive, or for being indifferent to, Melville's increasingly deliberate effort, allegedly most visible in the latest stage of his revisions (which brings Captain Vere and his conflicted consciousness to prominence) to "dramatize" the story, by which they mean to infuse it with and undecidable "ambiguity":

> The disagreements and prolonged contentions among what Melville might have called "the critical experts" are but the proper issue of his requiring every reader to "determine for himself." But the rhetorical question "Who in the rainbow can draw the line . . . ?" should be a warning to critics who find the lines of demarcation in the story easy to determine and who suppose Melville's own attitude was altogether clear cut. To Melville's mind, after all, the question was not simply the rightness or wrongness, sanity or insanity, of the captain's action, but also the very existence of a problematical world in which such a story as he had been so long developing and brooding upon was (in his guarded phrase) "not unwarranted." His story was an epitome in art, of such a world. (BB, pp. 38–39)

Despite the publication between 1970 and the present of a number of strong essays on *Billy Budd* that significantly deepened the few, admittedly thin, earlier commentaries that read the novel as Melville's ironically articulated "testament of resistance" — I am thinking especially of the important work of Edgar Dryden, Joyce Sparer Adler, and Brook Thomas, and most recently, Eve Kosofsky Sedgwick, Nancy Ruttenburg, Sharon Cameron, and Gregory Jay[29] — this conservative ideological perspective masked as anti-ideological seems to have remained in tact for the "Melvillians" — those critics and scholars who have dominated what has become the Melville industry. For example, in a summary analysis of *Billy Budd* criticism published in 1998, twenty-seven years after Hayford and Sealts's history, Robert Milder writes:

> Reductive and crudely argued, ironist readings [by which he means those that interpret the novel as a testament of resistance, not those of the New Critics, who identified irony with the autotelic work], were easy game for an incisive critic like [Edward H.] Rosenberry [who at-

tacked the "shoddy reasoning" of the ironists from the more "authentic" perspective of the "straight readers"], yet at the core of the ironist position was an emotional truth that could not easily be denied: *a feeling of outrage at Billy's execution as visceral and overwhelming as the acceptance critics' feeling of exaltation.* Nearly every reader shares both emotions to some degree, opposite though they are and resistant though they seem to thematic reconciliation. The preference for a straight or an ironic reading of *Billy Budd* depends partly on whether one responds primarily to the serenity of Melville's prose [*sic*] or to the horror or his action — and beyond that, perhaps, on the moral susceptibility that causes one reader to shiver at Billy's "God bless Captain Vere!" and another (as [Joseph] Schiffman says) to "gag." The humbling reality, in any case, is that Melville seems [*sic*] to contain both emotions not simply at once but *as one*, and that the history of the acceptance/resistance debate is the disheartening spectacle of two parties almost constitutionally unable to appreciate each other's hold on the truth *and thereby rise to the fullness of Melville's.*[30]

Despite his nonpartisan gesture, which both expresses sympathy for and antagonism to the two schools' perspectives, Milder's "higher," more disinterested, point of view, like that of Hayford and Sealts, whose edition of *Billy Budd* he seems to accept as definitive, turns out to be simply a more sophisticated variation of the "party" committed to the interpretation of *Billy Budd* as Melville's testament of acceptance. Milder's omission of reference, which is to say, his indifference, to the question of the politics of martial law (the state of exception) that pervades Melville's text — and cries out for attention, not least in the context of the Cold War era in which Milder is writing — is not alone in bearing witness to this. It is also testified to by his easy *equation* of Captain Vere's mental suffering (expressed in Billy's blessing) and the dreadful execution by hanging of the innocent sailor, an equation that sublimates the absolute power over life of the martial law the captain upholds in the name of the state and the absolute powerlessness — the bare life — of the common seaman impressed by violence, into a higher synthesis, which Milder, rather arrogantly, takes to be "the fullness of Melville's" "truth."[31]

Also writing as an member of an alleged saving remnant, this time bearing the vulnerable Word of Hayford and Sealts, Hershel Parker, in

1990 obscures the fact that it is the latter's definitive reading text, if not their genetic text, that, with minor and basically inconsequential exceptions, has been used by critics and scholars ever since its publication in 1962.[32] Parker's critique of the critics who followed Hayford and Sealts's edition of *Billy Budd* is ostensibly directed against their failure to attend to the latter's disclosure that Melville's text is unfinished, that is, thematically unresolved and, therefore, resistant to definitive, that is, ideological, interpretations. It is everywhere clear in his book, however, that his real criticism is directed against critical perspectives, emerging in the context of the protest movement during the Vietnam War — and theoretically emanating from Europe (the "Old World") — that was politicizing Melville's text, indeed, reading it (and his earlier fiction) as a radical political critique of a conservative society of law and order. Citing Sealts's retrospective account of the reception of his and Hayford's scholarship in 1986, Parker, in a humanistic argument that grossly dedifferentiates the New Criticism and the various other emergent theoretical perspectives, above all, the neo-Marxist, writes in 1990:

> As was already clear when Sealts wrote, the New Critical attitude to-
> ward authorial intention [the assumption of the autonomy of the liter-
> ary text] had dominated a succession of theoretical approaches to
> literature since the 1950s — including phenomenology, structuralism,
> and deconstruction. In the 1980s it conspicuously dominated the New
> Historicism, an approach which (contrary to its self-bestowed name)
> avoids historical, biographical, and textual research. This Marxist-
> derived approach denies that a literary work is created by an individual
> author's mind but instead sees a work as being "generated" by a social
> context. . . . These theorists acknowledge that their dread of being in-
> fluenced by the power of an individual creative artist forces them to de-
> vise strategies for being sure that they can control the text.[33]

Similarly, Parker's ostensible purpose in defending Hayford and Sealts's revisions of Weaver's and Freeman's editions (including the 1953 version containing the corrections made by Elizabeth Treeman) by way of his "Chapter-by-Chapter Reading of *Billy Budd, Sailor*" is to demonstrate that Melville left his text uncompleted and thus, like his colleagues, to conclude that any interpretation of such an "inherently problematical" text claiming to be decisive is a spurious imposition. "In this reading of the novel," he writes, "I will avoid the stance of an ideologue of the right or the left" (RBB, p. 98). In attending to his ideologically "neutral" argument from the perspective of poststructuralist theory's problematization of disinterested inquiry, however, one cannot help but perceive that Parker's avowed objective scholarship, like Hayford's and Sealts's, is everywhere, in fact, informed by a conservative ideology. This is manifest in his exaggeration of the alleged importance of the differences between Hayford and Sealts's "definitive" reading text and the earlier ones of Weaver and Freeman, an exaggeration that obscures the lopsided predominance of socially and politically conservative readings in the history of the criticism and commentary of *Billy Budd*.[34] It is also manifest in Parker's acceptance of his predecessors' arbitrary inclusion of the Nelson chapter, which, according to their and his own readings of the Genetic Text, was problematic both as to whether or not Melville intended to include it in the final version and, not least, as to the finality of its form; of their representation of the age in which Nelson flourished as a gloriously poetic one (as opposed to the narrator's prosaic present); and of Nelson as Melville's exalted model of the heroic leader. Above all, this political conservatism, like that of his Melvillean colleagues, is manifest in Parker's insistent — that is, labored — effort not simply to trivialize the politically fraught global historical context in which the terrible events on board the HMS *Bellipotent* occur by way of effacing the "Preface" that introduced the earlier editions of *Billy Budd*, the matter of which, as I have observed, is contained more or less intact in chapter 3 (and elsewhere) in Hayford and Sealts's edition, but also to represent these epochal historical events as patent manifestations of Melville's arrival in his old age at the anti-revolutionary "wisdom" of political conservatism:

> Here . . . for the first time [Parker is referring to the illegitimacy of the "Preface"] Melville dates the action to the summer of 1797 and defines what he had meant earlier by "hurried day," the time following the rebellion at Spithead (April) and the Nore (May). In this passage he defines the Great Mutiny in a voice like that of Edmund Burke, not Thomas Paine: the bluejackets who ran the British colors up the flagstaff with the union and cross wiped out had "by that cancellation" transmuted "the flag of founded law and freedom defined, into the enemy's red meteor of unbridled and unbounded revolt" [BB, p. 54].

Melville's point of view at this point is clear — that of a traditionalist, a deeply conservative man apprehensive at the thought that insurrection might shake England, *which was then "all but the sole free conservative" power "of the Old World."* We are told that some of the demands made by the mutineers at the Nore were deemed by the authorities as "not only inadmissible but aggressively insolent" [BB, p. 55]. Rather than focusing on the injustices toward sailors, Melville is interested in and appalled by, the French-inspired irrational combustion into which those grievances were ignited.[35]

Seemingly oblivious to the possibility that the phrases about the Great Mutiny Parker quotes from Melville's text to support his argument could be read as the opposite of what he says they mean — in my close reading of the novella in chapter 3, I comment at length especially on Hayford and Sealts's and Parker's appropriation of the narrator's invocation of British exceptionalism vis-à-vis the rest of Europe in behalf of their argument — he goes on to invoke Melville's telling comment "that the Great Mutiny is one of the suppressed episodes of [British] history, one about which information is hard to come by, even 'in libraries' " (BB, p. 55) to underscore how utterly shameful and degrading the Great Mutiny was to the national honor of the British empire. And, in explaining the narrator's reference to similar events "befalling states everywhere, including America," that "national pride along with views of policy would fain shade off into the historical background" — that is, would efface — he gives the following (patently incommensurate) example: "We know the sort of thing [Melville] had in mind from his comments in *Clarel* (pt. 4, canto 9, 'The Shepherds' Dale') about America's own national sins, memory of which had been suppressed — the North's blockade which kept medicines from the South during the Civil War" (RBB, p. 109). In so doing, Parker precludes the possibility, far more in keeping with Melville's lifelong ethics as well as his politics (Melville's devastating genealogical criticism of monumental history in *Israel Potter* is a propos here),[36] of reading the suppression of the Great Mutiny as the violent act of a politically reactionary imperial regime — authorized by the state of exception — intent on enforcing obedience from its oppressed subjects at all costs. Analogously, he disables the possibility of interpreting the obliteration of the event of the Great Mutiny from the annals of British history by the custodians of the national memory as an act of cultural repression intent on obliterating the memory of that politically reactionary violence.[37] These "caviling" possibilities, which, to use Melville's own language, are precluded by "sticking behind the secure Malakoff of confidence" rather than being "tempted forth to hazardous skirmished on the open ground of reason," are, as I shall show, in the next chapter, underscored when they are considered in the light of the terrifically ironic addendum to the "inside narrative" (the penultimate chapter of *Billy Budd)*, in which the singular events on board the *Bellipotent* are airbrushed from history by the official historians of the British Navy in the name of "the true light."

This same ideological anti-ideological perspective on the history of the criticism of Melville's novel is repeated in miniature form by the Melvillean scholar Donald Yannella, in his "Introduction" to *New Essays on Billy Budd*, published in 2002, in the prestigious Cambridge University Press series on the American novel.[38] Assuming the questionable role of spokesperson for a saving remnant that would conserve the essential Melville from marauding leftist barbarians, Yannella in this essay points, more overtly than his predecessors, to the "stream of politically charged readings" of *Billy Budd* that had "emerged in the past twenty-five years," that is, from "the framework, established by post-modernist, post-structuralist, 'critical theory' " (YI, p. 12; the quotation marks, I assume, imply fraudulence). Invoking Robert Milder's "sane" summary history — that " 'the warring factions of acceptance and resistance critics . . . subsume an ambiguous text to their characteristic ways of orienting the world and assigning it value' " — he adds that "many [of these] have unblushingly promoted political and social agendas, ideological positions — in short made Melville's text fit their own purposes, frequently with an intensity greater than their predecessors" (ibid.). In opposition to this degrading critical practice — another name for it would be "worlding" or, more radically, "profaning" — this spokesperson for an alleged saving humanist remnant invokes the civilized ideal of disinterestedness, understood from the New Critical perspective:

> This subjectivism is what the scholars in this collection seek to avoid.
> . . . The political and social implications of *Billy Budd* have dominated discussions among general readers as well as scholars . . . since the so-called New Criticism began to wane and presumably dissolve. . . . What

has all too often been lost by activist modern readers is that Melville was not an activist, nor was he a social, political, or behavioral scientist. He was a *literary artist* composing intellectually charged fiction and poetry about cultural issues which are markedly different from all but a handful of commentaries and treatises published by "soft" scientists.[39]

Like his predecessors, Yannella greatly overestimates the authority of the criticism that identifies the Melville of *Billy Budd* with political resistance. But what is especially striking about this latest, 2002, Melvillean version of the history of *Billy Budd* criticism is its manifest anachronism. In identifying Melville as "literary artist" (as if this precluded his work from being political or worldly in the Saidian sense) and then invoking the "disinterestedness" of the New Criticism against the "framework established by the postmodernist, post-structuralist, 'critical theory,'" Yannella's history makes clearer than its predecessors that for these Melvillean historians, as for the official historians who rewrote the history of the events on board the *Bellipotent*, the critical revolution that had decisively shown that disinterested inquiry, whether the Arnoldian or New Critical variety, was ideological had never happened.

In drawing on poststructuralist theory's demystification of the "disinterestedness" of the traditional humanist discourse that has dominated commentary on *Billy Budd*, I do not want to imply a blind commitment to that aspect of its practice that first gained prominence in the United States in the 1970s and early 1980s. I am referring to the deconstructive mode of interpretation that, in the very process of exposing the metaphysics — the perception of the things themselves from after or above them (*meta-ta-physica*) or panoptically — and, in so doing, the will to power informing the allegedly disinterested comportment towards being of classical humanism, on the one hand, and the principle of presence, of identity, of totality informing classical humanism's alleged adherence to difference, to individuality, and democracy, on the other, reduced its original polyvalent emancipatory potentialities by restricting them to the site of (an unworldly) textuality. Though the deconstructionists' dismantling of the world structured by metaphysical thinking was enabling in the sense of dis-closing or liberating the polyvalent possibilities that had been closed off by the metaphysical structuration of being (and the world) in dominance, this American version of deconstruction, as I observed long ago, reduced the temporality — the polyvalent be-*ing* — of being it disclosed to the disciplinary site of language, thus becoming a New Criticism in reverse.[40] In reducing the historicity of history to a free-floating textuality, in other words, it, like the "disinterestedness" of liberal humanist inquiry and the "objectivity" of the New Criticism, *equalized the radical imbalance of power relations* that always obtains in *this* world, metamorphosing the historical world into a no-place/no-time where, alone, all things are equal. In Edward Said's more political formulation, in opting for — and reducing to a rule — Derrida's notion that "Il n'y a pas d'hors text" (There is nothing outside the text), the American version of deconstruction unworlded the world.[41]

This stricture applies in some significant — and, in my mind, disabling — degree not only to the otherwise brilliant and deservedly prestigious "deconstructive" reading of *Billy Budd*, "Melville's Fist: The Execution of Billy Budd," by Barbara Johnson, but also to more recent Americanist readings of Melville's novella that have followed the general textualist directives of deconstruction (indeed, of Johnson's) reading such as those of Eve Kosofsky Sedgwick, Nancy Ruttenburg, and Sharon Cameron. As in the case of Johnson, these later critics demonstrate greater attunement to the radicality — the de-centeredness — of Melville's irony than both those Old Americanists who read the narrative straightforwardly, that is, identified the narrator with Melville, and those in the ironist camp who understood Melville's irony in the traditional liberal humanist sense of its meaning. In taking the deconstructivist notion of textual undecidability too literally, however, they not only equalize the inordinately — and quite visible — unequal power relations on board the *Bellipotent*; they also, necessarily — and like their traditionalist predecessors — de-historicize the evental historical context, thus rendering the Britain and France of the Napoleonic wars and the America of Melville's occasion allegorical.[42] Since Barbara Johnson's deservedly well-known deconstructive essay inaugurated and is exemplary of this more recent Americanist reduction to symmetry of the radically lopsided disparity between the powerful and the powerless, the elect and the preterite, I shall, for the sake of economy, restrict my critique of this politically disabling unworlding of the world of the *Bellipotent* to her essay.

Following her brilliant reading of Billy's stutter — that it " 'mars' the [traditional allegorical] plot in that it triggers the reversal of roles between Billy and Claggart," Johnson writes: "Yet in another sense this reversal does not mar the plot, it constitutes it. Here, as in the story of Eden, what the envious 'marplot' mars is not the plot, but the state of plotlessness that exists 'in the beginning.' What both the Book of Genesis and *Billy Budd* narrate is thus not the story of a fall but a fall into story."[43] By "the fall into story," Johnson is referring to that mode of language (writing) that, according to Jacques Derrida (and Paul de Man), the metaphysical West has historically subordinated to speech because it has "fallen away," become "separated from," the self-identical voice — the voice that hears and understands simultaneously (*s'entendre*) and is thus contaminated by aporias (gaps) and undecidability (*différance*). The "fall into story" enacted by *Billy Budd*, in other words, could be read as the fall from eternity into time and history. But this latter is not what Johnson concludes, since she reduces the historically specific context — the martial law or the state of exception under which the singular events that terminate in the execution of Billy Budd are enacted — to the functioning of plot understood from a deconstructive perspective, that is, as a writing that always already defers the presence it would bring to stand and thus renders it undecidable. "If all plots somehow tell the story of their own marring," she writes, "then perhaps it could be said that all plots are plots against authority, that authority creates the scene of its own destruction, that all stories necessarily recount by their very existence the subversion of the father, of the gods, of consciousness, of order, of expectations, or of meaning" (MF, p. 88).

Unlike most of her humanist predecessors, Johnson, to her credit, introduces history into the context by way of Captain Vere's "political" reading of the situation on board the *Bellipotent*, but in so doing, her intention is to identify history with textuality:

> The fundamental factor that underlies the opposition between the metaphysical Budd/Claggart conflict on the one hand and the reading of Captain Vere on the other can be summed up in a single word: history. While the naive and the ironic readers [Billy and Claggart, acceptance and resistance critics] attempt to impose upon language the functioning of an absolute, timeless, universal law (the sign as either motivated or arbitrary), the question of *martial* law arises within the story precisely to reveal the law as a historical phenomenon, to underscore the element of contextual mutability in the conditions of any act of reading. Arbitrariness and motivation, irony and literality, are pa-

rameters between which language constantly fluctuates, but only historical context determines which proportion of each is perceptible to each reader. Melville indeed shows history to be a story not only of events but also of fluctuations in the very functioning of irony and belief (MF, pp. 100–101).

Thus the purpose of Johnson's analysis of Captain Vere's judgment against Billy Budd at the court-martial — the decidable story into which the historical situation compels him even against his deepest feelings to put Billy and Claggart — is to show that Vere's externalization of ambiguities inhering in (textualized) history into binary opposites (into a decidable plot) constitutes a violence against *différance* similar to the violence of *all* plots. Johnson's intention, that is to say, is to show that historical judgment (*praxis*), like deciding about the meaning of a text, is essentially impossible:

> It would seem . . . that the function of judgment is to convert an ambiguous situation into a decidable one. But it does so by converting a difference *within* (Billy as divided between conscious submissiveness and unconscious hostility, Vere as divided between understanding father and military authority) into a difference (between Claggart amd Billy, between Nature and the King, between authority and criminality). A difference *between* opposing forces presupposes that the entities in conflict be knowable. A difference *within* one of the entities in question is precisely what problematizes the very *idea* of an entity in the first place, rendering the "legal point of view" inapplicable. In studying the plays of both ambiguity and binarity, Melville's story situates *its* critical difference neither within nor between, but in the *relations between the two* as the fundamental question of all human politics. (MF, p. 106)

From her infinitely negative textual perspective, then, Johnson sees Claggart and Billy and Vere and Billy *as equals* or, to put it alternatively, is blinded to the possibility that the "difference *between* opposing forces" in the *historical world* can also activate the recognition of the radical inequality of power relationships and thus the will to redress this murderous imbalance of power. Her anti-universal universalist deconstructive problematic reduces the imbalance of power that obtains between Billy, on the one hand, and the sociopolitical constituency composed of Claggart, Captain Vere, the British Navy, and the British state, on the other, to the same, thus canceling each's singularity out. As in the case of Rousseau in Derrida's reading, Claggart becomes "Claggart," Billy becomes "Billy," Vere becomes "Vere," and so forth. Johnson's textual frame of reference positively reduces to invisibility the very visible singular reality that Billy, as his brutal impressment suggests, doesn't stand a chance in the political "plot" — the narrative of the sovereign exception — that, like an animal, he's trapped in. In other words, it renders her necessarily blind to the possibility that Melville can *both* challenge the principle of presence — take his lead from the "marplot" — the *dia-bolos* (the one who throws apart) — *and* still make moral and political judgments about historically specific injustices.

In espousing a mode of reading that does not judge, that is, in disabling the ability to make judgments, Johnson, as Brook Thomas has argued in one of the most powerful essays on *Billy Budd* I've read, is, in fact, like her disinterested humanist predecessors, making a judgment, one that is complicit with the existing structure of power:

> It has been my aim in this essay to use the encounter between deconstruction and *Billy Budd* to show that deconstruction's strategy of closer than close reading [the reference is to Paul de Man's famous deconstructive critique of the New Criticism] is not enough. Rather than giving a more sensitive reading of man's fate, deconstruction works to seal man's fate by confining man to an ahistorical, textual world. Man becomes truly impressed. The ragged edges of *Billy Budd* do not disappear into textuality; they lead outward into history, the realm in which the reader lives and must judge. The text of *Billy Budd* deconstructs the ground of its own textual authority not to render the reader silent but to appeal for a judgment. It is through our acts of judgment that the text of *Billy Budd* in turn judges us. What the encounter of *Billy Budd* with deconstruction shows is that to adopt a judgment of silence is to reveal a conservative ideology, for, as the execution of Billy Budd makes clear, to defer a judgment [as Barbara Johnson does] is ultimately to defer to the existing system of authority.[44]

Let me put Thomas's damaging point alternatively, in a way that not only brings the argument of this chapter back to its beginning but also goes far to explain why I have emphasized the earlier phases of the history of *Billy Budd* criticism. Invoking the ambiguous words on ambiguity of the narrator that have become standard in this criticism — "Who in the rainbow can draw the line where the violet tint ends and the orange tint begins?" — in her conclusion, Johnson writes: "As a political allegory, Melville's *Billy Budd* is thus much more than a study of good and evil, justice and injustice. It is a *dramatization* of the twisted relations between knowing and doing, speaking and killing, reading and judging, which make *political understanding and action so problematic*" (MF, p. 108; my emphasis). In overdetermining the term "dramatization" in the process of affirming that Melville's real purpose in *Billy Budd* is to disclose the undecidability of historical events, that is, the impossibility of political judgment, Johnson's "advanced" deconstructive rhetoric strikes a familiar chord, which, as we have seen, runs from its simple expression by early British critics of the 1920s, epitomized E. L. Grant Watson, through its more sophisticated articulation by humanists such as Newton Arvin and Warner Berthoff, to its fullest existentialist version by Paul Brodtkorb Jr.,[45] that, in the process of revising his text, Melville was not only seeking to dramatize the various allegorical perspectives, but also, in so doing, to announce his acceptance of the ambiguities of the way things are in the world as his last will and testament. Despite its avowed intention — and the uncommon richness of its reasoning — Johnson's essay — and those of Sedgwick, Ruttenburg, and Cameron, which it patently influenced — thus in the end betrays its complicity with the politically conservative acceptance school of *Billy Budd* criticism.[46]

In sum, for all the commentators and critics who have invoked one form are another of the denouement's undecidable ambiguity, not only humanist or New Critical, but also however inadvertently, deconstructionist or New Americanist, Melville's resistance to such narrative closure in *Billy Budd* (indeed, in all his major work) was intended to affirm his achievement in his late phase of the higher, serenity-producing wisdom of ideological neutrality and his antipathy to lowly and crass ideological partisanship: an unworldliness, if not otherworldliness, that perceives engagement in and with the world as a manifestation of immaturity or even barbarism. Their disinterested problematics precludes them from perceiving that Melville's refusal of the call of closure ("the symmetry of form"), that is, his commitment to the "jagged edges" endemic to "Truth uncompromisingly told" (128), could have been intended, on the contrary, to undermine the decisiveness — and sovereign decisionism — of narrative closure — *and the civilized brutality against any gesture of deviation, real or imagined, that its optimistic exceptionalist politics mandates*. I am referring, more specifically, to the eviscerating closure enacted by the politically reactionary — pacifying — account, "doubtless for the most part written in good faith," of the destabilizing affair triumphantly and decisively announced to the (British) world by its officials (or, in Adorno's apt phrase, its culture industry): "The criminal paid the penalty of his crime. The promptitude of the punishment has proved salutary. Nothing amiss is now apprehended aboard H.M.S. *Bellipotent*" (BB, p. 131).

Billy Budd: A Meditation on American Exceptionalism and the State of Exception

As I have been implying throughout this chapter, my perspective on *Billy Budd* is, in a general way, in solidarity with what has come to be called all too reductively by the literary historians "the criticism of resistance": the criticism that represents the late Melville of *Billy Budd* as continuous with rather than antithetical to the ironic and titanic Melville of his prime. I mean the Melville of *Moby-Dick*, *Pierre*, *Israel Potter*, "Bartleby, the Scrivener," "Benito Cereno," and *The Confidence-Man*, who was ferociously critical of both the emergent optimism inherent in metaphysical ontologies and the hegemonic worldly practices they justified, particularly, the providential Puritan Calvinism that gave rise to the nationalist/capitalist/imperialist politics of American exceptionalism. This ironist resistance criticism by and large has been of two kinds. One, epitomized by Lawrence Thompson, Leonard Casper, and most forcefully, Edgar Dryden,[47] has overdetermined the site of ontology (i.e., the opposition between "chronologicals and horologicals," adopted from Plinlimon's pamphlet in *Pierre*) — Melville's resistance to the providential history of (American) Puritanism and/or its secular version (Manifest Destiny) — and, in so doing, has generalized the historical events on board the *Bellipotent* in terms of Melville's relationship to the Protestant interpretation of mortal human experience at the expense of the sociopolitical meaning of the historical occasion. The other, epitomized by Joseph Schiffman, Phil Withims, and, above all and at its best, Brook Thomas,[48] has overdetermined the sociopolitical site — Melville's resistance to naval law, and the sociopolitical structure that is its corollary — at the expense of the ontological site. In countering the dominant conservative criticism of acceptance from their respective disciplinary perspectives, both overlook the polyvalency of the being that Melville's story is addressing: the indissoluble relationality between the ontological and the sociopolitical sites in the world of the *Bellipotent*. The one overlooks its sociopolitics in favor of "man's" quarrel with God. The other, more important, proceeds in its critique along liberal ameliorist or reformist lines to suggest that Melville's purpose in pointing to the injustice perpetrated against Billy and "the populace" is, as it was in *White-Jacket*, to effect changes in the hegemonic legal system that would mitigate such injustices.

Despite this consequential difference, in other words, both these progressive exponents of the resistance thesis, no less than their opponent conservative adherents of the acceptance thesis and the deconstructionist exponents of undecidability, have strangely marginalized, if not entirely annulled, the *essential* — and, to reiterate, quite visible — structural conditions of Melville's (anti)narrative: the martial law established by the globalization of the imperial war between Britain and France or, more precisely, the ontologically grounded permanent state of exception that, as I shall underscore, penetrates the symbolic life of the body politic of the *Bellipotent* right down to its capillaries. I say "strangely marginalized" because the vast majority of the criticism, both the acceptance and the resistance types, was written during the period of the Cold War when the United States became (for the first time since the Civil War) overtly a national security state characterized, as the McCarthy phenomenon testifies, by the abrogation of civil rights, the establishment of a tacit police state and its reign of fear, the enabling of "criminal" types to influence the polity, and the reduction of human life perilously close to bare life under the aegis of the state of exception. Given this fraught global historical context, it is not difficult to conclude that the blindness of both camps to the exceptionalist law that "structures" *Billy Budd* is, like the blindness of Captain Amasa Delano to the conditions that "structure" life on board the *San Dominick* in "Benito Cereno," the result of the "oversight" intrinsic to their mutually, however vestigially, held American exceptionalist problematic. I mean by this the critical frame of reference that has prevailed throughout the criticism and commentary of those who have come to be called the "Old Americanists"[49] and, with a few exceptions, continues, unfortunately, to limit, if not entirely disable, much of the welcomed discourse on "America" of both non-Americanist critics such as Barbara Johnson and "New Americanists" such as Eve Sedgwick, Nancy Ruttenburg, and Sharon Cameron.[50]

It is no accident, I suggest, that the one reading of *Billy Budd* that acknowledges the decisive importance of the global historical conflict that produced the state of exception on board the *Bellipotent* — and thus is enabled to point fundamentally to Melville's uncanny anticipation of the contemporary global occasion precipitated by the 9/11 attacks on the American "homeland" and the Bush administration's declaration of its global war on terror — is by a French critic, Alain Brossat, who is identified with that recent manifestation of poststructuralist theory (Alain Badiou, Jean-Luc Nancy, Jacques Rancière, and Giorgio Agamben, for example) that has bridged the gap between the ontological, textual, and the political sites that the disciplinary system has disablingly separated. I quote Brossat at some length not only to suggest the force and the freshness of his insight but also to anticipate a further reference to his essay in the next chapter:

> We insist on the context [produced by the conquerors] in which this limit [that blocks the discursive possibilities that "would permit rendering the division and the opposition between masters and servants the object of a deliberative process"; i.e. a politics]. . . . Melville himself put this political dimension of his novel in relief, insisting — with accents that sometimes evoke the Burke of *Reflections on the French Revolution* — on the unforgivable character of the confrontation that opposes, at this end of the eighteenth century, not only two powers, two ambitious continentals, but indeed, two principles, two doctrines, two visions of history and of man. In the register of maritime metaphors mobilized by the novelist, this takes the form of the death struggle between a *monarchie flotante* and a *republique flottante*. His emphasis is equally placed on the state of emergency, the suspension of all rights to "those below" [*ceux d'en bas*], established on his Gracious Majesty's ships, following, notably, three recent mutinies during which the red flag had been hoisted. On the *Bellipotent*, then, a kind of martial law reigned, the sailors being treated by the officers like stubborn cattle, constantly suspected of sympathy for the French Revolution and enthusiasm for the Rights of Man. They are beaten, hazed, punished, threat-

ened, badly fed and submitted to a veritable dictatorship exercised on their spirits as well as on their bodies. The first act of [Benjamin] Britten's opera [*Billy Budd*] underscores with especial force this condition of bare life [*vie nue*] to which the impressed naval plebs were compelled, submitted to a debasing discipline, and terrorized. But Melville too puts the emphasis on the relation between the state of exception (total war) and the dictatorial regime pitilessly exercised by the masters. "At short notice an engagement might come on. When it did, the lieutenants assigned to batteries felt it incumbent on them, in some instances, to stand with drawn swords behind the men working the guns."[51]

It is true, as Hayford and Sealts and Parker reiterate — and the contradictory history of the criticism of *Billy Budd* confirms — that the fact that Melville left his manuscript unfinished precludes easy affirmations of the story's meaning. But the status of its incompleteness is, like that of the doubloon in *Moby-Dick*, such that it encourages — indeed, demands — rather than prohibits interpretation. We are, that is, left with no other choice than to undertake, in Althusser's phrase, a *symptomatic reading* of this unfinished text. And such a reading will show that *Billy Budd* is pointing not simply to something fundamentally different from the political conservatism that the adherents of the acceptance thesis — including those affirming the text's undecidability — but also to something more radical than the political amelioration espoused by the adherents of the resistance thesis. By attending fundamentally to the fraught global context in which the particular events on board the *Bellipotent* are indissolubly embedded, it will show that in addressing the question of the justice of Vere's execution of Billy Budd, the late Melville, probably with his dissatisfaction at his earlier treatment of the issue in *White-Jacket* in mind, was struggling to bring into his late, "catastrophic," consciousness something consonant with that ontological radicality he inaugurated in *Moby-Dick*, particularly in his destructuring of Captain Ahab's onto-imperial reduction of the ineffable white whale to a "practically assailable" Moby Dick[52] and developed into its penultimate form in *The Confidence-Man*. I mean a political condition that implicates the ontology of American exceptionalism (God's or History's election of America as redeemer nation) with a *permanent* state of exception that, in the name of a higher ("sacred") cause, strips Billy Budd, *the synecdoche of the innocent common sailor or, as the story has it, "the people,"* of his human rights and reduces him and the humanity he represents, in Giorgio Agamben's phrase, to bare life, that is, to a disposable body. In taking its point of departure from the global historical context that Hayford and Sealts's edition would put out of play, that is to say, a symptomatic reading will disclose that Melville's last work of fiction constitutes an uncannily proleptic critique of post–9/11 exceptionalist America, the "redeemer nation" that, in declaring its war on terror, has rendered the state of exception the rule.

CHAPTER THREE

Billy Budd
A Symptomatic Reading

Be it here, once and for all, understood, that no sentimental and theoretic love for the common sailor; no romantic belief in that peculiar noble-heartedness and exaggerated generosity of disposition fictionally imputed to him in novels; and no prevailing desire to gain the reputation of being his friend, have actuated me in anything I have said, in any part of this work, touching the gross oppression under which I know that the sailor suffers. . . .

Nor . . . is the general ignorance or depravity of any race of men to be alleged as an apology for tyranny over them. On the contrary, it can not admit of a reasonable doubt, in any unbiased mind conversant with the interior life of a man-of-war, that most of the sailor iniquities practiced therein are indirectly to be ascribed to the morally debasing effects of the unjust, despotic, and degrading laws under which the man-of-war's man lives.   — HERMAN MELVILLE, *White-Jacket*

Things fall apart; the centre cannot hold;
Mere anarchy is loosed upon the world,
The blood-dimmed tide is loosed, and everywhere
The ceremony of innocence is drowned;
The best lack all conviction, while the worst
Are full of passionate intensity.
     — W. B. YEATS, "The Second Coming"

The Narrator's Identity

Who is the narrator of *Billy Budd*? Given the astonishing indifference to or the willful marginalization of this question in most previous criticism of the novella, asking this admittedly difficult question should not be taken as an impertinence. Indeed, one of the fundamental and, in my mind, immensely productive, lessons about reading that the poststructuralist revolution has taught us is that an author is never in total command of his/her representation, that his/her agency is always in one degree or another adulterated by a system of discourse — an ideology that has become hegemonic, a construction that has become naturalized — and that, therefore — and here I invoke Louis Althusser's particular version of this lesson — reading must be "symptomatic," a *lecture symptomale.*[1] Granted, this "lesson" has been called into question in the wake of Edward Said's influential and justified critique of the poststructuralists' radical "textualization" of the "worldliness" of the literary text. But this admission should not diminish the urgency of the question: "Who is the narrator of *Billy Budd*? For, besides the poststructuralist imperative, what makes this question especially necessary is the inescapable fact that Melville left his tale unfinished. In other words, he left his readers, not simply with a text in which the conflicts or ambiguities are apparently unresolved, but, beyond that, with the uncertainty as to whether or not he even intended to resolve them. Seen in this obscured light, Melville's novella leaves us no other choice but to read it symptomatically. Every reading I refer to in the previous chapter, especially those associated with the "testament of acceptance," has been, in fact, a symptomatic (and ideological) reading. The difference between them and the one I undertake in this chapter is a difference in the degree of awareness. Despite the lip service paid to the incompleteness of Melville's text, the vast majority of earlier studies, as I have shown, were undertaken in the name of disinterested inquiry into a completed and therefore self-identical, that is, nameable, text. Mine, on the other hand, like the recent deconstructionist readings, is undertaken in full awareness of its ambiguities, its ultimate unnamability. It is, therefore, an openly interested (ideological) reading, but one, unlike those of the deconstructionists, that attends as faithfully as possible, not simply to the ambiguities *as such* (*as if they were equal in authority*), but to the different degree of power or weight that accrues to each side of the ambiguity in the process of the telling.

The first ambiguity has to do with the national identity of the narrator of *Billy Budd* — given that the story, although ostensibly about naval warfare between Britain and France, was written by an extremely self-conscious American writer. Significantly, none of the vast number of critics of the novella, British and American, have addressed this fundamental question, as, for example, many have done in writing about Henry Adams's chapters on Britain's policies during the American Civil War in *The Education of Henry Adams*. As I noted in chapter 1, a few have suggested that Melville was alluding to contemporary events in America, particularly the social unrest epitomized by the Haymarkets Riots of 1886.[2] But such references have been marginal to these critics' essentially allegorical readings of the tale and, more important, have been cited independently of the question of the ideological identity or, to put it another way, the reliability of the narrator. What I want to suggest as point of departure of my inquiry into the question of the narrator's identity is that he is fundamentally "American." He is, I mean, a narrator who, whatever the degree of the self-certainty of his American perspective, is writing a story about an earlier epochal "event" of Old World history addressed to a late-nineteenth-century American audience deeply inscribed by the myth of American exceptionalism and, as noted in chapter 1, highly receptive, especially in the context of the anxiety-provoking closing of the frontier, to the new jeremiads proselytizing in behalf of extending America's errand in the wilderness into the Pacific, that is, for the renewal of its flagging divinely or historically ordained global imperial calling.

That my attribution of "Americanness" (in this particular contrastive sense) to the narrator is a viable one is, as I have shown in chapter 1, borne witness to by the three strategically located and highly resonant references to America he makes in the process of telling his story (a fourth to which I shall return in the appropriate place, occurs in one of the codas): at the beginning (chapter 3), when, in recalling the expunging of the Great Mutiny from official British history, he invokes the analogy of similar erasures by American historians (BB, p. 55); in the middle (chapter 8), when, in referring to the "eclipsing menace mysterious and prodigious" posed by "Napoleon's unexampled conquest," he recalls that "there were Americans who had fought at Bunker Hill" who read "the ultimate schemes of this French portentous upstart from the revolutionary chaos" as the fulfillment of the judgment prefigured in the Apocalypse (BB, p. 66); and, not least, at the end (chapter 21), in the drumhead court scene, when, in recalling Captain Vere's appeal to the Nore mutiny in behalf of his preordained argument for the execution of Billy Budd, he invokes the analogous future, pre–Mexican War, example of the commander of the USS *Somers*, who, in the name of the security of the American ship's community, ordered "the execution at sea of a midshipman and two sailors as mutineers designing the seizure of the brig" (BB, pp. 113–114).

When it is acknowledged that the narrator is not an objective observer, but an "American" — one deeply conscious of the determinative history of the relationship between the "Old World" and the "New," particularly between Britain and the United States, and, not least, of the origins of the American exceptionalist ethos — then it is also reasonable to conclude that his reason for telling the story of Billy Budd lies primarily in the *exemplary* character of the historical occasion in which it is embedded, precisely the history that the editors of the "definitive edition" of *Billy Budd* — and the vast majority of criticism and commentary, old and new — have reduced to mere "background," if not entirely excised. For why would such a self-conscious American wish to tell a story whose context is the Old World, indeed, an epochal moment in its history, since its impact was global, if not to remind his contemporary readers — Americans highly aware of the Gilded Age's capitalist momentum to "incorporate" the United States and to extend its imperial reach into the Pacific — of this highly fraught relational history?

Of course, this identification of the narrator as an American who is speaking to Americans about a global event that affects their country's cultural and political identity does not entirely answer the question "Who is the narrator?" But it does tell us, against the tendency to read him as an allegorist of the universal human predicament, that his story is "politically" motivated, that is, worldly. It enables the reader, that is, to perceive the story he tells, not as one in the Aristotelian tradition, in which the end (in both senses of the word: termination and ideological goal) is present from the beginning, but as the harbinger of a new anti-Aristotelian form, one in which, as Charles Olson via Robert Creeley put this emancipatory gesture much later, "form is never more than the extension of content."[3] To put it in the terms of Melville's novella, it enables us to perceive that the measure of the narrator's story is not the domesticating Orphic measure by which Captain Vere acts, but, rather, the errant measure of its "occasion" (immediately from *occasus*, "the setting of the sun," and its cognate *occidere*, "to fall," especially, "to set" or "to wester," from which the English word Occident comes; and ultimately from *cadere*, "to perish," "to die"). In other words, identifying the narrator as an American enables us to perceive the story, despite its retrospective perspective, as an explorative process, essentially similar in manner to Ishmael's errant narrative of Captain Ahab's "fiery pursuit" of the white whale,[4] by which he symptomatically arrives, without arriving, at a radical indictment of "measured forms" that inform existing power relations: not simply of the tyrannical Old World states, in which the state of exception is the norm, but also of exceptionalist democratic America, in which its exceptionalism — *the structurally inherent need for a perpetual enemy*, that is, for national security, as the dominant way of life — far from differentiating the New (the open) from the Old (the closed) World, renders it complicit with its avowed opposite.

The Role of the Historical Context

Following the symptomatic directive suggested by identifying the narrator as a worldly American deeply interested in the resonant relationship between the Old World of a century before and the New World of his present historical occasion, let me retrieve, by way of a repetition (in the Heideggerian sense), the thesis concerning the historical context in which the story of Billy Budd is embedded that I offered as a "forestructure"[5] in chapter 1: the postrevolutionary struggle between Britain and France for control of the world's oceans, which, in betraying the French Revolution, inaugurated the modern imperialist era and its concomitant: the perpetual national security state. This is the historical mise-en-scène of the impressment, dehumanization, and hanging by the neck of an innocent common sailor, Billy Budd, according to the inexorable dictates of martial law. As I have argued, any reading of *Billy Budd*, however theoretically sophisticated, that effaces or even marginalizes this very worldly global setting travesties Melville's text, since it pervades the body of the story right down to its capillaries. Even if, as Harrison Hayford and Merton Sealts and, later, Hershel Parker, assert, it was Melville's intention to delete the historical "Preface," such a deletion would not radically affect the dominant role this fraught global history plays in the determination of the events involving the fate of Billy Budd.[6] It is, as it were, an *informing presence* from the beginning, which, in invoking the "Great Mutiny," establishes the *Bellipotent*'s reason for being where and what it is; through the middle, which articulates the conditions that produces the particular kind of policeman that Claggart is and that enables his machinations against Billy; to the (non)end, which provides the logical/legal context that "justifies" Captain Vere's terrible judgment against this innocent young sailor. Equally important—indeed, in a way that underscores its tremendous significance—its starkly intransigent reality is *there* in the second coda, now, as I shall show, as a spectral presence that haunts the very official representation of the events on board the *Bellipotent*. To put it succinctly, this pervasive global history is one that, in representing the war between Britain and France as an epochal struggle for control of the high seas, also establishes security—the physical safety of the abstract whole over the singularity of its parts, the sacred over the profane, arbitrary order over dissent, tyranny over freedom, the bare body over the political being—as the essential value system of the ship of state.

In the face of the predominant tendency of *Billy Budd* criticism (including that of those I have been calling the critics of undecidability) to marginalize the "Preface" (or, in some cases, to read it as testimony to Melville's conservative turn in his old age)—and given the visible presence of this history in the story[7]—it becomes both reasonable and necessary at the outset of a symptomatic reading to retrieve it from the margins, if not the oblivion, to which it has been relegated:

> The year 1797, the year of this narrative, belongs to a period which, as every thinker now feels, involved a crisis for Christendom not exceeded in its undetermined momentousness at the time by any other era whereof there is record. The opening proposition made by the Spirit of that Age involved rectification of the Old World's hereditary wrongs. In France, to some extent, this was bloodily effected. But what then? Straightway the Revolution itself became a wrongdoer, one more oppressive than the kings. Under Napoleon it enthroned upstart kings, and initiated that prolonged agony of continual war whose final throe was Waterloo. During those years not the wisest could have foreseen that the outcome of all would be what to some thinkers apparently it has since turned out to be—a political advance along nearly the whole line for Europeans.
>
> Now, as elsewhere hinted, it was something caught from the Revolutionary Spirit that at Spithead emboldened the man-of-war's men to rise against real abuses, long-standing ones, and afterwards at the Nore

to make inordinate and aggressive demands — successful resistance to which was confirmed only when the ringleaders were hung for an admonitory spectacle to the anchored fleet. Yet, in a way analogous to the operation of the Revolution at large, the Great Mutiny, though by Englishmen naturally deemed monstrous at the time, doubtless gave the first latent promptings to most important reforms in the British navy.[8]

This "Preface," not unlike the more diffuse representation of this epochal history, is patently not, as some commentators have maintained, an expression of Melville's politically conservative turn in his old age, a preconceived end that will determine our understanding of the minute particulars of the middle.[9] Nor, on the other hand, is it an expression of Melville's political commitment to the revolutionary dynamics of the French Revolution as other liberal commentators have concluded. To arrive at such simplistic readings, one is compelled to annul not only many of its contradictory details, but also the matter it highlights: the "crisis of Christendom not exceeded in its undetermined momentousness of any other era of which there is record." What is at the absent heart of this "Preface" — *and, I suggest, of the "inside narrative" proper* — is, rather, as the paradoxes in which the American narrator expresses this history — "its undetermined momentousness" — suggest, the French Revolution: an "event" (*événement*) in Alain Badiou's "situationist" (or my "occasionalist") sense of the word, in which what does not count in the prevailing regime of truth comes to visibility. I repeat the passage from Badiou's *Ethics* I quoted in a general context in chapter 1 in order underscore its relevance for this particular exegetical moment:

> We might say that since a situation is composed by the knowledges circulating within it, the event names the void inasmuch as it names the not-known of the situation.
>
> To take a well-known example: Marx is an event for political thought because he designated, under the name "proletariat," the central void of early bourgeois societies. For the proletariat — being entirely dispossessed, absent from the political stage — is that around which is organized the complacent plenitude established by the rule of those who possess capital.
>
> To sum up: the fundamental ontological characteristic of an event is to inscribe, to name, the situated void of that for which it is and event.[10]

In de-centering not only the truth discourse of "Christendom" but also the traditional politics of Europe—the tyrannical monarchical Old World (the divine right of kings that Christianity sponsored), the French Revolution, the "Preface" tentatively suggests, in a way that cannot help but recall the American Revolution, opened up the possibility of an utterly new *anti-foundational* ontological, social, and political dispensation, one in which the nobody of the old regime of truth becomes, in Badiou's term, "some-one": "a human animal among others, which nevertheless finds itself *seized* and *displaced* by the eventual [*événementiel*] process of a truth" (E, p. 91),

But this epochal event was immediately betrayed by a sleight of hand concerning its terms that Badiou calls "a simulacrum of truth": "when a radical break in a situation, under names borrowed from real truth-processes [disclosed by the event], convokes not the void but the 'full' particularity or presumed substance of that situation" (E, p. 73), that is, its de-differentiating plenary totality. The revolutionary "Spirit of that Age"—whose "opening proposition" was "the rectification of the Old World's wrongs"—was, in other words, transformed, first, into a reign of terror in France in the name of compassion for the multitude and, then, in the Napoleonic moment, into a global imperial war between France and England, which, in the name of civilized humanity, reduced the revolting "multitude" (BB, p. 50) even further to cannon fodder. It was, the narrator tells us, this "Revolutionary Spirit," ignited by the French Revolution, that "emboldened" the "man-of-war's men at Spithead" and, later at the Nore, to "rise against *real* abuses, long standing ones," which, in turn, enabled the dominant culture to demonize the mutiny—interpret it as a threat to England's security—and to justify the ruthless execution of its ringleaders as an "admonitory spectacle before the anchored fleet." It was, that is to say, this crisis of Christendom—this "undetermined momentousness"—precipitated by the "Revolutionary Spirit," that precipitated the particular events comprising his story.

The narrator's attitude towards this inaugural history seems ambivalent: the Revolution itself became "a wrongdoer, one more oppressive than the kings," yet it turned out to be "a political advance along nearly the whole line for Europeans." The Great Mutiny was "deemed monstrous at the time" by the dominant culture in England, yet it "gave the first latent promptings to most important reforms in the British navy."

Admittedly, in chapter 3 of the Hayford and Sealts edition, which, following those that introduce, first, the idea of the "handsome sailor" and, then, Billy Budd (his impressment from the merchant ship *Rights-of-Man*), contains the historical content, does not mention this "crisis of Christendom," and thus, rather than enforcing its eventual character, appears to support the view that Melville had abandoned his earlier political radicality for a more conservative perspective. Indeed, in this early chapter, the narrator appears at first to sympathize with the dominant British culture that ruthlessly put the mutiny down:

> It was the summer of 1797 [when the *Bellipotent*, having joined the Mediterranean fleet, was on a scouting mission]. In the April of that year had occurred the commotion at Spithead followed in May by a second and yet more serious outbreak in the fleet at the Nore. The latter is known, and without exaggeration in the epithet, as "the Great Mutiny." It was indeed a demonstration more menacing to England than the contemporary manifestoes and conquering and proselytizing armies of the French Directory. To the British Empire the Nore Mutiny was what a strike in the fire brigade would be to London threatened by general arson. In a crisis when the kingdom might well have anticipated the famous signal that some years later published along the naval line of battle what it was that upon occasion England expected of Englishmen [Nelson's famous declaration at Trafalgar]; *that* was the time when at the mastheads of the three-deckers and seventy-fours moored in her roadstead — a fleet the right arm of a Power then all but the sole free conservative one of the Old World — the bluejackets, to be numbered by the thousands, ran with huzzas the British colors with the union and cross wiped out; by that cancellation transmuting the flag of founded law and freedom defined, into the enemy's red meteor of unbridled and unbounded revolt. Reasonable discontent growing out of practical grievances in the fleet had been ignited into irrational combustion as by live cinders blown across the Channel from France in flames. (BB, p. 54)

On closer examination, however, such a straightforward conclusion becomes untenable. For one thing, the narrator distances himself from the negative interpretation of the mutiny by attributing it, first, to the abstraction "England," and then, more tellingly, to the "British Empire," thus suggesting that the loyalty expected of "Englishmen" "on occasion" by

"England" was a coerced loyalty, a loyalty demanded by the exponents of British imperialism (including Admiral Nelson) and justified by representing itself as *exceptionalist* — "a Power then all but the sole free conservative one of the Old World" — and appealing to national security. This suggestion of an alternative reading is enforced by the following comment by the narrator: "The event [The Great Mutiny] converted into irony for a time those spirited strains of [Charles] Dibdin — a song-writer *no mean auxiliary to the English government at that European conjuncture* — strains celebrating, among other things, the patriotic devotion of the British tar: 'And as for my life, 'tis the King's!' " (BB, p. 55; my emphasis)[11]

Following the directive offered by this irony, we are enabled to read what the narrator goes on to say about the historical context — particularly the future representation of events of the Great Mutiny by *official history* — quite differently from the way it has been hitherto read:

> Such an episode in the Island's grand naval story her naval historians naturally abridge, one of them (William James) candidly acknowledging that fain would he pass it over did not "impartiality forbid fastidiousness." *And yet his mention is less a narration than a reference, having to do hardly at all with the details. Nor are these readily found in the libraries.* Like some other events in every age befalling states everywhere, including America, the Great Mutiny was of such character that national pride along with views of policy would fain shade it off into the historical background. Such events cannot be ignored, but there is a considerate way of historically treating them. If a well-constituted individual refrains from blazoning aught amiss or calamitous in his family, a nation in the like circumstances may without reproach be equally discreet. (BB p. 55; my emphasis)

The narrator, in this signaling passage, seems to sympathize with the official historians' tendency to repress — *to prevent from becoming part of the national archive* — events such as the Great Mutiny that would undermine the moral authority of a government that represented its violence as justified by its benign intent. At the beginning, he refers to the naval historians' desire to "abridge" the episode of the Great Mutiny as "natural," and, at the end, he reiterates his apparent sympathy by invoking the analogy between "a well-constituted individual" who suppresses the disclosure of a calamity in the family with such official historians.[12] But in the very act of apologizing for one of these official historians' desire to "pass [the event of the mutiny and its suppression] over," he also points emphatically to something radically different. He makes visible the violation of the truth of the history that is entailed by such an excision of its differential "details" in the name of national security or, as in the case of the British historian William James, whose "impartiality" forbade outright effacement, passing reference to, rather than a detailed narration, of them.

It is, to anticipate, precisely this alternative truth that is struggling to rise into the narrator's consciousness against the "truth" of his hegemonic discourse that will emerge in the opening close of *Billy Budd*. This radical violation of historicity, to be more specific, which is foreshadowed (though not registered, as far as I know, by any of the criticism devoted to *Billy Budd*) at the beginning of the narrator's tale in his reference to the paradoxical censoring of history by official history in behalf of the "higher cause" of national security, will be *dis*-closed with ironic force in the first of the three codas the narrator appends to the story. I mean, of course, the official "account of the affair," "doubtless for the most part written [like William James's history] in good faith" (BB, p. 130), that would bring the awful — and politically dislocating — events on board the "ship of [the exceptional] state," *Bellipotent*, to it decisive and locating *closure* — and peace.

And what I have said about the narrator's perspective at this early stage in his narration on the historical context in which the story of Billy Budd takes place applies as well to the "digressive" encomium to Nelson that, not accidentally, immediately follows. Since I have offered an extended reading of this "err[ing]" from the "main road" into an irresistible "bypath" in chapter 2, it will suffice simply briefly to summarize what I said there, adding comments only on aspects of the narrator's apparent encomium that are pertinent to this juncture of my argument. What I emphasized there, it will be recalled, was the excessiveness of the narrator's celebration — and monumentalization — not only of the beauty of old wooden warships, the romance of such naval warfare, and the glory it enabled its commanders to achieve, as opposed to the utilitarian ("Benthamite") nature of modern ironclads and the pedestrian reality of modern naval warfare, but also of the gloriousness of Nelson's crown-bestowing death:

At Trafalgar Nelson on the brink of opening the fight sat down and wrote his last will and testament. If under the presentiment of the most magnificent of all victories to be crowned by his own glorious death, a sort of priestly motive led him to dress his person in the jeweled vouchers of his own shining deeds; if thus to have adorned himself for the altar and the sacrifice were indeed vainglory, then affectation and fustian is each more heroic line in the great epics and dramas, since in such lines the poet but embodies in verse those exaltations of sentiment that a nature like Nelson, the opportunity be given, vitalizes into acts. (BB, p. 58)

In claiming that this ironic reading of the narrator's encomium to Nelson is a viable one, I invoked an earlier and singularly different, but resonantly echoing allusion to Nelson's attire on the day of his death made by Melville, here, however, devoid of ambiguity, in "Cock-A-Doodle-Do," his Voltairean satire of the Panglossian American optimism, so fundamental to *The Confidence-Man*,[13] enabled by its exceptionalist ethos, which monomaniacally crows the benignity of the world even in the midst of the Jobian dung heap to which it has been reduced by the capitalization of America. I repeat the passage to underscore its relevance — particularly its identification of the cock with the phallus — at this juncture of my argument:

A cock. More like a golden eagle than a cock. A cock, more like a Field-Marshall than a cock. A cock, more like Lord Nelson with all his glittering arms on, standing on the Vanguard's quarter-deck going into battle, than a cock. A cock, more like the Emperor Charlemagne in his robes at Aix la Chapelle, than a cock.

Such a cock!

He was of a haughty size, stood haughty on his haughty legs. His colors were red, gold, and white. The red was on his crest alone, which was a mighty and symmetric crest, like unto Hector's helmet, as delineated on antique shields. Hs plumage was snowy, traced with gold. He walked in front of the shanty, like a peer of the realm; his crest lifted, his chest out, his embroidered trappings flashing in the light. His pace was wonderful. He looked like some noble foreigner. He looked like some Oriental king in some magnificent Italian Opera.[14]

The rhetorical excess of *Billy Budd*'s narrator, as I noted, is (not incidentally, like the official history of William James) reminiscent of the monumentalist historiography that Foucault's Nietzschean genealogy in the parodic mode delegitimizes. It inadvertently discloses not only the narrator's romantic nostalgia but also his *tendency to monumentalize* history, which is to say, to *forget* the actualities at the origin of the "glorious truth" the memorial monument celebrates: the reduction of the crew of the man-of-war (understood as ship of state) to bare life and their wholesale slaughter in the name of a "higher" or "sacred" cause: imperial Great Britain's control of the global seaways.[15]

Given the irony of Melville's portrait of the hero of Trafalgar, then, it will be seen, though this goes unobserved by the editors of the "definitive text" and the critics who follow them, that it is not accidental that the next chapter (5) begins abruptly — and in a deflating way — with a pointed return to the larger historical context in which Billy's story is embedded (including a reference to the Nelson of that year of the war) — to the very "evental" matter they would efface: the "contingencies present and to come of the convulsed continent"; the impressment of civilians on which the British fleet, "insatiate in demand for men," depended; the crisis-provoking mutinies at Spithead and Nore, which, although "put down, lurkingly survived them" and continued to arouse apprehension of "some return of trouble sporadic or general"; and, not least, the vigilant state policing of the people in the name of "security": "So it was that for a time, on more than one quarter-deck, anxiety did exist. At sea, precautionary vigilance was strained against relapse. At short notice an engagement might come on. When it did, the lieutenants assigned to batteries felt it incumbent on them, in some instances, to stand with drawn swords behind the men working the guns" (BB, p. 59).

It is no accident, in other words, that what immediately follows the narrator's portrait of Nelson is a return to the epochal global situation, which, in determining life on board the microcosmic HMS *Bellipotent* down to its capillaries, reduces humans to bare life — epitomized by the arbitrary impressment of civilians and holding them at sword's point — under the ruthless aegis of what I have been calling "the permanent state of exception."

Claggart and Vere: Allegory or Worldliness?

It is into this degrading, global historical situation that the narrator introduces the other two characters that are central to the "inside narrative" on board the *Bellipotent*, first "the Honorable Edward Fairfax Vere," the captain of the ship, and then Claggart, its master-at-arms. In so doing, he provides symptomatically an interpretive directive that, if it does not entirely counter the traditional allegorical reading of *Billy Budd*, does at least justify the (onto)political reading I am undertaking. Consonant with his inaugural ambivalent attitude towards the French Revolution, the narrator appears to be generally sympathetic with Captain Vere's political conservativism, though this is not absolute. In the first of the two chapters that introduce Captain Vere, the narrator emphasizes his aristocratic background, but makes it clear that his advancement in the British Navy "has not been altogether owing to influences connected with that circumstance," that, on the contrary, he had earned his rank: "He had seen much service, been in various engagements, always acquitting himself as an officer mindful of the welfare of his men, but never tolerating an infraction of discipline; thoroughly versed in the science of his profession, and intrepid to the verge of temerity, though never injudiciously so. For his gallantry in the West Indian waters as flag lieutenant under Rodney in that admiral's crowning victory over De Grasse, he was made a post captain" (BB, p. 60).

Seen in the light of the history-oriented directive I have underscored, however, this way of putting Vere's character, renders his advancement, in fact, a matter of conscientiousness and competence, not of an imaginative uniqueness, brilliance, and heroism that would confirm his authority, a conscientiousness and competence marked by his disciplinary intolerance of errancy. It suggests, in other words, that, however intelligent, well read, and well-meaning he is, Captain Vere's decisions as a naval officer are not those of a free agent, but are ultimately determined by a hegemonic discourse that he has deeply internalized.

Indeed, we might say, after Edward Said, Vere's decisions are not so much the consequence of disinterested inquiry, as the narrator seems to think, as of "the textual attitude," that distancing perspective on "the swarming, unpredictable, and problematic mess in which humans beings live" derived "from what books—texts—say" that Cervantes, Voltaire, and Flaubert mercilessly satirize in *Don Quixote, Candide,* and *Bouvard et Pécuchet,* respectively.[16] In the next chapter, for example, the narrator observes of Vere:

He had a marked leaning toward everything intellectual. He loved books, never going to sea without a newly replenished library, compact but of the best. . . . With nothing of that literary taste which less heeds the thing conveyed than the vehicle, *his bias was toward those books to which every serious mind of superior order occupying any active post of authority in the world naturally inclines*: books treating of actual men and events no matter of what era — history, biography, and unconventional writers like Montaigne, who, free from cant and convention, honestly and in the spirit of common sense philosophize upon realities. *In this line of reading he found confirmation of his own more reserved thoughts — confirmation which he had vainly sought in social converse, so that as touching most fundamental topics, there had got to be established in him some positive convictions which he forefelt would abide in him essentially unmodified so long as his intelligent part remained unimpaired. In view of the troubled period in which his lot was cast, this was well for him. His settled convictions were as a dike against those invading waters of novel opinion social, political, and otherwise, which carried away as in a torrent no few minds in those days, minds by nature not inferior to his own.* While other members of that aristocracy to which by birth he belonged were incensed at the innovators mainly because their theories were inimical to the privileged classes, Captain Vere, disinterestedly opposed them not alone because they seemed to him insusceptible of embodiment in lasting institutions, *but at war with the peace of the world and the true welfare of mankind.* (BB, pp. 62–63; my emphasis)

If, as, in fact, we are encouraged to do by Melville's subversive text, we read the narrator's particular characterization of Vere in the context of the global history in which it is embedded, we cannot help but perceive that not too far below the surface of its sympathy, as my emphases clearly suggest, there is the shadow of a darker Captain Vere. More specifically, its directive enables us to see a Vere — a "bookish gentleman" (BB, p. 63) — who has derived "convictions," not from "social converse," but from the books he has read. However intelligent, knowledgeable about the world, disinterested (unlike most of his social class), and humane, ("Starry") Vere is nevertheless deeply inscribed by and inexorably fixated on the "Truth" of a world structured in domination: a world of perpetual war represented as "peace" and an "impressed" humanity represented as the "true welfare of mankind." The "Truth" of Vere's world, in other words, is the truth of a world, justified discursively by the exceptionalist myth that Britain was the "sole free conservative" power "of the Old World," that lies behind the state of exception or, to be more precise, is at the mercy of the *system of authority* — the lawless law — that reigns on board the *Bellipotent* in the unmovable name of national security.

Similarly, when we reconstellate the fraught global historical context into the narrator's introductory characterization of John Claggart, from which it has been excised, we are enabled to perceive that the master-at-arms of the *Bellipotent* is not simply Satan, the allegorical principle of evil or "Natural Depravity" (BB, p. 75), as virtually all the criticism and commentary of *Bill Budd* maintains,[17] but as the epitome of the particular kind of policeman who is endemic to the polity variously called the police state, the national security state, *l'état de siège*, or the state of the state of exception. I am not simply referring to the narrator's telling genealogy of the current function of the office of master-at-arms, which culminates in an emphasis that pits the higher authority of the state against the lowly populace: "But very long ago, owing to the advance in gunnery making hand-to-hand encounters less frequent and giving to niter and sulphur the preeminence over steel, that function ["the instruction of the men in the use of arms, sword, or cutlass] ceased; the master-at-arms of a great warship becoming a sort of chief of police charged among other matters with the duty of preserving order on the populous lower gundecks" (BB, p. 64). I am also calling attention to the following, more particular passage about the identity of Claggart retrieved from the oblivion to which Melvillean criticism has consigned it and reconstellated into the central or "inside" story. It is a passage, not incidentally, which, in the act of inaugurating the middle, crisis-instigating phase of the inside story, returns to that aspect of the global historical context that discloses the unjustifiable corruptness and corrupting practices of the British state enabled by the state of exception, the civilized state Captain Vere is defending:

> But the sailor's dogwatch gossip concerning him [Claggart] derived a
> vague plausibility from the fact that now for some period the British
> navy could so little afford to be squeamish in the matter of keeping up

muster rolls, that not only were press gangs notoriously abroad both afloat and ashore, but there was also little or no secret about another matter, namely, that the London police were at liberty to capture any able-bodied suspect, any questionable fellow at large, and summarily ship him to the dockyard or fleet. Furthermore, even among voluntary enlistments there were instances where the motive thereto partook neither of patriotic impulse nor yet of random desire to experience a bit of sea life and martial adventure. Insolvent debtors of minor grade, together with the promiscuous lame ducks of morality, found in the navy a convenient and secure refuge, secure because, once enlisted aboard a King's ship, they were as much in sanctuary as the transgressor of the Middle Ages harboring himself under the shadow of the altar. (BB, pp. 65–66)

Following this meditation on a rumor concerning the origins of Claggart's malignant presence on board the *Bellipotent*, one, not incidentally, that suggests the indissoluble relationship between the global struggle for control of the high seas, the security state, the government's inhumane impressment policies, and the criminal policing this condition entails, the narrator, while admitting to uncertainty about the truth of "such [state] sanctioned irregularities" (BB, p. 66), nevertheless goes on to recall something he had once seen in print and then heard repeated to him by "a Baltimore negro, a Trafalgar man" that gave weight to his surmise:

It was to this effect: In the case of a warship short of hands whose speedy sailing was imperative, the deficient quota, in lack of any other way of making it good, would be eked out by drafts culled direct from the jails. For reasons previously suggested it would not perhaps be easy at the present day directly to prove or disprove the allegation. But allowed as a verity, how significant would it be of England's straits at the time confronted by those wars which like a flight of harpies rose shrieking from the din and dust of the fallen Bastille. (BB, p. 66)

Despite the state-damning tenor of his account of the British government's irregular, that is, cruel illegal or lawless, practices at the time of the Napoleonic wars, the narrator, as the simile he uses to refer to the French Revolution suggests, seems in the end to express sympathy for them. From his chronologically distant vantage point he observes:

That era appears measurably clear to us who look back at it, and but read of it. But to the grandfathers of us graybeards, the more thoughtful of them, the genius of it presented an aspect like that of Camoëns' Spirit of the Cape [of Good Hope], an eclipsing menace mysterious and prodigious. Not America was exempt from apprehension. At the height of Napoleon's unexampled conquests, there were Americans who had fought at Bunker Hill who looked forward to the possibility that the Atlantic might prove no barrier against the ultimate schemes of this French portentous upstart from the revolutionary chaos who seemed in act of fulfilling judgment prefigured in the Apocalypse. (BB, p. 66)

But how reliable is this apparent justification of the "sanctioned irregularities" the narrator has enumerated immediately before? Read in the larger context of the chapter, his inflation of the fear — the national insecurity — instigated by invoking a "mysterious and prodigious" menacing enemy who "seemed in act of fulfilling judgment prefigured the Apocalypse" — makes his justification sound like a rationalization ultimately intended to obscure the terrible social and political consequences of the sovereign government's imposition of the state of exception. And this possible reading is underscored, when, after his invocation of the Napoleonic wars, the narrator returns to the mysterious character of Claggart:

It was no gossip, however, but fact that though, as before hinted, Claggart upon his entrance into the navy, was, as a novice, assigned to the least honorable section of a man-of-war's crew, embracing the drudgery, he did not long remain there. The superior capacity he immediately evinced, his constitutional sobriety, *an ingratiating deference to superiors, together with a peculiar ferreting genius* manifested on a singular occasion: all this, capped by *a certain austere patriotism*, abruptly advanced him to the position of master-at-arms.

Of this maritime chief of police the ship's corporals, so called, were the immediate subordinates, and compliant ones; and this, as is to be noted in some business departments ashore, almost to a degree inconsistent with entire moral volition. His place put various converging wires or underground influence under the chief's control, capable when astutely worked through his understrappers of operating to the mysterious discomfort, if nothing worse, of any of the sea commonality. (BB, p. 67; my emphasis)

Despite the narrator's apparent defense of Britain's sanctioned irregularities, what comes through with considerable force here, at the end of the chapter that inextricably relates the historical "background" and the "inside story" of the *Bellipotent and foreshadows the dreadful fate of Billy Budd under Claggart's unrelenting malevolent gaze*, is something that drastically qualifies, if it does not entirely contradict, his exculpatory reasoning. It is not only the reduction of "the people" to bare life and a (moderately) free society—a society of rights emphasized by the arbitrary and crassly conducted abduction of Billy Budd from the *Rights-of-Man*—to a (secret) police state, but also the transformation of the moral conditions of a civilized law enforcement in such a way as to render the amoral criminal, drawn for the underworld, the agent of policing the multitude.

What comes through, in other words, is the image of the fear-oriented world of the amoral secret police state that was enabled—indeed, compelled—by the chain of ontological, moral, cultural, social, legal, and political reductions precipitated by the dominant British culture's establishment of the state of exception ostensibly in the name of defending "civilization"—the world of freedom, law, and order against the "menacing" atheistic irrationality of the "Revolutionary Spirit" but, in fact, as I have been suggesting, in behalf of the British empire's control of the high seas. And it is this "austere" civilization, this world of the secret police enabled by the state of exception that saturates the "inside story" right down to the last detail. I mean the events that have their beginning in Billy's "[finding] himself getting into petty trouble occasionally about such matters as the stowage of his bag or something amiss in his hammock, matters under the police oversight of the ship's corporals of the lower decks, and which brought down on him a vague threat from one of them" (BB, pp. 68–69); their middle in the scene in which Billy, shocked into speechlessness by Claggart's accusation that he has been fomenting a mutiny, delivers his speechless death blow to the head of his glib accuser; and their opening close in Captain Vere's execution of Billy in the name of securing the *Bellipotent* and the multitudinous world it represents against the specter of revolt: "the peace of the world and the true welfare of mankind," as Vere represents them, that the "invading waters of novel opinion social, political, or otherwise" was threatening to overwhelm. To anticipate, the narrator's reference to Claggart's underlings—the clandestine network (the "converging wires or underground influence" under his control) that "operat[ed] to the mysterious discomfort, if nothing worse, of any of the sea commonality" — is, especially if we register his tellingly dislocating American analogy — remarkably proleptic of the rise, in democratic America, of the security state during the Cold War, particularly in the so-called McCarthy era, and then, in an even more manifest way, in the period of the George W. Bush presidential administration, when, in Yeats's words, the "best lack[ed] all conviction" and "the worst [were] full of passionate intensity."

It is true, of course, that after returning to the inside story, specifically to the question of Claggart's apparently impenetrable motives for his being "down on" Billy Budd, the narrator, picking up on a comment made to him long before by "an honest scholar, my senior," distinguishes the master-at-arm's labyrinthine being as "exceptional" and "phenomenal" (BB, p. 75) (i.e., not that of a normal person) and then sharply subordinates the knowledge about human behavior *attained by participating in the world (of politics)* to that intuitive knowledge endemic to recluses such as the Hebrew prophets or, as he prefers in order to avoid the charge of "being tinctured with the biblical element" (BB, p. 75), to visionary philosophers like Plato. From this perspective, he suggests, such exceptional men as Claggart are characterized by their "Natural Depravity," a depravity, it seems, that is not the consequence of one's worldly circumstances, but "according to nature." And it is, of course, this definition of natural depravity — "not engendered by vicious training or corrupting books or licentious living" (BB, p. 76), a depravity that seems to efface the historical conditions, the very fraught worldly context, the narrator had invoked earlier to account for Claggart's machinations against Billy — that the great majority of critics have adopted to justify their reading of *Billy Budd* as an allegorical psychomachia.

What these critics who derive this de-historicized allegorical interpretation of the master-at-arms' character from the narrator's meditation miss, however, is his subtle, but decisive qualification of his initial Platonic attribution of "Natural Depravity" to such "phenomenal men." Because this definition savors of a universalist Calvinism, he modifies it to apply "to individuals" and then goes on to assert that it is endemic to "civilization," which, as the qualifier he deliberately uses makes clear, can only mean actually existing British civilization: "At any rate, for notable instances, since these [peculiarly depraved individuals] have no vulgar alloy of the brute in them, but invariably are dominated by intellectuality, one must go elsewhere [than the gallows and jail to find them]. *Civilization, especially if of the austerer sort, is auspicious to it. It folds itself in the mantle of respectability*" (BB, p. 75; my emphasis). Thus what seems at first to be an allegorization of the character of the master-at-arms, turns out in fact to be a verification of his historical worldliness. It is the "austere" civilization of Britain under the aegis of the state of exception, not nature as such, that has reduced his human potential to a depraved monomaniacal rationality, remarkably similar to that of Captain Ahab, that functions as

> an ambidexter implement for effecting the irrational. That is to say: Toward the accomplishment of an aim which in wantonness of atrocity would seem to partake of the insane, he will direct a cool judgment sagacious and sound. These men are madmen, and of the most dangerous sort, for the lunacy is not continuous, but occasional, evoked by some special object; it is protectively secretive, which is as much as to say it is self-contained, so that when, moreover most active it is to the average mind not distinguishable from sanity, and for the reason above suggested: that whatever its aim may be — and the aim is never declared — the method and the outward proceeding are always perfectly rational. (BB, p. 76)

What immediately follows the narrator's tortured meditation on Claggart's civilizational evil is thus, not accidentally, a return to precisely the historical world, clandestinely organized and set in motion, puppet-like, by the chief of the secret police, that preceded it, now, as an enactment on board the *Bellipotent* of the sociopolitical imperatives of the state of exception. It is a world, in other words, that is far more *worldly* than that assumed by the critics who read Claggart simply as an allegorical figure of evil. I am referring to the episode, following Billy's accidental spilling of a bowl of soup at the feet of Claggart (chapter 10), in which we are given a resonant glimpse of the illegal policing methods Claggart's position as "chief of police" in a police state empowers him to utilize, initially to cause Billy discomfort and then to entrap him: above all, the use of the subordinate informer, whose identity and well-being are utterly dependent on the goodwill of his puppeteer boss:

From his chief's employing him ["Squeak . . . so nicknamed by the sailors on account of his squeaky voice and sharp visage *ferreting about the dark corners of the lower deck after interlopers*, satirically suggesting to them the idea of a rat in a cellar"] as an implicit tool in laying little traps for the worriment of the foretopman — for it was from the master-at-arms that the petty persecutions heretofore adverted to had proceeded — the corporal, having naturally enough concluded that his master could have no love for the sailor, made it his business, faithful understrapper that he was, to foment the ill blood by perverting to his chief certain innocent frolics of the good-natured foretopman, besides inventing for his mouth sundry contumelious epithets he claimed to have overhead him let fall. The master-at-arms never suspected the veracity of these reports, more especially as to the epithets, for he well knew how secretly unpopular may a master-at-arms, *at least a master-at-arms of those days*, zealous in his function, and how the bluejackets shoot at him in private their raillery and wit; the nickname by which he goes among them (Jemmy Legs) implying under the form of merriment their cherished disrespect and dislike. (BB, p. 79; my emphasis)

As the narrator's pointed identification of the master-at-arm's ferreting function and status in the eyes of the policed multitude with the historical circumstances of the Napoleonic wars — "those days" — clearly suggests, it is precisely this aggrandizement of secret policing under the state of exception that this episode focuses.

It is also this elaborated reference to the dehumanizing transformation of policing under the aegis of the state of exception — a gesture that deflects the reader's attention from the narrator's allegorical emphasis to the historico-political site — that is continued in the succeeding chapters that culminate in Billy's deadly assault on Claggart and the inevitable emergence of the question of justice under the aegis of martial law. It informs the afterguardsman's insidious temptation of Billy to mutiny in the name of the impressed sailors on board the *Bellipotent* and, after Billy's resistant threat, his insistent efforts by eye contact to draw Billy into an unspoken conspiratorial complicity. And its aura pervades Billy's puzzled visit to the old Dansker, who, unlike his interlocutor, for whom truth is a matter of surface, is knowledgeable — but prudent — from long experience about policing on board a man-of war under martial law and who thus discloses the actions of the afterguardsman as a subterranean plot instigated against him by "Jemmy Legs," but does not offer him advice or assistance:

> "Didn't I say so, Baby Budd?"
>
> "Say what?" demanded Billy.
>
> "Why, *Jemmy Legs* is *down* on you."
>
> "And what," rejoined Billy in amazement, "has *Jemmy Legs* to do with that cracked afterguardsman?"
>
> "Ho, it was an afterguardsman, then. A cat's-paw, a cat's-paw!" And then with that exclamation, whether it had reference to a light puff of air just coming over the calm sea, *or a subtler relation to the after-guardsman*, there is no telling, the old Merlin gave a twisting wrench with his black teeth at his plug of tobacco, vouchsafing no reply to Billy's impetuous question, though now repeated, for it was his wont to relapse into grim silence when interrogated in skeptical sort as to any of his sentitious oracles, not always very clear ones, rather partaking of that obscurity which invests most Delphic deliverances from any quarter.
>
> *Long experience had very likely brought this old man to that bitter prudence which never interferes in aught and never gives advice.* (BB, pp. 85–86; my emphasis)

More tellingly, this aggrandizement of the secret policing function incumbent on the declaration of the state of emergency and the establishment of the security state infuses and informs the narrator's account of Claggart's subsequent fatal meeting (after the aborted chase of the French frigate), with Captain Vere, in which he accuses Billy of fomenting mutiny on the *Bellipotent*. What has been entirely overlooked in all the commentaries, old and new, about the narrator's account of Claggart's accusation — and yet, as I have been underscoring, is quite visible and telling — is its nuanced but decisive disclosure of the subtle hold that this petty officer has come to have over the captain of the *Bellipotent*, however much the latter would resist it, a hold that has its source, as I noted earlier, in his knowledge of the "austere civilization" he is exploiting. I mean, specifically, his knowledge of the historical context in which the *Bellipotent* exists and of Vere's state of mind as it pertains to the threat of mutiny, which is to say, his certain *foreknowledge* of Vere's response to his accusation. It is a hold, not incidentally, that Claggart insidiously tightens by the rhetoric he uses in his encounter with his superior victim.

At first, Claggart, "with the air of a subordinate," "conscientiously" generalizes the particular threat to the security of the *Bellipotent* by way of invoking the mutiny at the Nore, above all, the destabilizing conditions and agents — traitors to the crown and impressed sailors — that had fueled the uprising. He informs Captain Vere that, during the *Bellipotent's* recent chase of a French frigate, he had become convinced "that at least one sailor aboard was a dangerous character in a ship mustering some who not only had taken a guilty part in the late serious troubles, but others also who, like the man in question, had entered His Majesty's service under another form than enlistment." Though Vere impatiently interrupts the master-at-arms by commanding him to be "direct, man; say impressed men," Claggart continues in this circumlocutory way, focusing insistently — and knowingly but always with apparently responsible diffidence — on the analogy with the Great Mutiny and, underlying that event, the inexorable authority of the state of exception:

> Claggart made a gesture of subservience, and proceeded. Quite lately he (Claggart) had begun to suspect that on the gun decks some sort of movement prompted by the sailor in question was covertly going on, but he had not thought himself warranted in reporting the suspicion so long as it remained indistinct. But from what he had that afternoon observed in the man referred to, the suspicion of something clandestine going on had advanced to a point less removed from certainty. *He deeply felt*, he added, *the serious responsibility* assumed in making a report involving such possible consequences to the individual mainly concerned, *besides tending to augment those natural anxieties which every naval commander must feel in view of extraordinary outbreaks so recent as those which, he sorrowfully said it, it needed not to name.*
>
> Now at the first broaching of the matter Captain Vere, taken by surprise, could not wholly dissemble his disquietude. But as Claggart went on, the former's aspect changed into restiveness under something in the testifier's manner in giving his testimony. However, he refrained from interrupting him. *And Claggart, continuing, concluded with this: "God forbid, your honor, that the Bellipotent's should be the experience of the ——*" (BB, pp. 92–93; my emphasis)

Throughout this colloquy, the narrator informs us, Captain Vere feels an antipathy for his master-at-arms' obsequiously patriotic manner, indeed, a certain suspicion about the latter's testimony by innuendo and, not least, as his sudden interruption of Claggart suggests, his repeated implicit comparison of the *Bellipotent*'s present precarious occasion with the mutiny at the Nore. Nevertheless — and tellingly — he continues to listen to someone he intuits to be an "informer" (BB, p. 93), a "false witness" (BB, pp. 95, 96), and, above all, to intimate a deep anxiety over the parallel in the very process of trying to minimize its importance. In so doing, he implicitly betrays precisely that in him which gives his devious subordinate a power over him: the deeply inscribed ethical code that has its raison d'être in the sacredness of the "law" under the aegis of the state of exception.

This implicit revelation of the real stakes involved in the allegation of mutiny on board the *Bellipotent* is underscored in what immediately follows. When Captain Vere impatiently orders the master-at-arms to name "the dangerous man aboard" (BB, p. 94), the latter replies, " 'William Budd, a foretopman, your honor'," and then goes on to assert that a "man trap" lies behind his mask of innocence, one motivated by a deep resentment of his impressment. And he does this by way of (mis)representing that previously recounted occasion of Billy Budd's arrival on board the *Bellipotent* as evidence of the threat he posed to the security of the ship from the beginning. It is a revisionist historiographic strategy, not incidentally, that, as I have suggested, is a central target of Melville's irony in this story as well as in many of his others that address the question of the cultural memory:[18]

> "Did Lieutenant Ratcliffe happen to tell your honor of that adroit fling of Budd's, jumping up in the cutter's bow under the merchantmen's stern when he was being taken off? [The reference is, of course, to Billy's apostrophe, 'And good bye to you, old *Rights-of-Man*' (BB, p. 49)] It is even masked by that sort of good-humored air that at heart he resents his impressment. You have but noted his fair cheek. A man-trap may be under the ruddy-tipped daisies." (BB, p. 94)

Vere, the narrator tells us, had heard of Billy's "adieu" to the ship *Rights-of-Man* from Ratcliffe but had interpreted it favorably as the act of "a spirit that could take an arbitrary enlistment so merrily and sensibly" (BB, p. 95). Later, after observing the young sailor's conduct, he had decided to recommend him for promotion to "the captaincy of the mizzentop." "In sum," the narrator concludes, "Captain Vere had from the beginning deemed Billy Budd to be what in the naval parlance of the time was called a 'King's bargain', that is to say, for His Britannic Majesty's navy a capital investment at small outlay or none at all" (BB, p. 95). Bracketing for the time being the troubling reductive rhetoric Vere's uses to assess Billy's worth, it will suffice to say that, despite his sympathy for Billy and his visceral dislike of Claggart and deep suspicion of his witness, he is visibly incapable, try as he might, of breaking the hold his subordinate's gaze has on him: "Captain Vere again heard him out; then for the moment stood ruminating. The mood he evinced, Claggart — himself for the time liberated from the other's scrutiny — steadily regarded with a look difficult to render: a look curious of the operation of his tactics, a look such as might have been that of the spokesman of the envious children of Jacob deceptively imposing upon the troubled patriarch the blood-dyed coat of young Joseph" (BB, p. 96).

Vere brings the confrontation to an "end" by deciding to put the accuser to the test of being confronted by the accused, but, disablingly, in a closed setting. In so doing, he succumbs, in the very act of resisting, to Claggart's policing strategy — the insidious strategy based on his knowledge of Vere's deeply inscribed commitment to the "truth" of the (lawless) law of the security state and its extreme disciplinary imperatives. As I have observed, one of the essential realities of the state of exception is that it enables the criminal to all too easily become the policeman, the unruly, the ruler.

Since this paradox is at the heart or my reading of *Billy Budd*, it is worth pursuing at greater length even at the risk of digressing. Earlier, in chapter 2, I cited the French critic Alain Brossat's essay "L'inarticulable," written in the aftermath of 9/11, that reads *Billy Budd* (and Benjamin Britten's opera) as proleptic of the state of exception established by the George W. Bush administration's declaration of its "war on terror." Whereas my emphasis in treating the state of exception falls on the masters' reduction of human (political) life to bare life, Brossat focuses on the necessarily spontaneous violent response of the inarticulate — those who have been dispossessed of a political voice by the masters of the earth (Billy Budd's fist; Al-Qaeda's attack on the World Trade Center). Though I find his easy identification of Billy and the inarticulate of the world with Al-Qaeda somewhat problematic, I am in absolute agreement with his identification of Claggart as the real power on board the *Bellipotent* — the "master of masters" — and analogously, if only by implication, the "criminal" element as the real power in the post–9/11 United States.

This identification has been severely contested by the American political theorist John Brenkman in a recent substantial essay on *Billy Budd* entitled "The Melvillean Moment."[19] Sympathetic with Brossat's association of Billy with the plebs, who "are caught in two wars at once, the war between nations and the 'immemorial' one between 'patricians and plebeians,' " Brenkman goes on to say that Brossat "squanders this insight by oversimplifying the shape of power on the *Bellipotent*. He makes Claggart the epitome of rule on the ship, the 'master of masters.' Claggart's tyranny, dishonesty, and persecution of Billy becomes the very image of the ship's governance."

Brenkman goes on to refute this claim by underscoring the difference between Claggart's monomaniacal tyranny and Captain Vere humane sympathy with Billy just before the moment when, according to Brossat, the alleged difference between the masters and the servants — the powerful and articulate and the weak and inarticulate — irrupts in what, following Walter Benjamin, he calls "mythic violence." Vere's fatherly council to Billy — "There is no hurry, my boy. Take your time" — Brenkman affirms, "implies no such alignment of the repressive power and speech on the one side and silence, powerlessness, and hyperviolence on the other":

> The captain has had Billy brought to his cabin in the first place because he doubts Claggart, and "therefore, before trying the accused, he would first practically test the accuser" (chapter 18). Brossat apparently wants nothing to do with this difference between Claggart and Vere because it does not gel with the equations underlying his argument: if the depraved master-at-arms is the equivalent of the warship's captain, and if the warship is the equivalent of the modern state, then the wartime state of emergency is the equivalent of democratic rule. (p. 36)

What Brenkman's vestigial American exceptionalist problematic, like that of most critics of *Billy Budd*, blinds him to, I suggest on the basis of my retrieval of the minute particulars of the policing environment necessarily produced by the state of exception, is precisely the stranglehold that Claggart, the master-at-arms, has on Vere's, the captain's, mind: his insidious insight into the higher or "sacred" cause that unerringly determines the latter's vision and action. And, more important, in so doing, he also misses Melville's profound — *and proleptic* — recognition that, as I have shown, under the conditions of the state of exception, the criminals, or, more accurately, the "promiscuous lame ducks of morality" (BB, p. 65) easily become the policemen.[20]

Seen in the dislocating light of the larger global historical context I have retrieved from the margins, the narrator's chapters of *Billy Budd* that have traditionally been invoked to justify the allegorical or universalist reading of Melville's story undergo, in Louis Althusser's phrase, a remarkable "change of terrain" very much like that undergone by the early chapters of "Benito Cereno" at the moment when Captain Amasa Delano's American exceptionalist frame of reference (his "problematic") is shattered by the revelation that the slaves have been in command of Don Benito's ship from the time he had boarded it.[21] These chapters come to be seen, that is, not as a prefiguration of the narrator's final encomium to Captain Vere's affirmation of law and order against revolutionary chaos (nor to Melville's testament of acceptance), but as his representation of events that, saturated with the ominous aura of the state of exception, lead inexorably to the preordained — "fated" — reduction of Billy's body to "inarticulate" naked life and its execution in the sacred name of the security of the ship of state.

The Drumhead Court and the Unerring Logic of the State of Exception

This fated, unjustifiable, and violent "end" is inexorably enacted in the final chapters that recount Vere's reaction to Billy's unintended killing of Claggart, his precipitous decision to hold a drumhead court immediately and behind closed doors (in secret), his imposition of his judgment on the recalcitrant court, and his execution of the innocent sailor. From the beginning to the end of this process, Vere is convinced of Billy's innocence and manifests deep, indeed, fatherly, sympathy for the young man. But from the beginning to the end, too, Billy's innocence is ruthlessly secondary in the captain's mind to the security of the ship he commands in the name of the king and imperial Britain's war against Napoleonic France. What is ontologically prior to Billy's living being, that is, is Captain Vere's deeply inscribed and unerring loyalty to the (lawless) law of the state of exception. This inexorably predetermined momentum should be rather obvious to an "informed gaze,"[22] but because it has been rendered invisible by the supervisory gaze of those critics who have subscribed to one version or other of the testament of acceptance thesis, it will be necessary to spell it out systematically in what follows.

When, for example, the narrator recounts Billy's deadly reaction to Claggart's accusation during their encounter in the captain's quarters, the first words Vere is given to utter in the aftermath of the death blow—they are spoken in a whisper, which is to say, to himself—are, "Fated boy, . . . what have you done?" Vere thus goes a long way towards verifying his criminal policeman's mesmerizing/paralyzing power over him: Claggart's commanding knowledge of Vere's essential identity and, therefore, his foreknowledge of the latter's response to his allegation of the threat of mutiny. And then, after Vere ascertains that Claggart is dead, the narrator, in a transformative moment of understanding that manifests itself as a dislocating question, goes on:

> Captain Vere with one hand covering his face stood to all appearance as impassive as the object at his feet. Was he absorbed in taking in all the bearings of the event and what was best not only now at once to be done, but also in the sequel? *Slowly he uncovered his face; and the effect was as if the moon emerging from eclipse should reappear with quite another aspect than that which had gone into hiding. The father in him, manifested toward Billy thus far in the scene, was replaced by the military disciplinarian.* (BB, pp. 99–100; my emphasis)

This decisive transformation of Captain Vere from caring father to undeviating military disciplinarian is underscored when, after having called the surgeon in to verify Claggart's death, he suddenly and "vehemently exclaim[s]," "Struck dead by an angel of God! *Yet the angel must hang!*" (BB, p. 101; my emphasis). And it culminates after Vere, having removed the dead body to a compartment opposite to that in which Billy is immured and categorically dismissed the surgeon, now deeply troubled by his superior's "desire for secrecy" but compliant as a subordinate in the context of martial law, Vere announces his abnormal decision to "call a drumhead court" in secret instead of referring the case to the Admiralty, a higher and *more public* authority (BB, p. 101).

Immediately following this marked double "eclipse"—the transformation of Captain Vere *and*, in some significant degree, of the narrator—the narrator focuses his narrative on that aspect of the captain's authoritarian decision, above all, his arbitrary insistence on a trial of an obviously innocent sailor to be held in secrecy, that seems not only irrational (as most commentary represents this moment), but morally and, above all, politically troubling to those who have become privy to the events ending in the death of Claggart:

> Full of disquietude and misgiving, the surgeon left the cabin. Was Captain Vere suddenly affected in his mind, or was it but a transient excitement, brought about by so strange and extraordinary a tragedy? [This question, not incidentally, applies not only to the surgeon, but to the narrator as well.] As to the drumhead court, it struck the surgeon as *impolitic*, if nothing more. The thing to do, he thought, was to place Billy Budd in confinement, and in a way dictated by usage, and postpone further action in so extraordinary a case to such time as they should rejoin the squadron, and then refer it to the admiral. He recalled the unwonted agitation of Captain Vere and his excited exclamations, so at variance with his normal manner. Was he unhinged? (BB, pp. 101–102; my emphasis)

Tellingly, the narrator goes on to characterize the surgeon's (and the other officers') hesitant response to the captain's dislocating fiat by invoking the reductive and corrupting imperatives of the state of exception—and, by ironic implication, the democratic (public) openness that is annulled by the security promised by the abrogation of common law ("usage"), including that which guarantees human rights: "No more trying situation is conceivable than that of an officer subordinate under a captain whom he suspects to be not mad, indeed, but yet not quite unaffected in his intellects. To argue his order to him would be insolence. To resist him would be mutiny" (BB, p. 102).

In commenting on the surgeon's tentative attribution of mental unhinging as the cause of the Captain's arbitrary decision, the narrator, it is true, rightly interrogates a binarist interpretation of sanity and madness (and, for that matter, any form of the dyad, identity/difference, that is reduced to the hierarchic binary that privileges order over chaos: "Who in the rainbow can draw the line where the violet tint ends and the orange tint begins? Distinctly we see the difference of the colors, but where exactly does the one first blendingly enter into the other? So with sanity and insanity" (BB, p. 102). But this crucial qualification should not be read, as it has been by Barbara Johnson, Eve Sedgwick, Nancy Ruttenburg, and Sharon Cameron, as evidence of Melville's final refusal to judge Vere in the name of undecidable ambiguity, a refusal that, as Brook Thomas in his critique of Johnson's reading of *Billy Budd*, has decisively shown, could easily be interpreted as a license for political paralysis.[23] In the next paragraph the narrator writes, "Whether Captain Vere, as the surgeon professionally and privately surmised, was really the sudden victim of any degree of aberration, every one must determine for himself *by such light as this narrative may afford*" (BB, p. 102; my emphasis). Taking our directive from this suggestion that we read this complex social text symptomatically, we see the metaphor of the colors of the rainbow used by the narrator undergo a metamorphosis. As I have been suggesting by way of bringing the hitherto marginalized martial law of the state of exception to center stage, we are enabled to tentatively conclude that, the narrator is, in fact, referring to the dedifferentiating arbitrariness — the allegorization — of Vere's judgment after his eclyptic transformation. I mean, specifically, his arbitrary substitution (similar, not incidentally, to that of the imperialist British historians of the Great Mutiny and, as we shall see, of the official naval chroniclers of the "inside narrative" of the *Bellipotent*), of an unworldly worldly absolute, not for ambiguity as such, but for the (unjust) *imbalance* of power relations that always pertains *in the world*. And he does this, I suggest, in the name of pointing both to the injustice incumbent on reducing the complex sociopolitical occasion to decidable allegorical abstractions and to the political paralysis incumbent on reducing the actually existing imbalance of power to utterly undecidable ambiguity, that is, to the state of equivalence.

Be that as it may, it is no accident that, after underscoring Captain Vere's transformation, the narrator returns to the larger historical occasion that, in the eyes of the dominant British culture (the "naval authority," for whom the aftermath of the "suppressed insurrections" was "very critical") justified the establishment of the state of exception:

That the unhappy event [the death of Claggart] which has been narrated could not have happened at a worse juncture was but too true. For it was close on the heel of the suppressed insurrections, an aftertime very critical to naval authority, demanding from every English sea commander two qualities not readily interfusable — prudence and rigor. Moreover, there was something crucial in the case.

In the jugglery of circumstances preceding and attending the event on board the *Bellipotent*, and in the light of that martial code whereby it was formally to be judged, innocence and guilt personified in Claggart and Budd in effect changed places. In a *legal view* the apparent victim of the tragedy was he who had sought to victimize a man blameless; and the indisputable deed of the latter, *navally regarded*, constituted the most heinous of military crimes. Yet more. The essential right and wrong involved in the matter, the clearer that might be, so much the worse for the responsibility of a loyal sea commander, inasmuch as he was not authorized to determine the matter on that primitive basis. (BB, pp. 102–3; my emphasis)

In depicting the difficult conditions in which Captain Vere finds himself — the tremendous determining force of the "outside" world on the "inside" world of the *Bellipotent* — the narrator, it is true, expresses a certain sympathy for his terrible dilemma, even as he emphasizes the exacerbation of the imbalance of power — the chilling chiasma — that the martial law (the "legal view," the situation "navally regarded") has produced. But as he proceeds to reflect on Vere's transformation, he increasingly underscores the dehumanizing consequences of the state of exception — consequences that seep into every aspect of life in the public realm (the body politic of the *Bellipotent*). I quote the narrator at length to underscore the transformation that he has undergone in the process of relating the events that begin with Captain Vere's response to Claggart's accusation:

Small wonder then that the *Bellipotent*'s captain, though in general a man of rapid decision, felt that circumspectness not less than promptitude was necessary. Until he could decide upon his course, and in each detail; and not only so, but until the concluding measure was upon the point of being enacted, he deemed it advisable, in view of all the circumstances, *to guard as much as possible against publicity. Here he may or may not have erred.* Certain it is, however, that subsequently in the confidential talk of more than one or two gun rooms and cabins he was not a little criticized by some officers, a fact imputed by his friends and vehemently by his cousin Jack Denton to professional jealousy of Starry Vere. *Some imaginative ground for invidious comment there*

was. The maintenance of secrecy in the matter, the confining all knowl-
edge of it for a time to the place where the homicide occurred, the quar-
terdeck cabin; in these particulars lurked some resemblance to policy
adopted in those tragedies of the palace which have occurred more than
once in the capital founded by Peter the Barbarian [i.e., St. Petersburg,
Russia]. (BB, p. 103; my emphasis)

In highlighting the narrator's repeated returns to the negative aspects in
his meditation on Vere's decision, against "usage," to convene the drumhead court immediately and to carry out the proceedings in secret—which
is to say, in a space which is closed off from public scrutiny and provides
immunity to judges that preside over it—I do not want to suggest that he
is anticipating an indictment of Captain Vere's person as such, as many
critics have concluded in restricting the "case of Captain Vere" to the issue
of universal morality versus expedience ("chronometricals" versus "horologicals"). Rather, I am suggesting that the target of his concern is wider
than Vere, the individual, and more "political" in scope. Given the inexorable conditions produced by the insistent impingement of the macrocosmic world on the microcosmic world of the *Bellipotent* (which are further
emphasized by the narrator's return to them—"the slumbering embers of
the Nore among the crew" that "overruled in Captain Vere every other
consideration" (BB, p. 104)—immediately after this paragraph), Vere remains a sympathetic figure. Melville's target, rather, as the resonant reference to Peter the Great as "Peter the Barbarian" suggests, is a "civilization" of the "austere" sort—the rule of (public) law of the "Power then [at
the time of the Napoleonic Wars] all but the sole free conservative one of
the Old World" (BB, p. 54)—that has been transformed into barbarism by
the imposition of secrecy, the sine qua non of the state of exception:
ultimately, a reign of terror that has legally reduced the multitude—its
lowly and powerless human victims—to bare life. It is a barbarism all the
more barbarous in that the inhumane logic of its permanent lawless law is
capable of harnessing a basically good and thoughtful man like Captain
Vere as an unwitting agent of its totalizing dehumanizing cause.

That such a "civilizational" reading of this climactic passage of *Billy
Budd* is a viable one is strongly enforced, I suggest, by recalling a strikingly
similar passage in Melville's *White-Jacket*, there, however, focusing on an
American naval vessel, unequivocally indicting the dehumanizing secrecy

that is intrinsic to martial law. It is a passage that, not incidentally, culminates in an overt reference to the *Somers* affair, which, it will be recalled,
some critics have said, instigated Melville's *Billy Budd* and, which, not
least, the narrator will invoke later in the chapter when he recounts the
drumhead court proceedings that terminate in the decision to execute Billy:

> What can be expected from a court whose deeds are done in the dark-
> ness of the recluse courts of the Spanish Inquisition? when that dark-
> ness is solemnized by an oath on the Bible? when an oligarchy of
> epaulets sits upon the bench, and a plebeian top-man, without a jury,
> stands *judicially naked at the bar*? . . . .
>
> Some may urge that the severest operations of the code are tacitly
> made null in time of peace. But with respect to several of the Articles [of
> War] this holds true, yet at any time any and all of them may be legally
> enforced. Nor have there been wanting recent instances, illustrating the
> spirit of this code, even in cases where the letter of the code was not al-
> together observed. The well-known case of a United States brig fur-
> nishes a memorable example, which at any moment may be repeated.
> Three men, in a time of peace, were then hung at the yard-arm, merely
> because, in the Captain's judgment, it became necessary to hang them.
> To this day the question of their complete guilt is socially discussed.[24]

But we need not appeal to a text published many years before to argue
that what is fundamentally at stake in the narrator's identification of
Vere's insistence on secrecy in the conduct of the "trial" with the terrorism
of the Spanish inquisition and Peter the Barbarian is the corruption of
civilization from top to bottom under the aegis of the state of exception.
For this thesis is decisively *enacted* immediately after this reference by the
drumhead court, a court — the first lieutenant, the captain of the marines,
and the sailing master — strategically chosen, secretly convened, and
single-mindedly determined by Captain Vere. From the beginning (as the
only eyewitness) and throughout the proceedings (as the presiding judge),
Vere affirms the essential innocence of Billy Budd and expresses his deep,
indeed, fatherly sympathy for him. That is to say, he acknowledges that,
from the moral point of view, Billy is innocent and should be exonerated.
But at no point in the process does Vere deviate from the "law" of the state
of exception. As the narrator says (in a reference to the religious fanatics
of the Inquisition serving God?), in inaugurating his account of the drama:

"But a true military officer is in one particular like a true monk. Not with more of self-abnegation will the latter keep his vows of monastic obedience than the former his vows of allegiance to martial law" (BB, p. 104).

This monkish comportment begins to assert itself openly when Billy, having been asked by the troubled captain of the marines why Claggart should have "so maliciously lied, since you declare there was no malice between you?" is unable to answer him and turns to Captain Vere for help. At this point, Vere, despite his natural sympathy for Billy and the compelling power of Billy's helpless appeal, intervenes in his capacity as judge of the court by deflecting the captain of the marines focus on the (natural) moral register to the political. Driven by the inexorable logic of martial law, he says:

> "The question you put to him comes naturally enough. But how can he rightly answer it?" — or anybody else, unless it be he who lies within there, designating the compartment where lay the corpse. But the prone one there will not rise to our summons. In effect, though, as it seems to me, the point you make is hardly material. Quite aside from any conceivable motive actuating the master-at-arms, and irrespective of the provocation to the blow, a martial court must needs in the present case confine its attention to the blow's consequence, which consequence justly is to be deemed not otherwise than as the striker's deed." (BB, p. 107)

Billy's response to this, to him, unexpected and enigmatic utterance, the narrator tells us in a metaphor that resonates with his reduction to bare life by Vere's disciplinary logic, is "an interrogative look toward the speaker . . . not unlike that which a dog of generous breed might turn upon his master, seeking in his face, some elucidation of a previous gesture ambiguous to the canine intelligence." The court's response is equally telling: they read in it "a meaning unanticipated, *involving a prejudgment on the speaker's part*," which "served to augment a mental disturbance previously evident enough" (p. 108; my emphasis). This last is, of course, a reference to the disturbed surgeon's earlier question following Vere's precipitous decision to convene a drumhead court: "Was he [Captain Vere] unhinged?" But here, in the context of Vere's relentlessly single-minded logic, it assumes a more definite meaning, one that recalls the narrator's identification of Claggart's as monomaniac (BB, p. 90) — and

Melville's devastating criticism of Captain Ahab's and the Indian-hater's metaphysically ordained single-mindedness in *Moby-Dick* and *The Confidence-Man*, respectively.[25]

Seeing that the members of the court are deeply troubled by his undeviating logic — a disquiet, the narrator says, exacerbated by "his phraseology, now and then . . . suggestive of the grounds whereon rested that imputation of a certain pedantry socially alleged against him" (BB, p. 109) — Vere repeats his monolithic argument, now, however, from his privileged position as the captain of the "threatened" ship, and thus in terms that explicitly relate it to the historical/political events — the "crisis" of the *Bellipotent*'s "security" — that has justified the overt declaration of the state of exception as the permanent law. I quote this climactic passage at length, first, to underscore the "law" of the state of exception — the unmovable "center elsewhere" that is "out of reach of freeplay," as it were,[26] that inexorably determines Vere's political argument, including, not incidentally, the authoritative words concerning the moral issue he puts into the mouths of his subordinates (and later into Billy's). I quote it as well to demonstrate the subtle (casuistical) way, epitomized by his reduction of those who would protect an innocent Billy's life from a degrading death on moral grounds to "casuists," in which his apparent argument becomes in the end an arbitrary final judgment: one that suppresses the aporias (doubts) that, opened to public scrutiny (the "political"), might undermine its higher — "paramount" — authority or, as one of the officers puts it in response, the "lateral light" on "what remains a mystery in the matter" that might be shed by the depositions of the members of "the ship's company":

> "Hitherto I have been but the witness, little more; and I should hardly think now to take another tone, that of your coadjutor for the time, did I not perceive in you — at the crisis too — a troubled hesitancy, proceeding, I doubt not, from the clash of military duty with moral scruple — scruple vitalized by compassion. For the compassion, how can I otherwise than share it? But, mindful of paramount obligations, I strive against scruples that may end to enervate decision. Not, gentlemen, that I hide from myself that the case is an exceptional one. Speculatively regarded, it well might be referred to a jury of casuists. But for us here, acting not as casuists or moralists, it is a case practical, and under martial law practically to be dealt with.

"But your scruples: do they move as in a dusk? Challenge them. Make them advance and declare themselves. Come now; do they import something like this: If, mindless of palliating circumstance, we are bound to regard the death of the master-at-arms as the prisoner's deed, then does that deed constitute a capital crime whereof the penalty is a mortal one. But in natural justice is nothing but the prisoner's overt act to be considered? How can we adjudge to summary and shameful death a fellow creature innocent before God, and whom we feel to be so? — Does that state it aright? You sign sad assent. Well, I too feel that, the full force of that. It is Nature. *But do these buttons that we wear attest that our allegiance is to Nature? No, to the King.* Though the ocean, which is inviolate Nature primeval, though this be the element where we move and have our beings as sailors, yet as the King's officers lies our duty in a sphere correspondingly natural? *So little is that true, that in receiving our commissions we in the most important regards ceased to be natural free agents. When war is declared are we the commissioned fighters previously consulted? We fight at command. If our judgments approve the war, that is but coincidence.* So in other particulars. So now. For suppose condemnation to follow these present proceedings. *Would it be so much we ourselves that would condemn as it would be martial law operating through us? For that law and the rigor of it, we are not responsible.* Our vowed responsibility is in this: That however pitilessly that law may operate in any instances, we nevertheless adhere to it and administer it. (BB, pp. 110–11; my emphasis)

When Captain Vere realizes that his appeal to duty to the king over natural inclination, responsibility to the dictates of the monarch over free will, does not appease the uneasiness of the court's members, he modifies his argument against the (female) heart to include "private conscience." In the process, he also modifies his particular appeal to duty to the king to include overtly the larger and finally more substantial obedience to the "imperial" imperatives of the martial law (the state of exception) and the security state precipitated by Britain's global war against Napoleon:

"But something in your aspect seems to urge that it is not solely the heart that moves in you, but also the conscience, the private conscience. But tell me whether or not, occupying the position we do, private conscience should not yield to that imperial one formulated in the code under which alone we officially proceed? . . . .

"To steady us a bit, let us recur to the facts. — In wartime at sea a man-of-war's man strikes his superior in grade, and the blow kills. Apart from its effect, the blow itself is, according to the Articles of War, a capital crime. (BB, p. 111)

At this point the officer of the marines emotionally interrupts the captain's unerring line of thought to remind him that "Budd purposed neither mutiny nor homicide." In response, Vere underscores his invocation of martial law against conscience, including its justification of impressment, an allusion that cannot help but evoke the memory of Billy's arbitrary enlistment into the ranks of the *Bellipotent* from the *Rights-of-Man*, not to say, the anti-Burkean author of the pamphlet from which it drew its name:

> Surely not, my good man. And before a court less arbitrary and more merciful than a martial one, that plea would largely extenuate. At the Last Assizes it shall acquit. But how here? We proceed under the law of the Mutiny Act. In feature no child can resemble his father more than that Act resembles in spirit the thing from which it derives — War. In His Majesty's service — in this ship indeed — *there are Englishmen forced to fight for the King against their will. Against their conscience, for aught we know.* Though as their fellow creatures some of us may appreciate their position, yet as navy officers what reck we of it? . . . *War looks but to the frontage, the appearance. And the Mutiny Act, War's child, takes after the father.* Budd's intent or non-intent is nothing to the purpose.

And when the faltering junior lieutenant, in a last desperate effort to save Billy from hanging, asks Captain Vere whether or not the court could "convict and yet mitigate the penalty," Vere, now decisively and with absolute finality, returns to the *political context*: to what I have been asserting from the beginning as the indissoluble relationship between the "outside" story (the insurrections at Spithead and the Nore instigated by the "Revolutionary Spirit") and the "inside" story (the events on board the *Bellipotent*), that is, to the hierarchic relation between "them" and "Us," the erratic "multitude" under aristocratic/imperial disciplinary rule:

"Gentleman, were that clearly lawful for us under the circumstances, consider the consequences of such clemency. *The people*" (meaning the ship's company) "have native sense; most of them are familiar with our naval usage and tradition, and how would they take it? Even could you explain to them—which our official position forbids—they, *long molded by arbitrary discipline, have not that kind of intelligent responsiveness that might qualify them to comprehend and discriminate.* No, to *the people* the foretopman's deed, however it be worded in the announcement, will be plain homicide committed in a flagrant act of mutiny. What penalty for that should follow, they know. But it does not follow. *Why?* [author's emphasis] they will ruminate. *You know what sailors are.* Will they not revert to the recent outbreak at the Nore? Ay. *They know the well-founded alarm—the panic it struck throughout England. Your clement sentence they would account pusillanimous. They would think that we flinch, that we are afraid of them—afraid of practicing a lawful rigor singularly demanded at this juncture, lest it should provide new troubles.* What shame to us such a conjecture on their part, and how deadly to discipline. You see then, whither, prompted by duty and law, *I steadfastly drive.* But I beseech you, my friends, do not take me amiss. I feel as you do for this unfortunate boy. But did he know our hearts, *I take him to be of that generous nature that he would feel even for us on whom in this military necessity so heavy a compulsion is laid.*" (BB, pp. 112–13; my emphasis)

In the eyes of Captain Vere, in sum, as these speeches insistently and chillingly testify in both what they say and leave unsaid, Billy (and the common sailors), despite his innocence in the face of a life and death charge, is as *nothing* or a *nobody* in comparison to the safety of his ship and his nation, irregardless of the morality or immorality of the latter's motives and practice. Nowhere in his eloquent and masterfully strategic address to the officers of the drumhead court does he invoke the question of the reality of the threat, to say nothing about the exceptionalist motives of the king (the dominant imperial culture) he (and his officers) so dutifully would obey. Despite Vere's sympathy, Billy is finally only an afterthought to Vere's monolithic commitment to the unerring disciplinary (biopolitical) imperatives of the state of exception, and his shipmates, the anonymous erratic vehicle of threat. They literally do not count in an accounting (value) system that privileges the security of the abstract national whole. This is what I meant when, earlier, I said that Billy does not stand a chance. He and his fellow sailors (the multitude) are, in Alain Brossat's apt term "the inarticulate" in a world in which language is utterly controlled by the masters.

Despite their abiding doubts, the members of the drumhead court capitulate in the end to Vere's inclusive judgment, partly because of his earnestness, partly in deference to his superior intelligence, but also, as the narrator tellingly puts it, partly because of his "closing appeal to their [collective] instinct as sea officers: in the forethought he threw out as to the practical consequences to discipline, considering the unconfirmed tone of the fleet at the time, should a man-of-war's man's violent killing at sea of a superior in grade be allowed to pass for aught else than a capital crime demanding prompt infliction of the penalty" (BB, p. 113). This egregious reduction in the name of vocation — a higher calling — that is, is further testimony to the insidious moral and sociopolitical effects of the state of exception.

If, then, we are attuned to the narrator's overdetermination of those aspects of sociopolitical life on board the *Bellipotent* that render it a police state by what precedes Captain Vere's justificatory discourse — his commitment to the security state in the name of the state of exception — it is difficult not to read it as a *political* argument that, whatever the benign motives behind it, not only legitimates those sociopolitical conditions, but also establishes a corrupt moral environment that enables less righteous leaders to take advantage of them with impunity. Read in terms of the preceding context established by the narrator, in other words, Vere's "steadfast" commitment to his calling — the ruthless biopolitical imperatives of martial law over the life of the innocent and utterly helpless Billy Budd or, more to his point (if we take his remarkably low opinion of the ordinary seamen that man the man-of-war he commands seriously) over the "the people" — provides license to the executive agency (as opposed to the "people" and/or the representatives of the people) to abuse its monolithic power. In a way that is remarkably proleptic of the entire Cold War and post–9/11 American occasion, it enables the executive deliberately to institute a climate of fear in the body politic, the establishment of the practice of secret policing, the production of the informant mentality, the denial of human rights to the accused, the inflicting of torture to elicit "confession," the abrogation of free speech and public trial by a jury of peers, all in behalf of disciplining — of biopoliticizing — the "volatile" multitude. All of which is to say that Vere's domesticated Ahabian affirmation of the illicit law of the state of exception, despite his unquestionable probity and his fatherly sympathy for Billy, opens the door to the formation of a polity in which politics is reduced to biopower and the "people" of the body politic to "bare life": to what, a hundred years later, Giorgio Agamben, following Michel Foucault and Hannah Arendt, has called, in its limit situation, the polity of "the [concentration] camp" in his meditations on the state of exception in the wake of its increasing presence in modern democratic societies:

> [T]he birth of the camp in our time appears as an event that decisively signals the political space of modernity itself. It is produced at the point at which the political system of the modern nation-state, which was founded on the functional nexus between a determinate localization (land) and a determinate order (the state) and mediated by autocratic rules for the inscription of life (birth or nation), enters into lasting crisis, and the State decides to assume directly the care of the nation's biological life as one of its proper tasks. . . . The state of exception, which was essentially a temporary suspension of the juridico-political order, now becomes a new and stable spatial arrangement inhabited by the bare life that more and more can no longer be inscribed in that order. The growing dissociation of birth (bare life) and the nation-state is the new fact of politics in our day, and what we call *camp* is this disjunction. To an order without localization (the state of exception, in which law is suspended) there now corresponds a localization without order (the camp as permanent space of exception). The political system no longer orders forms of life and juridical rules in a determinate space, but instead contains at its very center a *dislocating localization* that exceeds it and into which every form of life and every rule can be virtually taken. The camp as dislocating localization is the hidden matrix of the politics in which we are still living, and it is this structure of the camp that we must learn to recognize in all its metamorphoses into the *zones d'attentes* of our airports and certain outskirts of our cities. The camp is the fourth, inseparable element that has now added itself to- and so broken — the old trinity composed of the state, the nation (birth), and land.[27]

The American Reference

On the basis of the narrator of *Billy Budd*'s invocation of the *Somers* Affair (1842), I claimed pointedly in chapter 1, it will be recalled, that he is an American recounting the story of the *Bellipotent* as a cautionary tale in the face of a contemporary American global political initiative — the expansion, in the late nineteenth century, of the American frontier into the Pacific — bearing remarkable similarities to that of Britain in the period of the Napoleonic wars a century earlier. It is no accident, despite its appearance as a chronological anomaly, that the narrator invokes this earlier, resonantly symbolic American event immediately following Captain Vere's speech to the officers of the drumhead court in the form of a commentary on its dire conclusion:

> Not unlikely they [the members of the court] were brought to something more or less akin to that harassed frame of mind which in the year 1842 actuated the commander of the U.S. brig-of-war *Somers* to resolve, under the *so-called* Articles of War, *Articles modeled upon the English Mutiny Act*, to resolve upon the execution at sea of a midshipman and two sailors as mutineers designing the seizure of the brig. Which resolution was carried out though in a time of peace and within not many days' sail of home. An act vindicated by a naval court of inquiry subsequently convened ashore. History, and here recited without comment. True, the circumstances on board the *Somers* were different from those on board the *Bellipotent*. But the urgency felt, well-warranted or otherwise, was much the same (BB, pp. 113–114; my emphasis)

The narrator refers to his interpolation of the *Somers* Affair as history "recited without comment." But the narrative context, beginning with the impressment of Billy Budd from the *Rights-of Man* and culminating in Vere's call for his execution — and the rhetoric he uses to abstain from comment, which recalls the tendency of official historians to efface contradictory concrete particulars — insinuates something far more decisive. Immediately, as the terms I have underscored suggest, the narrator's laconic comment points dramatically to the disturbing contradiction inhering in the fact that the legal code of an American naval vessel — a vessel of a democratic republic claiming exceptionalist status — in peacetime, no less, is modeled on "the English Mutiny Act," on a law that is intrinsic to a fundamentally tyrannical, indeed, an imperial regime that, for that reason, is perpetually at war and, therefore, in which the state of exception is permanent. That this is what Melville, if not entirely the narrator, is implicitly drawing attention to in alluding to the *Somers* Affair is strongly suggested by recalling the previously cited chapters in *White-Jacket* on the genealogy of the legal system that obtained in the American Navy, which culminate in his exemplary angry republican invocation of the *Somers* executions:

> As the Articles of War form the ark and constitution of the penal laws of the American Navy, in all sobriety and earnestness it may be well to glance at their origin. Whence came they? And how is it that one arm of the national defences of a Republic comes to be ruled by a Turkish code, whose every section almost, like each of the tubes of a revolving pistol, fires nothing short of death into the heart of an offender? How comes it that, by virtue of a law solemnly ratified by a Congress of freemen, the representatives of freemen, thousands of Americans are subjected to the most despotic usages, and, from the dock-yards of a republic, absolute monarchies are launched, with "glorious stars and stripes" for an ensign? By what unparalleled anomaly, by what monstrous grafting of tyranny upon freedom did these Articles of War ever come to be so much as heard of in the American Navy?
>
> Whence came they? They cannot be indigenous growth of those political institutions, which are based upon that arch-democrat Thomas Jefferson's Declaration of Independence? No: they are an importation from abroad, even from Britain, whose laws we Americans hurled off as tyrannical, and yet retained the most tyrannical of all.[28]

It is, in short, hard to believe that the Melville who could point so angrily at such an ironically grotesque contradiction earlier in his life would, as so many critics have concluded, reverse his judgment at the end of it.

But, I submit, the analogy to which the narrator draws our attention is not restricted to that between the *Somers* Affair and the events on board the *Bellipotent*. If it is assumed that the narrator is not an American, then this analogy would seem to be more or less pointless (as it has been for most commentators). If, however, he is seen to be an American, then the historical analogy can be read as one addressed to a contemporary American audience, that is, as an analogy that points not only to the events of 1797 on board the *Bellipotent* but also to a further analogy with the American present. I mean, as I have argued in chapter 1, with the last (Gilded Age) decades of the nineteenth century, when, in the wake of the incorporation of America by capitalism, the announcement of the closing of the frontier, and the consequent threat to the covenant — all deep and abiding concerns of Melville's earlier texts, as I have shown elsewhere — exceptionalist America began to consider the possibility of expanding its "empire of liberty" into the Pacific. Understood in this estranging light, the narrator's allusion to the peacetime executions on the *Somers* at the end of his account of Captain Vere's justification for hanging Billy Budd precipitates a further sea change. Under its pressure, the American occasion of the late 1880s, the years when Melville was writing *Billy Budd*, comes from the margins, where it has been relegated, to center stage. I mean, more specifically, the time when, under the emergent polyvalent pressure to enlarge the U.S. Navy into a global one, a massive pressure epitomized by the influential proselytizing of the naval historian Alfred Thayer Mahan,[29] Melville's contemporary, the United States, in imitation of exceptionalist Britain's imperialist effort at the end of the eighteenth century to gain control of the global seaways, began to globalize its interests — and in the process, insofar as the globalization of imperialism means the permanent threat of war, to normalize martial law: the state of exception that, as in the cases of the *Somers* and the *Bellipotent*, produced a cultural and sociopolitical environment (the national security state) that enabled and "justified" the summary execution of accused mutineers without trial by jury.

Billy as Bare Life

It is true, of course, that the narrator's conjectures about what transpired in a closeted interview between the executor and the about-to-be executed victim after the "court's decision" tend to minimize the severity of Vere's judgment, if not entirely exonerating him:

> Captain Vere in end may have developed the passion sometimes latent
> under an exterior stoical or indifferent. He was old enough to have
> been Billy's father. The austere devotee of military duty, letting himself
> melt back into what remains primeval in our formalized humanity, may

in end have caught Billy to his heart, even as Abraham may have caught young Isaac on the brink of resolutely offering him up in obedience to the exacting behest. But there is no telling the sacrament, seldom if in any case revealed to the gadding world, wherever under circumstances at all akin to those here attempted to be set forth two of great Nature's nobler order embrace. There is privacy at the time, inviolable to the survivor; and holy oblivion, the sequel to each diviner magnanimity, providentially covers all at last. (BB, p. 115)

Indeed, these conjectures of the narrator, as I have noted in chapter 2, became the point of departure for Warner Berthoff's eloquent canonical reading of *Billy Budd* as Melville's final encomium to the magnanimous humanist soul.

As I have shown by way of retrieving and focalizing the historical context, however, what is at stake in *Billy Budd* is not "privacy" as such — neither the personal fates of Vere and Billy nor the implications of their fates for humanism; it is, rather, the metaphysically grounded *sociopolitical system* — the state of exception authorized by an exceptionalist ontology and its privileging of the politics of biopower — that determines the thought and practice of the polity. Vere, as I have noted, is fundamentally (by nature) a good man. But his private feelings — the feelings that would save the innocent young boy, not simply from death, but from an ignominious death, are utterly overpowered by his "obedience to the exacting behest" of the call of a "higher," sovereign authority. Seen in this way, the analogy the narrator draws between Vere's relation to Billy and the Old Testament Abraham's relation to Isaac becomes ironic. Minimally, it points to the immense difference between the benign, life-oriented world envisioned by the Old Testament God who imposes his "exacting behest" on Abraham and that death-oriented world envisioned by the sovereign who declares the state of exception. But it is also possible — and more likely — that in this analogy, Melville, if not the narrator, is ironically condemning both worlds, theological and secular, insofar as they appeal to the sovereignty of a "*higher* cause" that, in reducing politics to biopower, rescinds the *political life* (*bios*) in favor of bare life (*zoē*) when it opts for the security state of the state of exception.[30]

Seen in the dislocating light shed by reading the novella in the context of the Napoleonic Wars, Billy, too, undergoes a metamorphosis. Those positive, sympathy-provoking characteristics that have been a constant of *Billy Budd* criticism—his childlike innocence, his nobility, his youthful good humor, his personal integrity, his acceptance of his impressment by the British navy, and, above all, his (doglike) loyalty to Captain Vere— come to be seen, as I have been suggesting, not as negatives per se—as in the case of Vere, there is no gainsaying that Melville wants us to have a genuine empathy for him—but as the ironically disabling political effects of a world organized according to the bio-disciplinary imperatives of the state of exception. In the process of the narration, we do not experience Billy's execution as a redemptive sacrifice to a sacred cause as the sacral system alleges. Rather, we bear witness to his inexorable metamorphosis from the disciplined docile body he was at the beginning of his forced sojourn on board the *Bellipotent* into the bare life (*zoē*)[31]—*the life voided of the political*, or, to invoke Billy's fatal stutter, *of speech* in the light of Hannah Arendt's distinction between *homo faber* and the *vita activa*[32]— that is the exclusive/inclusive condition of the biopolitically organized polis (which has become a concentration camp—or an Abu Ghraib— where "it is permitted to kill without committing homicide") under the aegis of the state of exception.

This reduction of Billy to bare life or, what in my mind is the same thing, disposable reserve, I suggest, is the ironic burden of the scene involving Billy's interview with the chaplain, in which the narrator, commenting on Billy's childlike indifference to the ministrations of the good "minister of Christ" who receives "his stipend from Mars" (BB, p. 120)[33] compares Billy, first to the childlike and docile British barbarians "captured by the Roman legions and, as *"living trophies," "made to march in the Roman triumph of Germanicus,"* and then to those "later barbarians, young men probably, and picked specimens among the earlier British converts to Christianity, at least nominally such, taken to Rome (*as today converts from lesser isles of the seas may be taken to London*), of whom the Pope of that time, admiring the strangeness of their personal beauty so unlike the Italian stamp, their clear ruddy complexion and curled flaxen locks, exclaimed 'Angles' (meaning *English*, the modern derivative), 'Angles, do you call them? And is it because they look so like angels?' " (BB, p. 120; my emphasis). The narrator's later remarks about Billy's indifference to the chaplain's ministrations, it is true, could be interpreted as an indirect gesture of resistance, a possibility enhanced by his comparison of

Billy's polite listening to the chaplain with the Tahitian savage's reception of the Christian missionary's proselytizing efforts: "Out of natural courtesy he received, but did not appropriate" (BB, p. 121). But this should not obscure the version of Billy's childlike/barbarian behavior I am thematizing by way of attending closely to the specific and the general contexts (the narrator's comparisons and the culminating events on board the *Bellipotent*): the version that understands the speechless childlike or barbarian, that is, pre-civilizational, behavior *of a civilized adult* as the debilitating effect of the "civilized" — biopolitical — state of exception. It is this terribly irony — this naked speechlessness in the face of the sacred sovereignty of the state of exception — too, that is enacted in Billy last words: "God bless Captain Vere!"

The "People," Surveillance, the State of Exception

After offering his ambiguous conjectures about the closeted interview between Captain Vere and Billy Budd, the narrator returns to the culminating events on board the *Bellipotent* following the drumhead court's prescribed decision to hang Billy: Vere's convening of the ship's crew to inform them of the master-at-arms' death, of the sentencing of the perpetrator to death by hanging by the summary court, of the time of the execution, and, in the aftermath of his announcement, the crew's "confused murmur" that is "pierced and suppressed by shrill whistles of the boatswain and his mates" (BB, p. 117). What is pertinent to my argument about the narrator's account of the moment prior to his narration of the execution of Billy Budd, is its insistent focus on the officers' systematic avoidance of "the word mutiny" (BB, p. 117) and, above all, their deliberate appeal to the dictates of disciplinary "usage" to prevent public dialogue and minimize the possibility of a reaction on the part of the sailors, whom the narrator, tellingly at this tense time, reverts to calling "the people" or "the populace" (BB, p. 123):

> In this proceeding as in every public one growing out of the tragedy,
> strict adherence to usage was observed. Nor in any point could it have
> been at all deviated from, either with respect to Claggart or Billy, with-
> out begetting undesirable speculations in the ship's company, sailors,
> and more particularly men-of-war's men, being of all men the greatest

sticklers for usage. For a similar cause, all communication between Captain Vere and the condemned one ended with the closeted interview already given, the latter being now surrendered to the ordinary routine preliminary to the end. His transfer under guard from the captain's quarters was effected without unusual precautions — at least no visible ones. If possible, not to let the men so much as surmise that their officers anticipate aught amiss from them is the tacit rule in a military ship. And the more that some sort of trouble should really be apprehended, the more do the officers keep that apprehension to themselves, though not the less unostentatious vigilance may be augmented. In the present instance, the sentry placed over the prisoner had strict orders to let no one have communication with him but the chaplain. And certain unobtrusive measures were taken absolutely to insure this point. (BB, pp. 117–118)

As always, in other words, it is the systematic secreting of the realities by way of the suppression of knowledge endemic to the disciplinary surveillance logic of the state of exception that the narrator is pointing to in this penultimate moment of his story. Or, to put this disclosure alternatively — in a way that foreshadows the unconcluding postscripts — it is the specter of mutiny, which has its source in the uprisings at Spithead and the Nore, that, paradoxically, is increasingly revealed to preside menacingly over the life of the body politic of the *Bellipotent* by the very systematic disciplinary martial logic — the oversight of a regulatory surveillance — that would annul its presence.

This secretive and corrupting security regime obtains at the time of the execution of Billy Budd and in its immediate aftermath. It is important to register its inexorably insistent presence at this crucial moment, especially in the face of a history of *Billy Budd* criticism that has virtually effaced it in the name of the testament of acceptance thesis, on the one hand, or of undecidability, on the other. The narrator's account of the scene of the execution is, it is true, fraught with the language of pity endemic to classical tragedy, even of the cathartic apotheosis that accompanies it, but this should not deflect attention from the biopolitical context, which, as I have shown, he has also established as the mise-en-scène of the execution. The "populace" is summoned by Captain Vere to view the spectacular execution as testimony of the undeviating rigor of martial law. Billy is "for special reasons" (BB, p. 123) — which can only mean the better to control the crew should it rebel — ordered hanged from the mainyard rather than the foreyard, from which such executions were generally carried out in that era. After the hanging and its immediate ambiguous repetition of Billy's blessing to Captain Vere, when the "ship's populace" begins to "murmur,"[34] the officers summarily disperse the assembled sailors to forestall their metamorphosis into a "mob":

> The seeming remoteness of [the sound's] source was because of its murmurous indistinctness, since it came from close by, even from the men massed on the ship's open deck. Being inarticulate, it was dubious in significance further than it seemed to indicate some capricious revulsion of thought or feeling such as mobs ashore are liable to, in the present instance possibly implying a sullen revocation on the men's part of their involuntary echo in of Billy's benediction. But ere the murmur had time to wax into clamor it was met by *a strategic command*, the more telling that it came with abrupt unexpectedness: "Pipe down the starboard watch, Boatswain, and see that they go."
> Shrill as the shriek of the sea hawk, the silver whistles of the boatswain and his mates pierced that ominous low sound, dissipating it; and yielding to the mechanism of discipline the throng was thinned by one-half. For the remainder, most of them were set to temporary employments connected with trimming the yards and so forth, business readily to be got up to serve occasion by any officers of the deck. (BB, p. 126)

Most tellingly of all, it is this regime of security that is irrevocably highlighted by the narrator in his account of the aftermath of Billy's burial at sea ("the closing formality" [BB, p. 126] of the ritual of execution intended to bring the crisis to closure) when the reassembled populace, struck by the symbolic clamorous seafowl scavenging for the flesh of his body, begin murmuring anew, that is, to metamorphose into a "multitude." On this climactic occasion, the Captain orders "the drum beat to quarters" — the synecdochal disciplinary instrument of martial law, now, as the narrator puts it, in full consciousness of the inaugural historical context (the "outside" story) of which the dreadful events on board the *Bellipotent* (the "inside" story) are an indissolubly related "termination":

True martial discipline long continued superinduces in average man a sort of impulse whose operation at the official word of command much resembles in its promptitude the effect of an instinct.

The drumbeat dissolved the multitude, distributing most of them along the batteries of the two covered gun decks. There, as wonted, the guns' crews stood by their respective cannon erect and silent. In due course the first officer, sword under arm and standing in his place on the quarter-deck, formally received the successive reports of sworded lieutenants commanding the sections of the batteries below; the last of which reports being made, the summed report he delivered with the customary salute to the commander. All this occupied time, which in the present case was the object in beating to quarters at an hour prior to the customary one. That such variance from usage authorized by an officer like Captain Vere, a martinet as some deemed him, was evidence of the necessity for unusual action implied in what he deemed to be temporarily the mood of his men. *"With mankind," he would say, "forms, measured forms, are everything; and that is the import couched in the story of Orpheus with his lyre spellbinding the wild denizens of the wood." And this he once applied to the disruptions of forms going on across the Channel as the consequences thereof.* (BB, pp. 127–128; my emphasis)

With this resonant gesture of multiple closure, the narrator's story proper comes to its seemingly resolved end. The crew is mustered; "the band played a sacred air;" the chaplain performs his customary morning's service; the "drums beat the retreat; and toned by music and religions rites subserving the discipline and purposes of war, the men in their wonted orderly manner dispersed to the places allotted them when not at the guns." And to emphasis this biopolitical, discipline-induced return to serenity, the narrator adds that a similar peace was observable in nature: "And the circumscribed air in the clearness of its serenity was like smooth white marble in the polished block not yet removed from the marble-dealer's yard" (BB, p. 128). But, as I have been suggesting, the peace that comes with Captain Vere's climactic disciplinary gesture to bring the disconcerting events culminating in the hanging of Billy Budd to "closure" is acutely ironic. In this passage, the narrator, in fact, decisively discloses — against the prevailing allegorical view — the fundamental centrality of the state of exception to his tale by way of drawing the outside (political) and the inside (private) story together or, rather, by revealing that the events extending from the French Revolution and the ensuing global war between Britain and France through the Great Mutiny at Spithead and the Nore to the threat of mutiny on board the *Bellipotent* and the execution of Billy Budd are indissolubly related: *constitute the "inside narrative" of the Melville's subtitle.*

Orpheus's Lyre: Narrative and Anti-Narrative

But this decisive disclosure that the general historical context and the particular narrative are one is not all. What should not be overlooked, as it consistently has been, is another related dimension of this implicit terminal disclosure, equally if not more important than the narrator's final integration of the outside and the inside story, that is, than his politicization of *Billy Budd*: a disclosure that sheds significant light not only on the difficult question of the ambiguities of the narrator's representation of the events on board the *Bellipotent,* but also on the curiously unstable form his complex narrative takes: above all, on the three codas that the narrator, like the narrator of "Benito Cereno," is compelled to append to his "inside narrative." I am referring to the metaphor he attributes to Captain Vere in order to focus this climactic passage's political meaning: the myth of Orpheus, which, as the narrator says, was a constant of Vere's political discourse. If, that is, we have been attuned to the historical/political theme by the narrator's insistent reference to the primacy of martial law in the determination of Billy Budd's terrible fate, then, we cannot accept interpretations such as those of Lawrence Barrett, John Gross, and Christopher Sten, among many other critics, who have invoked Vere's appeal to Orpheus's lyre — that is to say, *poiēsis* — to assert categorically that Melville's *Billy Budd* "repudiates revolution and defends fixed forms, tradition, order, and historical community."[35] Rather we are compelled to read this allusion to Orpheus's lyre as Vere's effort, as a traditional intellectual, to appropriate *poiēsis* to the British imperial project. In the sacred name of the security state enabled by the exceptionalist state of exception, Captain Vere, like the Roman Horace in "Dulce et decorum est," for example, invokes the "measured forms" of traditional literary narrative that reduces words into the Word as the ontological model for reducing the differences time disseminates to Identity (the many into the One), that is, for domesticating being — the production of docile bodies — from be- *ing* as such through the nomadic denizens of the woods (*sylvestres* [savages], as the Romans called animals and forest dwellers; "vagabonds," or "undomeciliated" as the American settlers called the native Americans).[36]

To put Vere's unyielding commitment to "measured forms" as determinative of everything pertaining to mankind in this way, that is to say, we cannot but recall, by contrast, the supreme theme of Melville's earlier anti-traditional fiction. I am referring to what I have elsewhere called its (creative) *errancy*[37] in order to underscore his willful "disruption of [measured] forms" — literary and political — that have their origin in the "center elsewhere" of Western metaphysics (thinking from after or above the things themselves), and whose destructive and projective dynamics is synecdochically articulated in his famous comments about the novel in *Pierre*:

> Like all youths, Pierre had conned his novel-lessons; had read more novels than most persons of his years; but their false, inverted attempts at systematizing eternally unsystemizable elements; their audacious, intermeddling impotency, in trying to unravel, and spread out, and classify, the more thin than gossamer threads which make up the complex web of life; these things over Pierre had no power now. Straight through their helpless miserableness he pierced; one sensational truth in him, transfixed like beetles all the speculative lies in them. . . . By infallible presentiment he saw, that not always doth life's beginning gloom conclude in gladness; that wedding-bell peal not ever in the last scene of life's fifth act; that while to the countless tribes of common novels laboriously spin vails of mystery, only to complacently clear them up at last; and while the countless tribes of common dramas do but repeat the same; yet the profounder emanations of the human mind, intended to illustrate all that can be humanly known of human life; these never unravel their own intricacies, and have no proper endings; but in imperfect, unanticipated, and disappointing sequels (a mutilated stumps), hurry to abrupt interminglings with the eternal tides of time and fate.[38]

What, in short, I am suggesting in thus underscoring Vere's climactic appropriation of the "measured forms" of traditional *poiēsis* in the name of the exceptionalist state and the state of exception and for the purpose not simply of disciplining the multitude on board the *Bellipotent* but also to express his absolutist negative judgment against the political "disruptions of forms going on across the Channel" is this: Whatever the narrator's, Melville's intention is to disclose both the polyvalent will to power over alterity—the differences ("details") that history always already disseminates—that inheres in the traditional literary and (monumentalist) historiographical representation of worldly events (narrative) and the positive possibilities of the details released by this dis-closure. That is to say, Vere's appropriation of Orpheus's "spellbinding" lyre at this "terminal" moment not only calls into question his own narrative—his representation of the events on board the *Bellipotent*—to the drumhead court, but also that of the official British naval historians of the Napoleonic war who, the narrator reminds us early in his text, would "abridge" "[s]uch an episode in the Island's grand naval story" as that of the Great Mutiny. I reconstellate this heretofore peripheral passage into this "terminal" "Orphic" context both to underscore the informing centrality of narrative and monumentalist history (to which I shall return below) in *Billy Budd*, and to demonstrate the pertinence of this motif for an American audience:

> Such an episode in the Island's *grand naval story* her naval historians naturally abridge, one of them (William James) candidly acknowledging that fain would he pass it over did not "impartiality forbid fastidiousness." And yet his mention is less a narration than a reference, having to do hardly at all with details. *Nor are these readily to be found in the libraries.* Like some other events in every age befalling states everywhere, *including America*, the Great Mutiny was of such character that national pride along with views of policy would fain shade it off into the historical background. (BB, p. 55; my emphasis)

The Narrative's "Ragged Edges"

That Melville's ultimate purpose in *Billy Budd* is, indeed, to de-structure the "Orphic" narrative/historiography whose "measured forms" are sanctioned by the "higher" binary logic of metaphysics (Identity/difference, One/many, Sacred/profane) underlying the sovereign state of exception is forcefully confirmed by the three chapters the narrator appends to the "completed" "inside story" proper. Like those appended by the narrator of "Benito Cereno" to his "inside story," they are additions he tellingly introduces by invoking the incommensurability of fictional representation and historical reality (the theme, I reiterate, at the very absent core of Melville's major fiction).[39] More tellingly, however, in introducing them, he repeats the very language he used to refer to Captain Vere's Orphic measure, this time without equivocation: "The symmetry of form attainable in pure fiction cannot so readily be achieved in a narration essentially having less to do with fable than with fact. Truth uncompromisingly told will always have its ragged edges; hence the conclusion of such a narration is apt to be less finished than an architectural finial" (BB, p. 128).

All three appendices, each in its own way, in fact, jarringly disrupt the apparent sense of an ending recorded by the narrator after quoting Captain Vere's invocation of Orpheus's spellbinding lyre. In the first, the narrator recounts the fatal wounding of Captain Vere in a sea battle with a French ship provocatively named the *Athée* (*Atheist*) shortly after the execution of Billy Budd. Here, he tells us, Vere's dying words, reported by his uncomprehending attendant to the officer of the marines were, "Billy Budd!, Billy Budd!" The narrator does not attempt to explain the meaning of these enigmatic words, offering only a negative surmise instead: "That these were not the accents of remorse would seem clear from what the attendant said to the *Bellipotent*'s senior officer of marines, who, as the most reluctant to condemn of the members of the drumhead court, too well knew, though here he kept the knowledge to himself, who Billy Budd was" (BB, p. 129). Because these words are three times removed from the speaker, to conclude that they are, indeed, a manifestation of Vere's fatherly regret for having killed his son would be precipitous. Yet the text offers no other positive alternative. What cannot be denied, however, is Vere's utterance itself. And that suggests that at the moment of his death he is being accosted by a phantasm from his immediate past that haunts his essential being — the essentialist self, that is, that has reduced the complex events of the *Bellipotent*'s world to a linear narrative in which Billy's lowly humanity is reduced to nothing (bare life) in the name of his obedience to the disciplinary imperatives of the metaphysical state of exception. (In repeating Billy's name, is Vere symbolically belatedly restoring the impressed and executed young sailor with the (political) life [*bios*] — his "some-oneness," as it were — he has denied him by reducing it to nothing [*zoē*]?) It could be said, that is, that at the moment of his death,

Vere is being confronted by the specter of the nothingness (the jaggedness) that, according to the post-"structuralists," haunts all measured forms.[40]

This spectral assault on the measured forms that have kept the peace on board the *Bellipotent* by arbitrary violence is even more pointedly enacted in the narrator's second appendix: an official "account of the affair" — a narrative with a vengeance — published a few weeks after the execution in "an authorized weekly publication," "doubtless for the most part written in good faith." It is an account, the narrator tells us pointedly, after quoting it, that "is all that hitherto has stood in human record to attest what manner of men respectively were John Claggart and Billy Budd" (BB, p. 131), testifying to the devastating efficiency of the measured forms of official historiography. I quote the whole of this summary narrative to underscore not only the violence it does to the previously narrated reality it is representing (the imbalance of power relations on board the *Bellipotent*), but also, in opposition to the editors of the definitive edition of *Billy Budd* (and those critics who have deliberately or inadvertently followed them), its assumption of the decisive importance of the "outside history" in determining the meaning of the events on board the ship:

> "On the tenth of the last month a deplorable occurrence took place on board H.M.S. *Bellipotent*. John Claggart, the ship's master-at-arms, discovering that some sort of plot was incipient among an inferior section of the ship's company, and that the ringleader was one William Budd; he, Claggart, in the act of arraigning the man before the captain, was vindictively stabbed to the heart by the suddenly drawn sheath knife of Budd.
>
> "The deed and the implement employed sufficiently suggest that though mustered into the service under an English name the assassin was no Englishman, but one of those aliens adopting English cognomens whom *the present extraordinary necessities* of the service have caused to be admitted into it in considerable numbers.
>
> "The enormity of the crime and the extreme depravity of the criminal appear the greater in view of the character of the victim, a middle-aged man respectable and discreet, belonging to that minor official grade, the petty officers, upon whom, as none know better than the commissioned gentlemen, the efficiency of His Majesty's navy so largely

depends. His function was a responsible one, at once onerous and thankless; and his fidelity in it the greater because of his strong patriotic impulse. In this instance as in so many other instances *in these days*, the character of this unfortunate man signally refutes, if refutation were needed, that peevish saying attributed to the late Dr. Johnson, that patriotism is the last refuge of a scoundrel.

"The criminal paid the penalty of his crime. The promptitude of the punishment has proved salutary. Nothing amiss is now apprehended aboard H.M.S. *Bellipotent*." (BB, pp. 130–131; my emphasis)

The arbitrary violence this retrospective narrative does to the complex truth of the events on board the *Bellipotent* to which we have borne witness is self-evident. What apparently is not for the majority of the critics, past and present, who have written on *Billy Budd*, especially those adhering to the testament of the acceptance school and, not incidentally, those adhering to the school of undecidability, is the essence of the "truth" that is violated by this summary retrospective narrative. For the critics of acceptance, as I have noted, this truth has to do with one version or another of allegory: the paradoxical triumph of good over evil in the very enactment of the triumph of evil over the good. For these critics in other words, the retrospective narrative, if it is referred to at all, is either an anomaly, the consequence of Melville's failure to return to it after introducing and working out the character of Vere, as in the case of Hayford and Sealts,[41] or, if it is seen to be integral, a banal generalization about "how the world will inevitably misconstrue complex human events."[42] The adherents of undecidability, on the other hand, productively reject this narrative reconciliation of the adherents of acceptance. Attuned to the story's jagged edges, they rightly read the violated "truth" as having to do with the hegemonic political binaries that the events on board the *Bellipotent* have deconstructed. But, as I have shown, in reducing the imbalance of power relations to the same, they render (political) judgment impossible — and, thus, the official narrative that constitutes this revelatory "appendix" irrelevant.[43] They thus inadvertently join with their implicit opponents. In overdetermining the allegorical and the political binaries at the expense of the historical and worldly aspects of *Billy Budd*, that is to say, the adherents of both acceptance and of undecidability, as I am suggesting, have been blinded to what I have shown to be the absolute oneness of the global historical context and the events on board the *Belli-potent* — to the fact that *this relationship constitutes the "inside narrative"* of Melville's subtitle, in opposition to the various "outside narratives" (such as those of the British historian William James) to which the narrator refers earlier in the process of his narration and, above all, to the one he appends following it.

As the reference to "the present extraordinary necessities of the service" testifies, the retrospective appendix is intended neither as a generalization about the human mind's penchant to misinterpret complex worldly events nor as an ironic articulation of its absolute opposite. It pointedly focuses attention on the concrete *political history* in which Billy Budd's "story" is embedded. Attending to this indissoluble relationship, we are enabled to see that the narrative proper and the appended "account of the affair" are not only "worldly," not allegorical or undecidable, documents but also that they are utterly symmetrical and antithetical. The appended narrative constitutes the fulfillment of the reductive violence of the logic of Vere's polyvalent "measured forms" (and of the official British historians of the Napoleonic war) that wreaks havoc on the innocent — and powerless — body of Billy Budd and annihilates the truth of the events on board the *Bellipotent*: the logic that has its origin in metaphysical ontology (representing the things themselves from above) and that, as such, enables the exceptionalist state of exception. More specifically, in representing the events on board the *Bellipotent* in such a way as to render Billy Budd the criminal and Claggart the victim, the appended narrative representationally reenacts — though now, in contrast, in a dramatically visible way — the violence of the reversal — the logical movement of the security state that makes the criminal the policeman — effected by Vere's undeviating adherence to the logical imperatives of the exceptionalist state of the exception. Like Vere's (and that of the official British historian to whom the narrator refers) representation of the events on board the *Bellipotent* in the name of the logic of the security state, the official retro-spective account culminating in the hanging of Billy Budd brings "peace" to the "murmuring" populace of the *Bellipotent* (and of the British Navy and ultimately of Britain): "the promptitude of the punishment has proved salutary. Nothing amiss is now apprehended aboard H.M.S. *Bellipotent*." But the violence against the truth precipitated by the unerrring logic of the state of exception of this account is so obvious that it throws the violence against Billy's body and against the truth of the main (narrator's) account into relief. In patently falsifying (doing violence to) the truth of the events on board the *Bellipotent*, this appended official narrative, however much "written in good faith," compels us to read the former (including the historical "background") as the "inside story" and the latter as an "outside story," that is, a narrative imposed on the things themselves from above: *meta-ta-physica*. That is, the excessively violent logic of the panoptically distanced outside story enables the reader to perceive the inside story of the *Bellipotent*, not as an allegory that ends in transcendent reconciliation — a "testament of acceptance" of the way things are, as it were — nor as an undecidable text that disables political judgment. On the contrary, this excess enables us to perceive it affectively but as an act of ontopolitical resistance: an ironic narrative of "jagged edges" that renders it an anti-narrative: the measure, as it were, of its evental global occasion. Put alternatively, the patent violence of the (mono)-logic of the outside story paradoxically *precipitates* Billy's story as the "end" — both the fulfillment and demise — of the logic of the exceptionalist state's state of exception. In fulfilling its logic, that is, the outside story in the end dis-closes the terrible truth of the events it has monographically tried to contain. More specifically, in self-de-structing it unwittingly projects the "inside story" as a *specter* that returns in the "end" from the oblivion to which it has been relegated by this conclusive logic to haunt the closure — the end — promised by the "measured forms" that justify the theory and practice of the state of exception — and to break its (sleep of) peace. The actual retrospective narrative of the affair, it will be recalled, concludes decisively not only with the assertion of peace on board: "Nothing amiss is now apprehended aboard H.M.S. *Bellipotent*" — but also with the narrator's assertion that its "truth" is "*all* that *hitherto* has stood in human record to attest what manner of men respectively were John Claggart and Billy Budd" (my emphasis). Taken together, could it not be said that, as in the case of Captain Ahab's "Naught's an obstacle; naught's an angle to my iron way!" Melville is ironically pointing precisely to this specter that *is* an obstacle, which not only haunts the truth of the official story but also threatens its peace?[44]

In short, in revealing its affiliation with monumental history, the official narrative — this outside story — discloses Melville's intention to be, in Foucault's Nietzschean terms, genealogy in the parodic mode:

The new historian, the genealogist, will know what to make of this masquerade [that of the traditional historians who offered the "confused and anonymous European" the possibility of "alternate identities" "more substantial than their own"]. He will not be too serious to enjoy it; on the contrary, *he will push the masquerade to its limit and prepare the great carnival of time where masks are constantly reappearing. No longer the identification of our faint individuality with the solid identities of the past, but our "unrealization" through the excessive choice of identities.* . . . "Perhaps, we can discover a realm where originality is again possible as parodists of history and buffoons of God." In this we recognize the parodic double of what the second of the *Untimely Meditations* called "monumental history": a history given to reestablishing the high points of historical development in a perpetual presence, given to the recovery of works, actions, and creations though the monogram of their personal essence. But in 1874, Nietzsche accused this history, one totally devoted to veneration, of barring access to the actual intensities and creations of life. The parody of his last texts serves to emphasize that "monumental history" is itself a parody. Genealogy is history in the form of a concerted carnival.[45]

This "revenant" — this hitherto visited that visits the visitor — to use the term Jacques Derrida coined to refer to the alterity that haunts the West's metaphysical obsession with identity[46] — is announced by the third appendix that concludes with the ballad "Billy in the Darbies." Taking their cue from the rhetoric the narrator uses to characterize the moment of the execution, the critics who have represented the novella as Melville's "testament of acceptance" have read its allusions to the crew's monumentalization of the spar on which Billy was hung, particularly their conversion of "a chip of it" into something resembling a Christian relic — "a piece of the Cross" (BB, p. 131) — as the apotheosis of Billy Budd. If, however, the reader has been attuned to the genealogical/parodic dynamics of the "jagged edges" these asymmetrical appendices are said to be, he/she will see that this third one is not oriented towards Billy's apotheosis, an ascendance into a transcendent realm beyond the anxiety-provoking contingencies of the fallen (occasional) realm, but, on the contrary, towards his (spectral) return to *this* conflicted secular world, indeed, to the political world that, on the analogy of the (worldly) binary that privileges transcendence over finitude, masters over slaves, the high over the low, the elect over the preterite, the sacred over profane, and the monuments to what *count* for the masters over the nonbeing of that which doesn't. This appendix, that is, does not privilege the dominant culture of the *Bellipotent* as the preceding official account does. Rather, this jagged edge, the last, it should be noted, privileges the crew *as* multitude. This telling reversal of the high and low binary is underscored by the narrator's commentary following the reference to the chip of the spar. However ignorant of the "*secret* facts of the tragedy" (my emphasis), we are pointedly told, Billy's lowly comrades deeply admired his innocent and unpresuming gentleness, instinctively feeling that he "was a sort of man as incapable of mutiny as of wilful murder" (BB, p. 132) and, consonant with their murmurings at the tense time of the hanging, knew that "the penalty . . . was inflicted from the naval point of view," that is, in the name of a higher — unworldly and dehumanized — martial law. This reversal — and the unappeasably disturbing sense of an unjustified loss it underscores — culminates with the narrator's commentary that introduces the ballad, "Billy in the Darbies"

> On the gun decks of the *Bellipotent* the general estimate of his nature and its unconscious simplicity eventually found *rude utterance* from another foretopman, one of his own watch, *gifted, as some sailors are, with an artless* poetic *temperament*. The tarry hand made some lines which, after circulating among the shipboard crews for a while, finally got *rudely printed* at Portsmouth as a ballad. The title given to it was the sailor's. (BB, p. 131; my emphasis)

And this reversal of the binary informing "the naval point of view," with its suggestion of menace, is enacted in the sustained ironic play of the metaphors of high and low that saturate the lines of this "rude utterance," now a mnemonic "relic" borne by Billy's comrades, from beginning to end. Following his precisely intense and life-affirming — imagist-like — articulation of his visual sense at the moment of his impending hanging:

— But, look:
Through the port comes the moonshine astray!
It tips the guard's cutlass and silvers this nook;
But 'twill die in the dawning of Billy's last day.

the condemned "rude" speaker goes on in the same acutely imagistic way to visualize what "they" — the abstract and dehumanized "naval point of view" — will make of him at the dawning of the day of his death:

> A jewel-block they'll make of me tomorrow,
> Pendant pearl from the yardarm-end
> Like the eardrop I gave to Bristol Molly —
> O, 'tis me, not the sentence they'll suspend
> Ay, ay, all is up; and I must up too,
> Early in the morning, aloft from alow.[47]

This "arising," however, is no redemptive resurrection or transfiguration in the traditional sacrificial sense, no vindication of the system that sentenced Billy to death, as it has too often been said of his hanging. It is, rather, a decisive descent — one often repeated by others of his kind:

> But Donald he has promised to stand by the plank;
> So I'll shake a friendly hand ere I sink.
> But — no! It is dead then I'll be, come to think.
> I remember Taff the Welshman when he sank.
> And his cheek it was like the budding pink.
> But me they'll lash in hammock, drop me deep.
> Fathoms down, fathoms down, how I'll dream fast asleep.

And it is the decisiveness of this descent — the utter unjustifiability of the higher logic that justified it — that, paradoxically, instigates, not the resurrection of the dead, but his spectral return to haunt that higher logic in the form of this earthy immaterial ballad that now circulates not only among the crews of the British Navy, but throughout the public domain.

In the end, that is, the second appendix, "the account of the affair" published in an "authorized" "naval chronicle of the time" — which constitutes the origin of the monumentalized history of "that time" (*in illo tempore*, as it were), as its echo of the official British naval histories referred to by the narrator suggests (their "abridgement" of the Great Mutiny) — is not only deflated (brought low) but also superseded by this "rude utterance" written by a common sailor, a member of the *Bellipotent*'s populace. More specifically, in thus decisively reversing the opposition between the high and the low — the elect and the preterite, the monumental and the irrelevant, what counts according to the world and what doesn't — that determines the truth of the outside narrative, this third appendix, which brings *Billy Budd* to its "close," minimally hints at a deep and dislocating dissatisfaction at the execution of a fellow member of the *Bellipotent*'s populace, a dissatisfaction that disrupts and thus gives lie to the peace promised by the execution (and affirmed with finality by the official "account of the affair" published in its aftermath). Maximally, it hints at an opening, a new beginning, indeed, an *up*-rising: the precipitation of a portentous aura, a spectral energy that menaces the exceptionalist state of exception that, according to the official account, seems to have decisively triumphed

The American Analogy

Let me finally return to the main argument of this symptomatic reading of *Billy Budd*: that Melville, in the last decade of the nineteenth century (the period appropriately called "the Gilded Age") and the waning years of his life, broke his forty-year silence to write this novella about an epochal European event in the eighteenth century as a cautionary tale addressed to an American public. In chapter 1, to be more specific, I argued that this sequestered Melville of the late 1880s, who had written critically about the complicity between America's exceptionalism and westward expansion (i.e., imperialism), was acutely aware of the United States's end-of-the-century initiative towards globalization. I mean, more specifically, by this last, the American momentum instigated by the closing of the western frontier and the rise of capitalism. This was epitomized by the naval historian Alfred Thayer's Mahan's extremely popular lectures proselytizing in behalf of the expansion of the U.S. Navy, emulating Great Britain's effort in the previous century (also undertaken and justified by its exceptionalist ethos vis-à-vis the rest of Europe), to gain control of the global seaways so as to establish imperial dominion over the planet. Equally important, I argued, Melville, as such stories as *Israel Potter*, "Benito Cereno," and, on a different but analogous register, "Bartleby, the Scrivener" and *The Confidence-Man* testify, was also aware of the dire consequences for a parliamentary or republican state of the fulfillment of such an expansionist momentum: the production of a permanent global crisis, the normalization of the state of exception, which is to say, the transformation of a republican polity into a security state; and the reduction of the human being as a *zōon logon echon* (animal endowed with language), that is, political man (in the Arendtian sense),[48] to bare life.

To justify this assertion that Melville, breaking his long silence, was writing *Billy Budd* with, above all, an American public in mind, it will be recalled, I identified the narrator as a late-nineteenth-century American author and invoked what I referred to as three strategically placed references to America in the main body of the narration: in chapter 3, where, in speaking of the "abridgment" of the knowledge of the "Great Mutiny" by official British historians of the Napoleonic wars, he invokes the analogy of *other states, "including America," that "would fain shade [such shameful events] off into* the historical background" (BB, p. 55); chapter 8, where, in explaining the British policy of impressment as a result of the national insecurity precipitated by the outbreak of the French Revolution, he implicates Americans, even those "who fought at the Battle of Bunker Hill," in the same fear (or hysteria) over the impending "Apocalypse" (BB, p. 66); and, most tellingly, chapter 21, where, in recounting Captain Vere's justification of his decision to hang Billy Budd, the narrator invokes the parallel with the executions on board the U.S. brig-of-war *Somers*. That these references to America are not irrelevant accidents, that, in fact, they constitute something like a *basso ostinato* that subsumes the overdetermined British events and relates them to the American motif is strongly suggested by one further and final allusion to America and Americans, this time, in a context that is unequivocally resonant with the exceptionalist state and the state of exception. I am referring to that place, entirely overlooked by previous critics of Melville's novella, in the appended official account of the affair on board the *Bellipotent* that characterizes the victim, Billy Budd, in terms of its typically exceptionalist rhetoric: "The deed and the implement employed sufficiently suggest that though mustered into the service under an English name the assassin was no Englishman, but one of those aliens adopting English cognomens whom the present extraordinary necessities of the service have caused to be admitted into it in considerable numbers" (BB, p. 130).

Admittedly, this identification of the alien assassin as an American, as opposed to, say a German or an Italian or a Dutchman or a Spaniard or a Portuguese, is a tenuous one, since an American name was, in the late nineteenth century likely (though by no means necessarily) to be an English name. On the other hand, there is no indication whatsoever in the narrative that Billy spoke with a foreign (non-English) accent. Given this and the fact that the British perceived the Americans in that postrevolutionary period as decadent hybrids, it is just as reasonable to believe that, in referring to the considerable number of "aliens" pressed into the service of the British Navy because of "the present extraordinary necessities," the author(s) of this official account were referring to those "upstart" Americans. I mean, more specifically, those "barbarian" Americans who, in falling away from the high ways of their civilized mother country, were, from the British exceptionalist perspective, no different from the decadent French and Spanish against whose brutal rapacity they invariably contrasted their "benign" imperial project.[49] If, then, the assassin of the "noble" and "patriotic" Englishman Claggart to which the appended account refers is an alien American, it can be said that this "outside" narrative patently reenacts in a microcosmic form the deadly imperatives of the more complex logic of the macrocosmic ("inside") narrative: the establishment, as we have seen, of the sovereign exception as norm; the national security state (with its penchant to blame aliens — "outside agitators" — for crises endemic to the polity and the elevation of the criminal to policeman); and the binary between sovereignty and bare life. And this in the name of a "sacred calling" or, as the narrator puts this exceptionalist British perspective against the "the [French] enemy's red meteor of unbridled and unbounded revolt" early in his story, "the flag of founded law and freedom" (BB, p. 54). More important, in rendering an (innocent) "American" its victim, the official ("outside") account paradoxically enables us to see that the "inside narrative" (understood as the indissoluble relationship between the events of the naval war between Britain and France and those on board the *Bellipotent*) ironically reenacts, now in inescapable visible form, precisely the reductive imperatives of the logic of American exceptionalism that had been the insistent object of Melville's exilic, nay-saying criticism in the great fiction of his mature years. I do not simply mean the "benign" exceptionalist logic that had its origins in the American Puritans' affirmation of their divinely ordained "election" (over the tyrannical and decadent "Old World") and thus the institutionalization of the need, intrinsic to election and the "calling" it mandates, of a *perpetual* frontier (i.e., a crisis or enemy) to *always already* renew their covenant and to rejuvenate their holy "mission in [the world's] wilderness." I also mean, to anticipate, this exceptionalist logic's revelatory (self-destructive) culmination in the period between the Cold War, when the United State, seeking global dominion for its capitalist version of democracy, normalized the state of exception and patently turned itself into a national security state, and the era of the George W. Bush and Richard B. Cheney administration, when, in the wake of 9/11/2001, the decisionist president of the United States declared his perpetual "war on terror" and, in the name of the American exceptionalist calling — and the machinations of his "master-at-arms" — began the process of institutionalizing the state of exception: the demolition of the system of checks and balances, the arbitrary transfer of sovereign power to the executive branch, and the establishment of a police state.

Melville's Late Style: A Testament of Refusal

Taken together, in short, the "jagged edges" represented by the three disclosive appendices to the main narrative of *Billy Budd*, unlike the retrospective of the traditional novel, do not confirm the peace (and the reader's repose) ostensibly established by Captain Vere's adherence to the machinery of martial law. Rather, they expose the fundamental aporia of that apparent reconciliatory closure: they precipitate the specter of Billy Budd that will return to haunt the exceptionalist logic and the state of exception that had justified his degrading reduction to bare life and his execution. In so doing, these asymmetrical addenda bear powerful witness to the essential argument of this book: that far from being the late Melville's "testament of acceptance" (or even his final affirmation of political undecidability) *Billy Budd* constitutes in essence a subversion of the traditional confidence-oriented perspective concerning aging that blithely expects — and demands — old men, in their accumulated wisdom, to reconcile themselves, like Job or Samson or Prospero, with the *apparent* contingency of being or with the injustices of the world and then to lie down and die in the peace of the knowledge of that higher synthesis. As such Melville's last fiction is, rather a testament, as I noted earlier, following the directives of Edward W. Said and Theodore Adorno, to the "late style." Its voice is, indeed, the voice of old age, but it is one that resurrects and exacerbates that brilliantly ironic subversive voice of the early works between *Moby-Dick* and *The Confidence-Man*. I mean the voice, epitomized by Bartleby's spectral "I prefer not to," that refused to be answerable to "America's

Calling" in the name of the occasional time of the always potential "now" and, ultimately, of the community of the commons.[50] Put alternatively, the late Melville did not capitulate to the oppressive imperative to acquiesce that necessarily informs the hegemonic American calling, that is, to the exceptionalism that was rapidly becoming the rule of his contemporary occasion. On the contrary, he maintained to the end his fidelity, to invoke Alain Badiou's apt ethical term, to the potential of the eventual void he bore increasing witness to in following the unerring itinerary of the logic of American exceptionalism to its self-destructive end, which is to say to the threshold of a radically new dispensation.[51]

The dominant culture of Melville's time, it will be recalled, "froze [his heretical voice] into silence."[52] And, as I have argued in *The Errant Art of Moby-Dick* and *Herman Melville and the American Calling*, after its return through the irresistible force of its dislocating and elusive art a half century later — at the time that came duplicitously, yet in an ironically appropriate way, to be called the Melville revival — the dominant culture tried again, however inadvertently, to silence its anxiety-provoking nay-saying, this time by the more nuanced and effective means of forcing its errancy into the American Renaissance narrative mould and, beyond that, into a cultural weapon in America's exceptionalist war against the global "Communist conspiracy."[53] But, as I have shown in this symptomatic reading of *Billy Budd* by way of disclosing its proleptic relevance to the contemporary global America occasion, Melville's voice, precisely in its refusal to speak the straightforward, means-and-end — and postponing — language of the American calling, continues to elude these efforts at inter-pellation and containment. Or, to put its negative dialectic positively, Melville's voice continues to haunt the pernicious myth of American exceptionalism. Like Billy Budd's specter, which returns to haunt Captain Vere and the exceptionalist state of exception whose dehumanizing imperatives he enacted in the name of national security, Melville's too refuses to be laid to rest. His ghost keeps returning to call the American calling to account.

CHAPTER FOUR

American Exceptionalism and the State of Exception after 9/11

Melville's Proleptic Witness

The camp is the space that is opened up when the state of exception begins to become the rule. In the camp, the state of exception, which was essentially a temporary suspension of the rule of law on the basis of a factual state of danger, is now given a permanent spatial arrangement, which as such nevertheless remains outside the normal order.

— GIORGIO AGAMBEN, *Homo Sacer*

"In feature no child can resemble his father more than that [Mutiny] Act resembles in spirit the thing from which it derives — War. In His Majesty's service — in this ship, indeed — there are Englishmen forced to fight for the King against their will. Against their conscience, for aught we know. Though as their fellow creatures some of us may appreciate their position, yet as navy officers what reck we of it? Still less recks the enemy. . . . War looks but to the frontage, the appearance. And the Mutiny Act, War's child, takes after the father. Budd's intent or non-intent is nothing to the purpose." — Captain Vere to the Drumhead Court in *Billy Budd*

The Uniqueness of Melville's View of the State of Exception

In the immediate aftermath of the terrorist bombing of the twin towers of the World Trade Center and the Pentagon on September 11, 2001, President George W. Bush, in his capacity as "commander in chief" of U.S. armed forces (not as president), declared his "war on terror," thus inaugurating a political momentum that, in the following years of his administration, bore witness to the virtual usurpation of political power by the U.S. government's executive branch from the Congress and the Supreme Court, a momentum undertaken with the tacit, if not wholehearted, consent of the other two branches of government[1] — and, it should not be forgotten, the ventriloquized media. The Bush administration did not only declare America's war on terror in the name of "homeland security." It also undertook this war against an unidentifiable (stateless) enemy, by way of its doctrine of "preemptive wars," to unilaterally invade alien polities — polities it represented as harboring terrorists and therefore categorically identified as "rogue states" that threatened the "peace" of the world — and then, in the name of America's messianic exceptionalist ethos, to employ its enormous militarily might to impose American-style democracies on them in behalf of world peace. That is to say, the Bush administration understood the American homeland as global in scope and its "war on terror" as a war intended to protect this global homeland.[2]

In the revolutionary process of the eight years of the Bush administration's tenure in office, the horrendously negative consequences, both abroad and at home, of this hubristic American global initiative became increasingly manifest. Abroad, to invoke only the most obvious of these, the United States's arrogant unilateral will to impose American-style democracies ("regime change") on Afghanistan and Iraq has culminated in its suspension of international law and the precipitation of seemingly unending civil wars in Afghanistan and Iraq that have borne witness not only to the killing and maiming of untold numbers of innocent civilians but also, as in the case of the Vietnam War, to the uprooting of untold numbers of noncombatants and their transformation into populations of homeless refugees. Further, instead of diminishing the threat of terrorism, this hubristic messianic American initiative to recreate the world in its image has exacerbated its potential, not least, by way of its violation of international law (the abrogation of habeas corpus, torture, and the obscenely inhumane practice euphemistically called "extraordinary rendition" by its perpetrators).[3] At home, the war on terror launched by the Bush administration in the name of homeland security has borne witness to the production of a pervasive climate of fear; the increasing conduct of government by secrecy and the falsification of historical reality;[4] the invasion of privacy by the executive branch; racial profiling; the branding of the undocumented as potential terrorists; the precipitation of the informer mentality; and, not least, the manipulation of the presidency by Claggart-like functionaries whose purposes are other than enhancing the public good. That all these lawless foreign and domestic initiatives of the executive branch of the

United States — and their imperial and anti-democratic consequences — have not been a matter of accident, but of a systematic effort by the presidency and the Justice Department has been made frighteningly manifest by the recent publication by the Barack Obama administration of the secret (illegal) plans drawn up and forcibly "legalized" by the President's Office of Legal Council (John C. Yoo, Jay Bybee, Robert J. Delahunty et al.),[5] and, in response to the urgings of Carl Rove, principal advisor to the president; Dick Cheney, vice-president of the United States; and Donald Rumsfeld, secretary of defense, among others, adopted by the Bush administration in the aftermath of 9/11. Based on the dubious assumption of the reality of a state of national emergency, it was a "legal" initiative, that gave the president the absolute authority ("plenary executive powers")[6] to deploy the military within the United States for the purpose of policing its citizenry (in violation of the Fourth Amendment and the Posse Comitatus Act of 1878);[7] to censor the media (i.e., annul the First Amendment); to represent any American citizen as an "enemy combatant" and to hold him or her in custody indefinitely and without recourse to the law; and to flout any international treaty, which is to say, to arrest, torture (use "enhanced methods of interrogating detainees"), and to render citizens of other countries to third-party jurisdictions.[8] In declaring a "war on terror" in the wake of 9/11, that is to say, the Bush presidency tacitly abrogated democratic law (the Constitution) in favor of establishing martial law — the sovereign lawless law of the state of exception — all, ostensibly, in the name of protecting the well-being of the abstraction — or, to appropriate Giorgio Agamben's more precise terms, the secularized sacred[9] — "the United States," a motive variously called "self-defense," "national security," "domestic security," and "homeland security." And insofar as the force that threatened the United States was an amorphous and nameless enemy — an enemy without an identifiable uniform and not associated with a state — it could be said that the Bush administration's unilateral declaration of "war on terror" in the aftermath of 9/11 was also a tacit announcement that rendered the state of exception permanent.

It has been primarily this momentous domestic/global initiative on the part of the U.S. executive branch — epitomized by the obscenely banal phenomenon now called alternatively Abu Ghraib or Guantánamo — that has reawakened the dormant memory of the Nazi concentration camps and the all too belated but welcomed interest of contemporary intellectuals in the question of the state of exception as it pertains to modern democracies. I am referring, above all, to the important work inaugurated by Giorgio Agamben in *Homo Sacer* by way of his retrieval of Michel Foucault's, Hannah Arendt's, Walter Benjamin's, Theodor Adorno's and, from a different perspective, the German National Socialist political theorist Carl Schmitt's writing on this most urgent question of our precarious contemporary occasion, specifically, to his claim that Western democracies, epitomized by the United States, are grounded in an ontology in which the state of exception — and the "camp" — is latent.[10] It is not my purpose in this brief concluding chapter on Melville's *Billy Budd* to undertake a full-scale rehearsal of Agamben's (and others') richly resonant and highly complex philological and historical analysis of the state of exception or to spell out his chilling representation of the polyvalent cultural and sociopolitical effects of its normalization in modernity. It will suffice, for my purpose, to say that, according to Agamben, the biopolitical (onto)logic informing the democratic nation-states achieves its fulfillment — its limit situation — in the permanent universalization of the concentration camp and its thanatopolitics (killing humans with immunity), however extreme such a characterization of the modern polity may seem:

> Along with the emergence of biopolitics, we can observe a displacement and gradual expansion beyond the limits of the decision on bare life, in the state of exception, in which sovereignty consisted. If there is a line in every modern state marking the point at which the decision on life becomes a decision on death, and biopolitics can turn into thanatopolitics, this line no longer appears today as a stable border dividing two clearly distinct zones. This line is now in motion and gradually moving into areas other than that of political life, areas in which the sovereign is entering into an ever more intimate symbiosis not only with the jurist but also with the doctor, the scientist, the expert, and the priest. . . . From this perspective, the [concentration] camp — as the pure, absolute, and impassable biopolitical space (insofar as it is founded solely on the state of exception) — will appear as the hidden paradigm of the political space of modernity.[11]

With this general diagnosis of contemporary political space, I basically agree.[12] What I do want to interrogate, however, is the tendency of the contemporary discourse on the state of exception — a tendency deriving from its unilateral appeal to Carl Schmitt's diagnosis of the modern liberal European nation-state (particularly the Weimar Republic) — to universalize the state of exception at the expense of its particular local manifestations. More specifically, I want to point out this discourse's failure to discriminate between the self-understanding of American democracy, on the one hand, and the modern "democracies" of Europe, on the other, a failure that, though it does not delegitimize its judgment, does, in its oversimplification, miss something fundamental about the source of the elusive power of the state of exception in its contemporary global American "democratic" setting.

Although Agamben traces the state of exception back to antiquity, particularly to the Romans' *Iustitium* ("suspension of the law"), his genealogy of its modern biopolitical avatar is instigated by the Bush administration's declaration of its "war on terror" (including its establishment of Abu Ghraib and Guantánamo) in the aftermath of 9/11 — or, more precisely, by the relationship he sees between this contemporary American political initiative and the Nazi regime:

> The immediately biopolitical significance of the state of exception as
> the original structure in which law encompasses living beings by means
> of its own suspension emerges clearly in the "military order" issued by
> the president of the United States on November 13, 2001, which autho-
> rized "indefinite detention" and trial by "military commissions" (not to
> be confused with the military tribunals provided for by the law of war)
> of noncitizens suspected of involvement in terrorist activities.[13]

Despite this genealogy, however, Agamben's commentary on the state of exception's modern allotrope, in fact, takes it theoretical point of departure from modern European history — the period between the French Revolution and the Napoleonic era, the very period, not incidentally, in which Melville sets *Billy Budd* (though he makes no mention of the global Napoleonic wars): "After being established with the Constituent Assembly's decree of July 8, 1791, [the state of exception] acquired its proper physiognomy as *état de siège fictif* [fictive state of siege] or *état de siège politique* [political state of siege] with the Directorial law of August 27, 1797, and finally, with Napoleon's decree of December 24, 1811."[14] As his "brief history of the state of exception" makes clear, Agamben treats its American manifestation, as nothing more than a continuation of the problematic that presides over its modern European occasion, suggesting a certain disabling blindness to the unique cultural origins of the American national identity and its particular form of democracy. To be specific, nowhere in his meditations on the state of exception (and, not incidentally, in those of Foucault, Arendt, Benjamin, Adorno, and Schmitt from which he draws) does he mention the founding myth of American exceptionalism (its onto-logical basis in the domain of the "sacred" — providential election — as it was understood by the Puritans and secularized in the postrevolutionary period) as a possible ground on which the contemporary democratic state of exception arises and derives its peculiar character and power. Nor, with the exception of Donald Pease, as far as I know, does any other commen-tator — European, Asian, African, American — who has addressed this urgent contemporary issue.[15] And this is where the American Herman Melville's fictional meditation on the state of exception in *Billy Budd* comes in as a directive for filling this crucial, disabling lack.

America's Version of the Friend/Foe Binary

Let me put this invocation of the late Melville succinctly, if all too broadly. As I have shown in my symptomatic reading of *Billy Budd*, Melville ul-timately intended his last work of fiction about an incident on board a British ship during the Napoleonic wars as a cautionary tale warning the United States against embarking on a domestic and foreign policy that, in imitating its former Old World mother country's arrogant imperialist effort to achieve global hegemony, would inevitably normalize the state of exception and produce the polity of the police state, right down to the establishment of the camp and production of bare life. In the process of writing *Moby-Dick*, *Pierre*, *Israel Potter*, and *The Confidence-Man*, as I have shown in chapter 3, Melville had become increasingly disillusioned with America's perennial — pre- and postrevolutionary — self-representa-tion as a benign, ontologically sanctioned — chosen — exceptionalist pol-ity and thus radically different from and superior to the decadent Old World and its tyrannical political system in its "youthful," vigorous, and optimistic sense of human potentiality and its dynamic democratic ideal-ism. By the time he began writing *Billy Budd* in the late 1880s, Melville had come to perceive America's unerring exceptionalism as a dangerous national fantasy that, despite the surface differences, obscured the secularized "New World's" essentially affiliative, if not filial, relationship with the Old World polities. To this late Melville, the United States at the end of the nineteenth century, precisely in its exuberant effort to fulfill the optimistic logic of its exceptionalist vocation, had paradoxically become the potentially surpassing dynastic heir of, not the superior antithesis to, the modern European political system: that polity which, after the Treaty of Westphalia, became the nation-state understood as the homeland of a (native) "people": self-identical, unique, superior, and, therefore, *always* dependent for its collective unity and strength on perceiving its neighbors as threatening enemies.[16] It is precisely to this paradoxical — and delegitimizing — analogy between the Britain of the end of the eighteenth century and the United States of the end of the nineteenth century that Melville draws his American readers' attention by way of his narrator's repeated reference to Britain's representation of its (self-renewing imperial) war against France over the control of the high seas (and eventually global humanity) as a benign, messianic effort of a civilized nation to, in Captain Vere's duplicitous terms, secure "the peace of the world and the true welfare of mankind"[17] against the alleged barbaric anarchy released by an inferior, civilization-destroying nation. It is, it will be recalled, a series of repetitions of the exceptionalist justification inaugurated in the beginning that embeds the story of Billy Budd in the larger context of the Nore Mutiny and the Napoleonic wars:

> To the British Empire the Nore Mutiny was what a strike in the fire brigade would be to London threatened by general arson. In a crisis when the kingdom might well have anticipated the famous signal that some years later published along the naval line of battle what it was that upon occasion England expected of Englishmen; *that* [Melville's emphasis] was the time when at the mastheads of the three-deckers and seventy-fours moored in her own roadstead — *a fleet the right arm of a Power then all but the sole free conservative one of the Old World* — the bluejackets, to be numbered by thousands, ran up with huzzas the British colors with the union and cross wiped out; by that cancellation transmuting the flag *of founded law and freedom defined*, into the enemy's red meteor of unbridled and unbounded revolt. Reasonable dis-

content growing out of practical grievances in the fleet had been ignited into irrational combustion as by live cinders blown across the Channel from France in flames. (BB, p. 54; my emphasis)

Melville, of course, was aware of the difference (within the affiliative continuity) between late-eighteenth-century British exceptionalism — its self-representation as the "Power then [at that time of crisis] all but the sole free conservative one of the Old World" during the Napoleonic wars — and America's exceptionalism in the 1880s. He knew, more specifically, that, whereas the exceptionalist mission of the British had its genealogical origins in the traditional European (Old World) nation-state, in which sovereign might — defeating the enemy — was privileged over the appeal to human rights and democracy in the pursuit of "civilizational progress," the exceptionalism of the American national identity and its benign mission had their origins in the memory of Old World tyranny and a sacred calling that, as Alexis de Tocqueville observed, in privileging the decentralization of sovereignty in the American Puritan polity, pointed toward democracy.[18] As an acute critical genealogist of the American national identity, however, Melville had also come to realize that endemic to America's sacred New World vocation was an imperative involving the imperial polity's weakness, vulnerability, and survival, a paradoxical imperative that cast a dark shadow on its benign claims, one that threatened, in the fulfillment of its "benign" logic, to transform the New World into the Old, indeed, to render its democracy ("Empire of Liberty," in Thomas Jefferson's apt phrase) more tyrannical than the tyranny of the Old World regimes.

To be more specific, the Melville of *Billy Budd* was acutely aware, in a way that most of his contemporaries were not, that the secular exceptionalist American national identity had its origins in the Puritans' providentially ordained "errand in the [New World] wilderness," and, above all, in their anxiety over the question of its fulfillment. I mean, more specifically, their realization that the perpetual renewal of their covenantal community and the rejuvenation of its sense of messianic mission — its collective duty to its "sacred" calling — in the face of the entropic effect of "profane" time (the recidivist threat of reverting to an unexceptionalist, decadent Old World) depended on the crisis afforded by a perpetual frontier: an always renewable, anxiety-provoking enemy (the raison d'être of the American jeremiad). Melville's awareness of this genealogy is especially reflected in his devastating parody of Daniel Webster's jeremiads on the occasions of the laying of the foundations of the Bunker Hill Monument (June 17, 1825) and of its completion (June 17, 1843) in *Israel Potter*.[19]

As *Moby-Dick*, *Pierre*, *Israel Potter*, and *The Confidence-Man* (particularly the sections on "The Metaphysics of Indian-hating") testify, the late Melville had also come to realize that this always theocratic (sacred) rejuvenating Puritan exceptionalist paradigm did not lose its formative power in the wake of the secularization of the American polity in the constitutional, postrevolutionary period. On the contrary, he had come to perceive this remarkably powerful paradigm, now, as in Tocqueville's influential work,[20] in the hegemonic form of a natural supernaturalism,[21] to be determinative throughout the period of Westward expansion. I means the period, aptly identified with "Manifest Destiny," that bore witness to the genocide of Native American "enemies," the imperial Mexican War, and the concomitant enclosure and incorporation of (agrarian) America — and, beyond that, as I have argued, to his own contemporary occasion that was bearing witness to the (en)closing of the frontier and the predictably renewed jeremiadic calls by such "American" historians as Frederick Jackson Turner and, even more ominously, Alfred Thayer Mahan for the extension — the opening — of the closed frontier beyond the Californian coast: for, that is, the globalization of America by means of its military might.

In calling his reluctant American readers' attention to the unlikely analogy between late-eighteenth-century (monarchical/parliamentary) British exceptionalism and late-nineteenth-century American (democratic/capitalist) exceptionalism in *Billy Budd*, the late Melville, in short, intended to disclose not only the United States's affiliative relationship with the Old World, but also *the unequivocally absolute relationship, however latent, between its unique version of exceptionalism and the permanent state of exception that abrogates the laws of democracy in favor of the global law of the exception in the name of securing them: the lawless (anomic) law that reduces the polity to the camp and human life to bare life*. Hidden within and informing America's alleged, moral, and political superiority over its former Old World master and its messianic errand in the "profane" global wilderness, he implied, was a binary (onto)logic — a "higher" (sacred) cause — the fulfillment of which would render the state of exception the rule. In the end, that is, Melville envisaged the United States's constitutional democracy metamorphosing, even against itself, into a constitutional dictatorship, and the "redeemer nation" the United States prided itself on being into a "crusading" nation: an imperial global policeman, indifferent to international law, policing polities it unilaterally deemed to be "rogue" or "outlaw" states. Under this disciplinary/biopolitical "regime of truth," not least, he foresaw the humanity, both domestic and foreign, over which this United States would preside being reduced, like Billy Budd, to disposable life: life, in Agamben's chillingly apt terms, that could be killed with immunity. From there, the concentration camp that Agamben has persuasively identified "as the hidden paradigm of the political space of modernity" becomes a black "visionary" possibility.

American Exceptionalism and the State of Exception That Becomes the Rule

In recalling the Puritan origins of the exceptionalist logic endemic to the American national identity, that is to say, the late Melville of *Billy Budd*, uncannily anticipates America's future as well: that undeviating messianic "progress" that bore witness to the United States's emergence as a global sea power during the Spanish–American War, a mere decade after Melville's death, and, in its long but undeviating wake — from World War I through World War II and the Cold War (Korea, Cuba, Vietnam, Nicaragua, and so on) — as an imperial global naval/military power that increasingly sought after unilateral hegemony over the world. I mean the relentless march that, following the end of the Cold War — and the temporary loss of America's necessary enemy — culminated in the George W. Bush administration's declaration of its unending war on (Islamic) terror after 9/11 in the name of its exceptionalist errand in the "world's wilderness": the search for and finding of not simply a new enemy in the face of the collapse of the Soviet Union — and consequent threat of peace — but a more appropriate one in that its undecidability would render *this* war — and the state of exception that the renewing emergency of war activates — permanent.

On January 29, 2002, President George W. Bush, in his capacity as commander in chief of the armed forces, delivered a State of the Union Speech to Congress and the nation following the "successful" invasion of Afghanistan, a "rogue state" or "outlaw regime." As the following unequivocal excerpts from this speech emphatically suggest, it is the peculiarly American global "calling," unilateral and ordained by a higher (sacred) cause, summarized above — the exceptionalist calling that, as Bartleby's synecdochical refusal to be answerable to it testifies, was diagnosed and resisted by Melville — that constituted the ominous gist of President Bush's remarks and the bipartisan applause he received. I quote at some length not only to underscore the affinity of Bush's arrogant and alarm-sounding biopolitical rhetoric with the traditional American jeremiad — its exceptionalist justification of the state of exception in the name of the American calling — but also its banalization of its original model:

> What we have found in Afghanistan confirms that, far from ending there, our war against terror is only beginning. Most of the 19 men who hijacked planes on September the 11th were trained in Afghanistan's camps, and so were tens of thousands of others. Thousands of dangerous killers, schooled in the methods of murder, often supported by outlaw regimes, are now spread throughout the world like ticking time bombs, set to go off without warning.
>
> Thanks to the work of our law enforcement officials and coalition partners, hundreds of terrorists have been arrested. Yet, tens of thousands of trained terrorists are still at large. These enemies view the entire world as a battlefield, and we must pursue them wherever they are (Applause.) So long as training camps operate, so long as nations harbor terrorists, freedom is at risk. And America and our allies must not, and will not, allow it. (Applause)
>
> Our nation will continue to be steadfast and patient and persistent in the pursuit of two great objectives. First, we will shut down terrorist camps, disrupt terrorist plans, and bring terrorists to justice. And second, we must prevent the terrorists and regimes who seek chemical, biological or nuclear weapons from threatening the United States and the world. (Applause.)
>
> Our military has put the terror training camps of Afghanistan out of business, yet camps still exist in at least a dozen countries. A terrorist underworld including groups like Hamas, Hezbolla, Islamic Jihad, Jaish-i-Mohammed — operates in remote jungles and deserts, and hides in the centers of large cities.

While the most visible military action is in Afghanistan, America is acting elsewhere. We now have troops in the Philippines, helping to train that country's armed forces to go after terrorist cells that have executed an American, and still hold hostages. Our soldiers working with the Bosnian government, seized terrorists who were plotting to bomb our embassy. Our Navy is patrolling the coast of Africa to block the shipment of weapons and the establishment of terrorist camps in Somalia.

My hope is that all nations will heed our call, and eliminate the terrorist parasites who threaten their countries and our own. Many nations are acting forcefully. Pakistan is now cracking down on terror, and I admire the strong leadership of President Musharraf. (Applause)

But some governments will be timid in the face of terror. And make no mistake about it: If they do not act, America will (Applause). . . .

We'll be deliberate, yet time is not on our side. I will not wait on events, while dangers gather. I will not stand by as peril draws closer and closer. The United States of America will not permit the world's most dangerous regimes to threaten us with the world's most destructive weapons. (Applause)

Our war on terror is well begun, but it is only begun. This campaign may not be finished on our watch — yet it must be and it will be waged on our watch.

We can't stop short. If we stop now — leaving terrorist camps in tact and terrorist states unchecked — our sense of security would be false and temporary. History has called America and our allies to action. And it is both our responsibility and Our privilege to fight freedom's fight. . . .

None of us would ever wish the evil that was done on September 11th. Yet after America was attacked, it was as if our entire country looked into a mirror and saw our better selves. We were reminded that we are citizens, with obligations to each other, to our country, and to history. We began to think less of the goods we can accumulate, and more about the good we can do.

For too long our culture has said. "If it feels good, do it." Now America is embracing a new ethic and a new creed. "Let's roll." (Applause) In the sacrifice of soldiers, the fierce brotherhood of firefighters, and the bravery and generosity of ordinary citizens, we have glimpsed what a new culture of responsibility could look like. We want to be a nation that serves goals larger than self. We've been offered a unique opportunity, and we must not let this moment pass. (Applause). . . .

This time of adversity offers a unique moment of opportunity — a moment we must seize to change our culture. Through the gathering momentum of millions of acts of service and decency and kindness, I know we can overcome evil with greater good. (Applause) And we have a great opportunity during this time of war to lead the world toward the values that will bring lasting peace. . . .

In a single instant, we realized that this will be a decisive decade in the history of liberty, that we've been called to a unique role in human events. Rarely has the world faced a choice more clear or consequential.[22]

It may be objected, of course, that President Bush's State of the Union address as commander in chief was more propaganda than policy and/or that its significance should be restricted to its immediate political context: that, in other words, its banal rhetoric is devoid of the kind of genealogical historical resonance I have attributed to it by way of suggesting that Melville's *Billy Budd* is proleptic of the Bush administration's jeremiadic initiative to normalize the state of exception by representing the war on terror as permanent. To disarm this possible objection I shall, therefore, briefly invoke the unequivocal analysis of the post-9/11 occasion undertaken by Samuel P. Huntington, a highly prestigious and influential neoconservative policy expert associated ideologically with the Bush administration, in his aptly entitled *Who Are We? Challenges to America's National Identity*,[23] published in 2004 in the wake of the stalling of the preemptive "missionary" initiative in Iraq and the exposure of the executive branch's prevarications concerning its justification for the invasion of Iraq.[24] For what Bush, as commander in chief, intimates about America's historical past (its exceptionalist Puritan origins) and future (the perpetual and self-renewing war on terror in the decisionist name of Homeland Security: the global Pax Americana), and the rhetorical strategy he employs to achieve this endless end (the American jeremiad), Huntington, this intellectual deputy of the dominant culture, spells out in the form of a systematic argument, one, in fact, that increasingly became American practice in the remaining years of the Bush administration.

Though the immediate cause of Huntington's proselytizing project was the faltering of America's covenantal collective will to "stay the course" inaugurated by the Bush administration's invasion of Afghanistan and then Iraq after 9/11, its more fundamental larger point of departure lies in what he represents as the "deconstruction" of the traditional American national identity in the 1960s and the ensuing emergence of divisive "subnational cultures."[25] Thus it is no accident that his anxiety-provoked — and anxiety-provoking — argument begins with the recuperation of the Puritan origins of the American national identity (the "who" and the "we" of the title of his book) and the calling endemic to their election by a sacred higher cause:

> The settling of America was, of course, a result of economic and other motives, as well as religious ones. Yet religion still was central. . . . Religious intensity was undoubtedly greatest among the Puritans, especially in Massachusetts. They took the lead in defining their settlement based on "a Covenant with God" to create "a city on a hill" as a model for all the world, and people of the Protestant faiths soon also came to see themselves and America in a similar way. In the seventeenth and eighteenth centuries, Americans defined their mission in the New World in biblical terms. They were a "chosen people," on an "errand in the wilderness," creating "the new Israel" or the "new Jerusalem" in what was clearly "the promised land." America was the site of a "new Heaven and a new earth, the home of justice," God's country. . . . The settlement of America was vested, as Sacvan Bercovitch put it, "with all the emotional, spiritual, and intellectual appeal of a religious quest." This sense of holy mission was easily expanded into millenarian themes of America as "the redeemer nation" and "the visionary republic."[26]

This theocratic exceptionalist Puritan sense of collective (convenantal) identity and the "calling" endemic to it,[27] according to Huntington's retrospective selective history of the United States, constituted the origin of what he calls the "Anglo-Protestant core culture" of America, which, despite its secularization in the postrevolutionary era and the periodic internal threats to its covenantal unity and vitality, has survived throughout American history until the contemporary occasion by way of a number of "Great Awakenings."

More specifically, as Huntington's invocation of Sacvan Bercovitch's cultural genealogy of the American national identity clearly suggests, these recuperative and rejuvenating "great awakenings" in the face of the threat of "backsliding" — the "murmurings" of the covenantal people, in the language of the Exodus story figurally appropriated by the Puritans — and of the consequent decay of the collective missionary zeal and disintegration of the convenantal polity were enabled by a unique structural mechanism intrinsic to the American Puritans' experience in the "New World" — what later came to be mythologized as "the Virgin Land": the divinely (later, History-) ordained myth of American exceptionalism. This unique structural mechanism was precisely the exceptionalism that, as Melville had learned, enabled the American Puritans not merely to distinguish their unique New World — both its youthful, always novel or future-oriented errand (vocation) and its covenantal, "democratic" polity — from the normal Old World's decadence and its past-oriented and tyrannical polity, in which the state of exception is an overt given. Because of these unique New World circumstances, this exceptionalism also provided the Puritans with the means of escaping the inevitable time-determined erosion and decline — the "overcivilization" — of all previous polities. I mean, of course, the always receding frontier — that is, *a perpetual foe* — and the covenantal anxiety (crisis/emergency) this always waning but never exhausted frontier always already aroused: the peculiar structural mechanism inherent in the American version of the exceptionalist myth that produced the peculiar logic of the cultural ritual that has come to be called the American jeremiad. I put this fundamental structural feature of the American national identity summarily in *American Exceptionalism in the Age of Globalization*. Foregrounding the "the frontier thesis" (elaborated by Frederic Jackson Turner at the end of the nineteenth century with the "closing of the frontier" — and critically alluded to by Melville in *Billy Budd*) that Sacvan Bercovitch minimized in his groundbreaking critical analysis of the American jeremiad, I wrote there:

> In pointing to Bercovitch's overdetermination of the unifying potentialities of the American jeremiad at the expense of its rejuvenating effects — the solidarity of the community in behalf of the errand at the expense of the renewal that would render its civil life immune to decay — I am not opting for the "frontier" thesis about the development of the American national identity. Rather, I am suggesting that Bercovitch's thesis about the role played by the American jeremiad needs to

incorporate and emphasize the "fact of the frontier" instead of minimizing it. Bercovitch is right in singling out the jeremiad as that cultural ritual that more than any other explains the development of the American national character and the elect's domestic and foreign policies. But this cultural ritual — this communal agency for the renewal of the commonweal's covenant with God — must, I suggest, be understood not simply in domestic terms (the solidarity of civil society), but also and simultaneously in terms of its "foreign" relations (the threatening Other beyond the American frontier). In the wake of the demise of the Puritan theocracy and the constitutional separation of church and states, the fact of the frontier came to dominate the discourse of an ever-westward expanding America, but it is the jeremiad — and the concept of providential/optimistic history on which it is founded — not in a purely secular form, as liberals have erroneously assumed, but in a religiosecular "natural supernaturalist" — form, that has determined the meaning of its various and fluid historical manifestations. And, as in the case of the Puritans, though increasingly as America rationalized and banalized the "wilderness," its purpose has been not to close the frontier and terminate the errand, but to keep it perpetually open, even after the farthest western reaches of the continent had been settled and colonized. Its purpose has been to *always already produce crisis and the communal anxiety crisis instigates* not simply to mobilize the national consensus and a flagging patriotism, but also to inject by violence the American body politic with antibiotics against decay.[28]

Given his recourse to the founding Puritan moment in his monumentalist history of the American national identity[29] — and to the American jeremiad for the projection of America's future — it comes as no surprise that Huntington invokes the enabling notion of the rejuvenating enemy in addressing the contemporary crisis of national identity ("Who Are We?") generated by the "deconstruction of America" (the "Anglo-Protestant core culture") in the wake of the turbulent 1960s, on the one hand, and the end of the Cold War, on the other. Like the exceptionalist logic of all his predecessor American Jeremiahs, theological and secular, in their confrontation with the possibility of peace, Huntington's compels him to read the end of this conflict as a threat to the exceptionalism that America has always invoked to distinguish itself from — and to escape the fate of — the decadent Old World. As such, not incidentally, his American invocation of the friend/enemy dyad should not be conflated, as it seems to have been by virtually every recent commentator on the state of exception, with that now popular European version that has its source in the German Hobbesian theoretician of jurisprudence Carl Schmitt:

> At the end of the twentieth century [with the implosion of the Soviet Union and the termination of the Cold War], democracy was left without a significant secular ideological rival, and the United States was left without a peer competitor. Among American foreign policy elites, the results were euphoria, pride, arrogance [the reference is to Francis Fukuyama's 1992 book *The End of History and the Last Man*] — and uncertainty. The absence of an ideological threat produced an absence of purpose. "Nations need enemies," Charles Krauthammer commented as the Cold War ends. "Take away one, and they find another." *The ideal enemy for America would be ideologically hostile, racially and culturally different, and militarily strong enough to pose a credible threat to American security.* The foreign policy debates of the 1990s were already over who might be such an enemy.[30]

It is at this point in Huntington's jeremiad that the attacks on the World Trade Center and the Pentagon on 9/11 come from the margins, where they have been lying in wait from the beginning, to center stage. In this chapter, tellingly entitled "America's Search for an Enemy," Huntington offers a rapid "objective" summary of the history of the policy debates over the qualifications of the various candidates for this bizarre status. And, then, in a rhetoric, analogous to the Puritans' response to God's calling, implying that History, not policy makers, determined America's new rejuvenating enemy, he brings his highly symmetrical narrative to a decisive and, to recall Melville, what can only be called a "measured" and euphoric "close": "The cultural gap between Islam and America's Christianity and Anglo-Protestantism reinforces Islam's enemy qualifications. And on September 11, 2001, Osama bin Laden ended America's search. The attacks on New York and Washington followed by the wars with Afghanistan and Iraq and the more diffuse 'war on terrorism' make militant Islam America's first enemy of the twenty-first century" (WAW, pp. 264–265).

With this History-granted culmination of America's search for an enemy, the jeremiadic logic of American exceptionalism comes to its bizarrely

paradoxical fulfillment. Al-Qaeda's attacks on American soil on 9/11 produced a civilizational (global) enemy adequate to America's exceptionalist
needs: the inauguration of a permanent threat to "homeland security" (the
normalization of the state of emergency); the consequent recuperation and
mobilization, at all costs, of the disintegrating covenantal consensus under
the aegis of "the Anglo-Protestant core culture"; and the rejuvenation of
the "America people's" eroding collective commitment to its History-
ordained messianic errand in the world's wilderness. In affirming the benignity of the massive threat posed by Islamic terrorism to American homeland security, in other words, Huntington's post-9/11 jeremiad announces
the advent of another Protestant-inspired "Great Awakening," one that
would be commensurate with his apocalyptic Manichaean "clash of civilizations." As in the case of George W. Bush's state of the union address, it
represents the horror of "Ground Zero" as an inaugural epochal moment:
"American identity began a new phase.... Its salience and substance in this
phase are being shaped by America's new vulnerability to external attack
and by a turn to religion, a Great Awakening in America that parallels the
resurgence of religion in most of the world" (WAW, p. 336). Seen in the light
of Huntington's previous diagnosis of the contemporary global occasion as
a Manichaean "clash of civilizations," the "salient" features of this "new
phase" of the American national identity he singles out can only mean,
analogous to Bush's identification of the 9/11 moment as "Ground Zero,"
the decisive and permanent mobilization of the American multitude (the
"profane" world), under the sovereign call of a higher ("sacred") cause,
into a nationalist biopolitical polity devoted exclusively (at the expense of
national and international law) and forever to the protection of the "vulnerable" global American homeland against an irreversibly evil and barbarian enemy. This is the fulfillment of Captain Vere's Orphic logic — his
"measured forms" — with a vengeance.

Reconstellated into the context of the discourse on the exception that
has become prominent in the wake of 9/11 and Bush's sovereign decision
to declare "war on terror," the unique and allegedly benign New World
exceptionalist myth informing Bush's all too typical speech and Huntington's retrospective historiography — this intrinsic need, embodied in
the rhetorical structure of the American jeremiad, for a perpetual frontier
or foe that will always already renew the covenant and rejuvenate the "the
people's" "errand in the wilderness" of the world — undergoes a discon-

certing but predictable sea change. It comes now to be seen—like the higher cause that determines Captain Vere's decision under the ironic light of the official ("outside") account of the affair on board the *Bellipotent*—as a powerful myth that (1) is informed by a metaphysical ontology (i.e., a naturalized supernaturalism or, in Schmitt's phrase, a "political theology") that understands the American nation's relation to history in terms of perpetual war (in the name of peace); that (2) represents the nation as a homeland that is always threatened by its Others, thus always instigating crises of national security; (3) that, in so doing, authorizes the sovereign executive not only to proclaim the state of exception that annuls the law in the name of protecting it but also to render the state of exception the rule; and that (4), in the process of the fulfillment of its measured logic, eventually transforms the profane plural polity into not only a national but also a global biopolitical police state—a totalized Abu Ghraib or Guantánamo—in which human being, both domestic and foreign, becomes, in Agamben's chilling phrase, bare life:

> He has been excluded from the religious community and from all political life: he cannot participate in the rites of his *gens*, nor . . . can he perform any juridically valid act. What is more, his entire existence is reduced to *a bare life stripped of every right by virtue of the fact that anyone can kill him without committing homicide*; he can save himself only in perpetual flight or a foreign land. And yet he is in a continuous relationship with the power that banished him precisely insofar as he is at every instant exposed to an unconditioned threat of death. He is pure *zoē*, but his *zoē* is as such caught in the sovereign ban and must reckon with it at every moment.[31]

To underscore the deadly dehumanizing effect on the lives of the preterite "populace" of the elect's effort to gain imperial control of the high seas, Herman Melville, as I have shown in my symptomatic reading of *Billy Budd* in chapter 3, represents the events culminating in the execution of the innocent Handsome Sailor on board the aptly named HMS *Bellipotent*, not as an afterthought, but as an integral part of the larger global war between England and France. I have also shown that his intention in doing so is to render this "asymmetrical" or "measureless" "inside narrative," retrieved from the oblivion to which it had been relegated by the official historians' retrospective symmetrical and measured narratives, a cautionary tale addressed to a late-nineteenth-century America: a Gilded Age United States that, in answer to its exceptionalist calling,[32] is preparing to embark on a national policy that would expand the closing frontier beyond its western continental border (i.e., globalize its "errand") and thus inaugurate a permanent state of emergency in which the state of exception would become the (global) rule and human beings would be stripped of their humanity. If these two related arguments are acknowledged, then it will also be seen that the cataclysmic end of the (onto)logic informing the American history I have summarized above—the benign American exceptionalist logic that was inaugurated by the American Puritans and brought to its culmination in the synecdochical post–9/11 discourse of President George W. Bush and Samuel P. Huntington—is precisely the cataclysmic end Melville anticipates in *Billy Budd*.

Thought in the context of the 9/11 occasion, then, the canonical *Billy Budd*, especially of those critics and commentators who subscribe in one way or another to the thesis that it is Melville's testament of acceptance, undergoes a remarkable estrangement. It not only comes to be seen as proleptically speaking the truth to the power of the American elect who exploited the so called "Ground Zero" occasion. It also comes to be seen as prefiguring the reemergence of the question of the state of exception as an urgent issue of contemporary democratic polities in the wake of the George W. Bush administration's declaration of war on terror, indeed, as a fictional meditation on the state or exception that contributes an insight to the diagnosis of this ominous political phenomenon of modern democracy, to which the theorists of the state of exception have been blinded by their failure to discriminate genealogically between the American nation-state and the European nation-states:[33] the remobilizing and rejuvenating function of the friend/enemy binary endemic to the American national identity, that is to say, the logical continuity between the American exceptionalist state and the state of exception that, unlike the era of the totalitarian regimes—Nazi, Fascist, Stalinist—is our contemporary global occasion.

Coda: Means without End

In *Billy Budd*, Melville discloses the shadow that haunts the benign messianic light of American exceptionalism. It is, in its ironic form, a negative critique of the myth's logic that does not overtly offer a positive alternative to a polity that, according to the ruthlessly unerring imperatives of the ontological friend/enemy opposition, ultimately reduces the humanity of human being to disposable bare life. But that negativity of the spectral revenant that haunts the American exceptionalist state invites thinking its positive possibilities. Melville, as I have shown, allows the monumentalist logic of exceptionalism to fulfill (realize) itself and in that liminal moment to self-destruct (unrealize itself): to disclose the reality this unerring logic has repressed (the unspoken threat implicit in the crew's "murmurings" that culminate after Billy's execution in the dislocating juxtaposition of the official ("outside") narrative with the spectral ballad penned by one of Billy's "rude" company. If we recall this Nietzschean-like genealogical strategy that "unrealizes" the "reality" of the exceptionalist regime of truth, we are, in other words, enabled to speculate about such a positive alternative polity.

The nexus of Melville's parodic/genealogical critique of the logic of American exceptionalism is, as I have shown, the frontier or, more precisely, the perpetual enemy to which this exceptionalist logic gives privileged status. In thus calling this binarist (Us against them) logic into question, Melville seems, on the surface, to adhere to precisely the universalistic — neutralizing and depoliticizing — liberal democratic ethos that constitutes the fundamental target of Carl Schmitt's theory of the political: the decisionist politics under the aegis of the sovereign exception that appears to be based ontologically on an irresolvable friend/enemy binary. I mean by this last, to put it all too briefly, a never-ending opposition that, according to Schmitt, protects man's ability to decide existentially against the metaphysically grounded liberalist imperative to neutralize and depoliticize the "political" (the decision-making intrinsic to the friend/enemy opposition) by universalizing it in the name of "humanity" — and "peace" — and, in the end, in thus privileging calculation, to dehumanize the human. As Schmitt puts it (in a way that anticipates the history of the United States in the post–World War II era):

For the application of such means ["of annihilation produced by enormous investments of capital and intelligence" endemic to the mechanized/calculative liberal enterprise], a new and essentially pacifist vocabulary has been created. War is condemned but executions, sanctions, punitive expeditions, pacifications, protection of treaties, international police, and measures to assure peace remain. The adversary is no longer called an enemy but a disturber of the peace and is thereby designated to be an outlaw of humanity. A war waged to protect or expand economic power must, with the aid of propaganda *turn into a crusade and into the last war of humanity* ["the war that will end all wars"]. This is implicit in the polarity of ethics and economics, a polarity astonishingly systematic and consistent. But this allegedly nonpolitical and apparently even antipolitical system serves existing or newly emerging friend-and-enemy groupings and cannot escape the logic of the political.[34]

But the reality is more complicated.

Melville's politics, *Billy Budd* implies, is, in fact, akin to Schmitt's antiliberal existentialism insofar as he espouses, against the dehumanizing violence that inheres in America's hubristic exceptionalist redemptive "errand" in behalf of "humanity" at large, a certain kind of irresolvable antagonism between politically imbalanced human groupings (the "populace" and the ship's officers, the preterite and the elect, the multitude and the national people) and, therefore, calls for continual decision — existential choice — however difficult that may be. But there the similarity with Schmitt ends. For Schmitt (and for the American exceptionalists, as President George W. Bush's post–9/11 State of the Union speech and Huntington's *Who Are We?* testify), the "friend" (the "us") in the secular friend/enemy binary is, in actual practice, like the identity vis-à-vis difference of metaphysics on which this binary is ultimately founded ("political theology"), ontologically prior to the enemy (the "them").[35] It is, therefore, a "sacred" principle that authorizes the latter's extermination, as Schmitt's commitment to the Nazis' idea of the nation-state makes clear.[36] For Melville, on the other hand, as opposed to the American exceptionalist (as Captain Vere's inexorable commitment to the sovereign higher cause is intended to bear witness),[37] the "theologically" ordained friend/foe opposition is rendered inoperative by way of his denying it a metaphysical (theological or naturalized supernatural) status. In decentering this Sacred/profane binary, to put it positively, Melville transforms the opposition understood as war to the death into a radically secular (i.e., profane), *intimate antagonism*, a *never-ending* dialectical belongingness of opposites in which the agonic *play* of the two always already produces differences that enhance and enrich the identityless identities of each. At the site of thinking, Heidegger, following Heraclitus, aptly called this paradoxical creative relationship a "loving strife" (*Auseinandersetzung*).[38] But it is, I think, Edward Said, who, in thinking the deracinated and exilic condition precipitated by the fulfillment of the incorporative logic of Western imperialism, constellates this ontological relationship into the cultural/political context and, in so doing, suggests most resonantly what the forgotten, but very much alive, Melville of *Billy Budd* was intuiting at the end of his exilic life in his genealogical meditation on the itinerary of the benign logic of exceptionalism, the itinerary that ends in the violence of the state of exception:

> [I]t is no exaggeration to say that liberation as an intellectual mission, born in the resistance and opposition to the confinements and ravages of imperialism, has shifted from the settled, established, and domesticated dynamics of culture to its unhoused, decentered, and exilic energies, energies whose incarnation today is the migrant, and whose consciousness is that of the intellectual and artist in exile, the political figure between domains, between forms, between homes, and between languages. From this perspective then all things are indeed counter, original, spare, strange. From this perspective also, one can see "the complete consort dancing together" contrapuntally.[39]

It was, then, neither the sacred politics of quiescence nor of reaction in the face of revolutionary change — the (non)politics that privileges might — that Melville endorsed in *Billy Budd*, as the majority of the Melvillean critics have implied or concluded. It was, rather, I submit, this politics of the "'complete consort dancing together' contrapuntally," in which the profane antagonists relate in loving strife, always — this nonutopian polyphonic politics, the measure of which is the measure of its occasion. Or, to put it in Giorgio Agamben's more radical terms, it was this vocationless "coming community," this community of "whatever being" that privileges the now over a futural end, *belonging as such* over *belonging to*,[40] and potentiality ("means without end") over power,[41] that was struggling to be born in the late Melville's imagination as, with increasing awareness, he followed the relentlessly *telos*-oriented logic informing the American exceptionalist calling to its deadly — and self-destructive — liminal end.

Chapter 1. Late Melville and His Historical Occasion:
Prolegomenon to a Rereading of Billy Budd, Sailor

1. See EA and HMAC.

2. I do not in this study invoke the substantial amount of poetry, including *Battle Pieces and Aspects of the War* (1866) and the great long poem *Clarel* (1876), that Melville wrote during this lengthy "silence." This may, understandably perhaps, be read as an unwarranted omission not too different from that to which I point in my criticism of the many *Billy Budd* critics who have omitted *Moby-Dick, Pierre,* "Bartleby," "Beneto Cereno," and *The Confidence-Man* from their discussions of *Billy Budd.* I do not think such an argument is ultimately valid, however. And this has to do precisely with my argument about the complex nature of Melville's "silence" during the long period between the publication of *The Confidence-Man* (1857) and the writing of *Billy Budd* (1885?–1891). To put it all too simply, Melville addressed his prose fiction to America at large; that is, it was a deliberate *public act* for him. His abandonment of fiction in favor of poetry after *The Confidence Man* was decisively passed over by the custodians of American cultural memory was essentially a bitterly reluctant but realistic and telling return to the private realm: the result, in other words, of his having been "frozen into silence" as one of them had demanded following the publication of *Pierre.* This inference is underscored by the fact that Melville not only privately financed the publication of these volumes of poetry but also published them in very limited editions. His decision to return to writing prose fiction in the last years of his life was, therefore, unlike writing the poetry, a decision — reminiscent of the late style — to break his "silence": to return one last time, now as a specter, to the public realm to speak the truth to power.

3. For a summary history of this archive, see Chapter 2.

4. Louis Althusser, "From *Capital* to Marx's Philosophy," in id. and Étienne Balibar, *Reading* Capital, trans. Ben Brewster (London: Verso 1979), p. 24. I expand on this aspect of the visualism (oversight) associated with Althusser's notion of the "problematic" later in this book. Suffice it to say here that the " 'changed

terrain'" (Marx's language) refers to the estranged world one comes to see after he/she has undergone a dis-location (*décalage*). For an extended analysis of Althusser's "problematic," see William V. Spanos, "Althusser's 'Problematic': Vision and the Vietnam War," in AE, pp. 35–46; and "'Benito Cereno' and 'Bartleby, the Scrivener': Reflections on the American Calling," in HMAC, pp. 105–166.

5. Herman Melville, *Billy Budd, Sailor (An Inside Narrative)*, ed. Harrison Hayford and Merton M. Sealts Jr. (Chicago: University of Chicago Press, 1962), cited as BB. "Very few critics writing on *Billy Budd* since 1962 have based any of their arguments on the Genetic Text as well as the Reading Text. In not using this evidence they have often proceeded with analyses which were simply not worth doing, wrong from the start," Hershel Parker asserts (RBB, p. 91). According to Parker, his reading was "the first study to try to answer any of Hayford and Sealts' questions. That odd circumstance leads me to design this book not only as a guide to Melville's last story but also as a guide to the Hayford-Sealts edition especially the 'Genetic Text'" (RBB, p. 8). It may be true that critics since 1962 have not consulted BB's "Genetic Text" in their interpretation of *Billy Budd*. But the fact is that virtually all have worked from its "Reading Text," which rejects and supersedes the notorious historical "Preface" included in the earlier versions of Raymond Weaver (1924, 1928) and F. Barron Freeman (1948).

6. "[I]t is important not to forget that the modern state of exception is a creation of the democratic-revolutionary tradition and not the absolutist one," Giorgio Agamben writes (SE, p. 5).

7. George Washington Peck, "Review of Herman Melville's *Pierre; or, The Ambiguities*," *American Whig Review*, November 1852, repr. in *Herman Melville: The Contemporary Reviews*, ed. Brian Higgins and Hershel Parker (New York: Cambridge University Press, 1995), pp. 131–142.

8. I am referring the those Americanists—Lionel Trilling, Richard Chase, Leslie Fiedler, Walter Bezanson, and R. W. B. Lewis, among others—who, following F. O. Matthiessen's lead in *American Renaissance: Art and Expression in the Age of Emerson and Whitman* (London: Oxford University Press, 1941), founded American literary studies as basically a Cold War instrument. See Donald Pease, "*Moby-Dick* and the Cold War," in *The American Renaissance Reconsidered: Selected Papers from the English Institute, 1982–1983*), ed. Walter Benn Michaels and Pease (Baltimore: Johns Hopkins University Press, 1985); "New Americanists: Revisionist Interventions into the Canon," in *New Americanist: Revisionist Interventions into the Canon, boundary 2*, 17, 1 (Spring 1990): 1–37; and Spanos, "Moby-Dick and the Canon," in EA, pp. 1–42.

9. "The hardheaded Dundee owner was a staunch admirer of Thomas Paine, whose book in rejoinder to Burke's arraignment of the French Revolution had then been published for some time and had gone everywhere" (BB, p. 48).

10. Thomas Paine, *The Rights of Man* (1791; London: Everyman's Library, 1969), pp. 224–225. I shall return later to the important post-nation-state critique of the traditional liberal understanding of human rights inaugurated by Hannah Arendt in *The Origins of Totalitarianism*, new ed. (San Diego: Harcourt Brace, 1979, 266–302) and developed by such contemporary thinkers as Alain Badiou in E and Giorgio Agamben, "Beyond Human Rights," in *Means Without End*, trans. Vincento Binetti and Cesare Casarino (Minneapolis: University of Minnesota Press, 2000), pp. 14–25.

11. I am referring to the occasion in *The Confidence-Man*, in which the Cosmopolitan, the ironic agent of American optimism, confronts an old man in the cabin whose faith has been deeply disturbed by his finding the pessimism of Ecclesiasticus 13 in the Bible. Invoking the prefigurative method of biblical exegesis that was fundamental to the American Puritans, the Cosmopolitan convinces the old man by way of his typical mode of indirection that his disturbance is "unwarranted," because Ecclesiasticus is an apocryphal book: "The uncanonical part should be bound distinct. And, now that I think of it, how well did those learned doctors who rejected for us this whole book of Sirach. I never read anything so calculated to destroy man's confidence in man. This son of Sirach even says—I saw it but just now: 'Take heed of thy friends'; not, observe, thy seeming friends, thy hypocritical friends, thy false friends, but thy *friends*, thy real friends—that is to say, not the truest friend in the world is to be implicitly trusted. Can Rochefoucauld equal that? I should not wonder if his view of human nature, like Machiavelli's, was taken from this Son of Sirach. And to call it wisdom—the Wisdom of the Son of Sirach! Wisdom, indeed! What an ugly thing wisdom must be! Give me the folly that dimples the cheek, say I, rather then the wisdom that curdles the blood. But no, no; it ain't wisdom; it's apocrypha, as you say, sir. For how can that be trustworthy that teaches distrust?" (C-M, p. 243). For an extended reading of this decisive passage in Melville's fiction, see Spanos, "Cavilers and Con Men: *The Confidence-Man: His Masquerade*," in HMAC, pp. 204–212.

12. BB, p. 25. RBB, pp. 47–50, emphatically supports Hayford and Sealts's conclusions about the "Preface." Indeed, Parker makes it the raison d'être of his study of the novella, clearly to delegitimize any politically radical reading.

13. See n. 4 above.

14. See also RBB, p. 89, where Parker quotes the passage from Hayford and Sealts's "Editors' Introduction" of the "definitive" text of *Billy Budd* to emphasize his solidarity with his colleagues.

15. What is misleading about Hayford and Sealts's (and, later, Parker's) invocation of Melville's commitment to the "ragged edges" of truth telling is that it implies, with critics such Warner Berthoff, Newton Arvin, and Robert Milder (see chapter 2), that Melville resisted the assertion of political views either because he

was in his humanist "magnanimity" — or had become so in his old age — above such petty matters or because he was too honest concerning the contradictions of mortal life to identify himself with a cause. As I argue in EA, Melville refused teleologies, philosophical and aesthetic, because they were ultimately totalitarian. This did not mean that the contradictions of earthly, especially worldly, life had equal weight and were therefore undecidable. On the contrary, he saw that in the real world the contradictions, that is, conflict or conflicting positions, were radically unequal, as, for example, in the case of Ishmael vis-à-vis Captain Ahab, or Bartleby vis-à-vis the lawyer, or Babbo vis-à-vis Captain Delano, or Israel Potter vis-à-vis Benjamin Franklin, and thus called, not for political quiescence, but for existential decision and resistance. It is Billy Budd's absolute lack of power in relation, not so much to Captain Vere as to the ship of state under the state of exception — the utter *helplessness* of this innocent, lowly ordinary seaman in a world organized in domination — that virtually all the commentary on Billy Budd has overlooked — and that I want to put back into play by way of retrieving the historical matter.

16. James Joyce, *A Portrait of the Artist as a Young Man*, ed. Chester G. Anderson (New York: Viking, 1968), p. 215. My emphasis.

17. I. A. Richards, *Principles of Literary Criticism* (London: Routledge & Kegan Paul, 1924), p. 250.

18. What I mean by this radical imbalance of power can, perhaps, be suggested by a contemporary example that the late Edward Said made it impossible for us to avoid: the power relations characterizing the struggle of the Palestinian people against an Israeli occupation supported by the United States. As Tony Judt puts Said's perspective on the "peace process" inaugurated at Oslo: "But the whole thing was deeply flawed. As Said reminds us, there were not two 'sides' to these negotiations: there was Israel, an established modern state with an awesome military apparatus (by some estimates the fourth strongest in the world today), occupying land and people seized thirty years earlier in war. And there were the Palestinians, a dispersed, displaced, disinherited community with neither an army nor a territory of its own. There was an occupier and there were the occupied. In Said's view, the only leverage that the Palestinians had was their annoying *facticity*: they were there, they wouldn't go away, and they wouldn't let the Israelis forget what they had done to them." Judt, "Foreword," in Edward W. Said, *From Oslo to Iraq and the Road Map* (London: Bloomsbury, 2004), p. xii.

19. In the characteristic words of John Middleton Murry, all these British admirers of *Billy Budd*, which was first published in England in 1924, represented the novel as the "last will and testament of a man of genius" (RBB, p. 58), a representation that culminated in TA, the essay that established the most prominent perspective of the Melville revival on the novel.

20. Herman Melville, *Billy Budd and Other Tales* (New York: Signet Books, 1961), pp. 7–8. This edition of the narrative is based on the text edited by Frederic Barron Freeman and corrected by Elizabeth Treeman (Cambridge, MA: Harvard University Press, 1956), pp. 7–8. My emphasis.

21. Hershel Parker, for example, writes of the historical matter of chapter 3 (like Hayford and Sealts, he rejects the "Preface" as "discarded" by Melville): "In this passage [Melville] defines the Great Mutiny in a voice like that of Edmund Burke, not Thomas Paine. . . . Melville's point of view at this point is clear — that of a traditionalist, a deeply conservative man apprehensive at the thought that insurrection might shake England, which was then 'all but the sole free conservative' power 'of the Old World.' . . . Rather than focusing on the injustices towards sailors, Melville is interested in, and appalled by, the French-inspired irrational combustion into which those grievances were ignited" (RBB, p. 109). See also the chapter on *Billy Budd* in Milton R. Stern, *The Fine Hammered Steel of Herman Melville* (Urbana: University of Illinois Press, 1957), pp. 206–239; and Larry J. Reynolds, "*Billy Budd* and American Labor Unrest: The Case for Striking Back," in *New Essays on Billy Budd*, ed. Donald Yannella (New York: Cambridge University Press, 2000), pp. 221–248.

22. For my analysis of the relationship between Melville and his narrator, see chapter 3. Here, it suffices to say two things that prior criticism has inadequately considered: (1) that the narrator is an American, and (2) that the incompleteness of Melville's manuscript demands a symptomatic reading, which is tantamount to saying that this American narrator is not entirely reliable.

23. E, p. 69.

24. I am indebted to Adam V. Spanos, "Strategy and Event: The Politics of Anticolonialism" (MA thesis, Dartmouth College, Hanover, NH, 2008), for directing me to Badiou's resonant concept of the "event."

25. This reading of the events of the year 1797 as a global "event" is further enforced by Melville's reference in the appended three chapters to the sea battle between the *Bellipotent* and the French ship *Athée* (*Atheist*), during which Captain Vere is killed (BB, p. 129).

26. IA, p. 202.

27. The quotations within the quotation are from BB, p. 55. See also Andrew Delbanco, *Melville: His World and Work* (New York: Knopf, 2005), in which, no doubt following Trachtenberg, he rightly (but contradictorily) observes that *Billy Budd*, "though set at sea in a distant past, was also a book about the time and place in which Melville was living when he wrote it," more specifically, about an America that, under the aegis of a rampant American capitalism in the 1880s, "stood on the verge of war with itself — a nation, as one contemporary observer put it, where 'workmen are denied the right of organization for self-protection,' and where,

when they try to organize, 'a hireling army . . . is established to shoot them down.' This was not a sensationalist claim. After Federal troops had been withdrawn in 1877 from the former Confederate states, soldiers were redeployed — sometimes as state militiamen, sometimes as mercenaries — to keep order among restive workers in the North. Private armies of 'security' guards patrolled America's railroad yards and factories, while one New York newspaper editorialized that what was needed was a New World Napoleon — someone who knew that 'the one way to deal with a mob is to exterminate it'" (p. 304). Delbanco might have added that it was during the period of Reconstruction that the "Posse Comitatus" Act, which prohibited the executive branch from deploying the military in domestic space, was passed in 1878 (and reaffirmed in 1894) to prevent the executive branch (Rutherford B. Hayes at the time of the railroad strike of 1877 and Grover Cleveland at the time of the Pullman strike of 1895) from violating the Fourth Amendment and rendering the state of exception the rule. After 9/11 and the George W. Bush administration's announcement of its "War on Terror" — and a state of exception — his Office of Legal Council, most notably John Yoo, undertook an initiative to legalize the right of the executive branch to govern independently of the Congress and the Supreme Court. One of these secret memoranda, recently released by the Obama administration, entitled "Authority to Use Military Force to Combat Terrorists Within the United States" (October 23, 2001), includes a reinterpretation of the Posse Comitatus Act to legalize this unconstitutional project. See Chapter 4 for my discussion of the relationship between Melville's *Billy Budd* and this initiative of the Bush administration to establish a state of exception. As in the case of Trachtenberg, however, Delbanco abandons this suggestive political interpretive orientation in favor of the more conventional one that represents *Billy Budd* as the old Melville's "testament of acceptance": "[B]y the time he composed *Billy Budd*, [Melville] was not so much outraged as resigned to the disjunctions between law and justice. *Billy Budd* was his farewell to what he had called, in *Pierre*, the 'beautiful illusions of youth'" (p. 312). For a recent example of the few readings of *Billy Budd* that view it as a tale reflecting on Melville's contemporary American occasion, in this case, the lynching pandemic during the Reconstruction era (without, however, addressing the question of the nationality of the narrator), see Gregory Jay, "Douglass, Melville and the Lynching of Billy Budd," in *Frederick Douglass and Herman Melville: Essays in Relation*, ed. Robert S. Levine and Samuel Otter (Chapel Hill: University of North Carolina Press, 2008), pp. 369–395.

28. Frederick Jackson Turner, *The Frontier in American History*, 2nd ed. (New York: Holt, 1953); Henry Nash Smith, *The Virgin Land: The American West as Myth and Symbol* (Cambridge, MA: Harvard University Press, 1950); Leo Marx, *The Machine in the Garden: Technology and the Pastoral Ideal in America* (New York: Oxford University Press, 1964); John F. Kasson, *Civilizing the Machine:*

Technology and Republican Values in America, 1776–1900 (1976; New York: Hill & Wang, 1999).

29. For a brilliant analysis of this epochal exhibition of the capitalist vision of the future of America, see IA, chapter 7, "White City," pp. 208–234.

30. Frederick Jackson Turner, "The Significance of the Frontier in American History," in id., *The Frontier in American History*, p. 1.

31. See Sacvan Bercovitch, *The American Jeremiad* (Madison: University of Wisconsin Press, 1978); and William V. Spanos, "American Exceptionalism, the Jeremiad, and the Frontier, Before and After 9/11: From the Puritans to the Neo-Con Men," in AE, pp. 187–241.

32. See Herman Melville, "The Encantadas, or Enchanted Isles," in *The Piazza Tales and Other Prose Pieces, 1839–1860*, ed. Harrison Hayford, Alma A. Mac-Dougall, and G. Thomas Tanselle (Evanston, IL: Northwestern University Press; Chicago: Newberry Library 1987), pp. 125–173. See also Rodrigo Lazo, "The Ends of Enchantment: Douglass, Melville, and Expansionism in the Americas," in *Frederick Douglass and Herman Melville*, ed. Levine and Otter, pp. 207–232. Lazo does not read Melville's early "Encantadas" in the context of westward expansion, nor does he point to the continuity of the matter of this earlier text (1854) with *Billy Budd*. But in focusing on Melville's critique of the American filibustering initiatives in Latin America, he provides important indirect evidence of Melville's abiding concern with the question of the closing of the frontier and, particularly, the role that the Caribbean (the waterway between the Atlantic and the Pacific oceans) played in the development of the American imperial project.

33. Mahan rose to the rank of rear admiral and was president of the Naval War College, where the young Theodore Roosevelt was his protégé.

34. "Adamastor, in the *Lusiads* of Luiz Vaz de Camões (1524–80), the Portuguese poet, is a monster, embodying the terror and danger of natural forces, who attempts to destroy Da Gama and his crew" (BB, p. 156).

35. Earlier critics who have claimed that the origin of *Billy Budd* is to be found in the *Somers* Affair include Charles C. Anderson, "The Genesis of *Billy Budd*," *American* Literature 12 (November 1940): 329–346, and Newton Arvin, both of whom take their point of departure from the fact that Melville's cousin Guert Gansevoort presided over the drumhead court that ordered the executions of the three alleged mutineers. But this historical origin does not come into play in their interpretations of the novella. Though Arvin, for example, points to the connection between the American and the British historical contexts (the alleged mutiny on board the *Somers* and the "famous Mutiny at the Nore," he goes on to observe: "All these, however, are matters of the surface; they have a genuine interest, but they say little about the real ['archetypal'] feeling of *Billy Budd*" (HM, p. 294).

36. See ISP, pp. 386–402. The quotation within the quotation is from Edmond

Jurien de la Gravière, *Guerres maritimes sous la République et sous l'Empire* (Paris: Charpentier, 1847). In the following paragraph Mahan again quotes Jurien de la Gravière to underscore his point: "The emperor, whose eagle glance traced plans of campaign for his fleets as for his armies, was wearied by these unexpected reverses. He turned his eyes from the one field of battle in which fortunes was faithless to him, and decided to pursue England elsewhere than upon the seas; he undertook to rebuild his navy, but without giving it any part in the struggle which became more furious than ever" (ISP, p. 47). See also ISP, pp. 386–402.

37. HS. It suffices at this point to say that, for Agamben, "bare life" is life that can be killed with impunity, and it is the condition to which human life is reduced in a state of exception.

38. For extended discussions of this global imperative of the myth of American exceptionalism, see EA, pp. 250–278; Spanos, "American Exceptionalism, The American Jeremiad, and the Frontier, Before and After 9/11" in AE; and HMAC, pp. 213–228.

39. See chapter 3.

40. On the notion of fidelity to the event, see E. After offering historical examples of the four sites (politics, love, science, and art) at which events occur (the French Revolution, the meeting of Eloise and Abelard, Galileo's creation of physics, and Haydn's invention of the classical musical style), Badiou adds: "From which 'decision,' then, stems the process of truth? From the decision to relate henceforth to the situation *from the perspective of its eventual (événémentiel) supplement.* Let us call this a fidelity. To be faithful to an event is to move within the situation that this event has supplemented, by *thinking* (although all thought is a practice, a putting to the test) the situation 'according to' the event. And this, of course — since the event was excluded by all the regular laws of the situation — compels the subject to *invent* a new way of being and acting in the situation" (E, pp. 41–42). For Badiou's discussion of infidelity to the event (i.e., "evil"), see *E*, pp. 67–71.

41. That this global emancipatory impulse was a constant of Melville's imagination is evidenced by his repetition on the first page of *Billy Budd* of his reference in *Moby-Dick* and *The Confidence-Man* to Anacharsis Cloots (1755–94), who presented thirty-six foreigners as a cross section of humanity to the French Constituent National Assembly on June 19, 1790, shortly after the outbreak of the French Revolution, as testimony to the common humanity of all mankind. In *Moby-Dick*, he refers to the crew of the *Pequod* — "isolatoes," now "federated along one keel" — as "An Anacharsis Clootz deputation from all the isles of the sea, and all the ends of the earth" (M-D, p. 121). In *The Confidence-Man*, he refers to the passengers on board the *Fidèle* as "an Anacharsis Cloots congress of all kinds of that multiform pilgrim species, man" (C-M, p. 9); and in *Billy Budd*, in

establishing the background for his account of the crew of the *Rights-of-Man* from which Billy was impressed, he refers to the crew of a similar ship he had encountered in Liverpool "half a century ago" (the reference is no doubt to his novel *Redburn*) as "made up of such an assortment of tribes and complexions as would have well fitted them to be marched up by Anacharsis Cloots before the bar of the first French Assembly as Representatives of the Human Race" *(BB,* 43). What is worth pointing out in the present context about Melville's globalized view of human emancipation is its striking similarity to Edward Said's repeated references to Aimé Césaire's lines from *Cahier d'un retour au pays natal* (1939; trans. as *Return to My Native Land*): "and no race has a / monopoly on beauty, on intelligence, on strength / and there is room for everyone at the convocation of conquest." Said, *Culture and Imperialism* (New York: Knopf, 1993), pp. 230–231.

42. BB, pp. 148–149. See Wendell Glick, "Expediency and Absolute Morality in *Billy Budd*," *PMLA* 68 (March 1953): 103–10; Laurence Barrett, "Differences in Melville's Poetry," *PMLA* 70 (September, 1955): 606–623; John B. Noone Jr. "*Billy Budd*: Two Concepts of Nature," *American Literature* 29 (November 1957): 249–262; Milton R. Stern, "Billy Budd," in *The Fine Hammered Steel of Herman Melville* (Urbana: University of Illinois Press, 1958), pp. 206–239; also 26–27. Merlin Bowen, *The Long Encounter: Self and Experience in the Writings of Herman Melville* (Chicago: University of Chicago Press, 1960), pp. 216–233. For other prestigious earlier exponents of this position, see EM, pp. 196–197, and Robert Milder, *Exiled Royalties: Melville and the Life We Imagine* (Oxford: Oxford University Press, 2006). Milder not only takes the Nelson chapter as straightforward, but also builds his entire reading of *Billy Budd* by way of identifying Melville's final attitude with that of Nelson (pp. 242–244). No New Americanist who has written on *Billy Budd* has addressed the issue of Melville's attitude to Nelson.

43. A telling instance in *Billy Budd* of this subtle politicizing transformation of the common sailors into the (lowly and dangerous) "people" inhabiting the ship of state (as opposed to its nationalist meaning) occurs in chapter 21, where Captain Vere unerringly defends—patently contemptuous of his referent—his unerring (Ahabian-like) decision to execute Billy Budd to the drumhead court. See pp. 112–115 above for further discussion of this locution.

44. That Melville, in this passage in *Billy Budd*, is indeed alluding ironically to the inordinately high price in blood paid by the preterite of the man-of-war for its "elect's" acts of "glory" is further suggested by another bitterly ironic reference to Nelson and Trafalgar in *White-Jacket*, his devastating criticism of governmentality in the U.S. Navy. Referring to the "precautions"—two life buoys always at the ready at the stern of the ship—adopted by the Navy (unlike "the merchant or whaling service") to save the life of anyone who falls overboard, the narrator writes:

"Thus deeply solicitous to preserve human life are the regulations of men-of-war, and seldom has there been a better illustration of this solicitude than at the battle of Trafalgar, when, after 'several thousand' French seaman had been destroyed, according to Lord Collingwood [second in command to Nelson], and, by the official returns, sixteen hundred and ninety Englishmen were killed or wounded, the Captains of the surviving ships ordered the life-buoy sentries from their death-dealing guns to their vigilant posts, as officers of the Humane Society" (Herman Melville, *White-Jacket; or The World in a Man-of-War* [New York: Modern Library, 2002], p. 72).

45. Herman Melville, "Cock-A-Doodle-Doo! Or, The Crowing of the Noble Cock Beneventano," in *Piazza Tales*, p. 282. See also *White-Jacket*, where the narrator, referring to the quarter-deck of a man-of-war in action as the most dangerous place, observes: "The reason is, that the officers of highest rank are there stationed; and the enemy have an ungentlemanly way of target-shooting at their buttons. If we should chance to engage a ship, who could tell but some bungling small-arm marksman in the enemy's tops might put a bullet through *me*: instead of the Commodore? If they hit *him*, no doubt he would not feel it much, for he was used to that sort of thing, and, indeed, had a bullet in him already. Whereas, *I* was altogether unaccustomed to having blue pills playing round my head in such an indiscriminate way. Besides, ours was a flag-ship, and every one knows what a peculiarly dangerous predicament the quarter-deck of Nelson's flag-ship was in at the battle of Trafalgar; how the lofty tops of the enemy were full of soldiers, peppering away at the English Admiral and his officers. Many a poor sailor, at the guns of the quarter-deck, must have received a bullet intended for some wearer of an epaulet" (*White-Jacket*, pp. 65–66; see also pp. 68–69).

46. Michel Foucault, "Nietzsche, Genealogy, History," in id., *Language, Counter-Memory, Practice: Selected Essays and Interviews,* ed. Donald F. Bouchard, trans. id. and Sherry Simon (Ithaca, NY: Cornell University Press, 1977), pp. 160–161; my emphasis.

47. The strongest of these displacing "allegorical" readings that take their point of departure from Melville's distinction between Horologicals and Chronologicals in *Pierre* is Hannah Arendt's in *On Revolution* (New York: Penguin Books, 1965), pp. 33–88. And this is because she embeds the allegorical struggle in the historical: the French Revolution.

48. See, e.g., TA.

49. HM, p. 292.

50. Edward W. Said, *The Late Style: Music and Literature Against the Grain* (New York: Pantheon Books, 2006), p. 13.

51. In invoking the term "profane" against "sacred," I am pointing to Melville's anticipation of Giorgio Agamben's rendering "inoperative" of the tradi-

tional Western binary in which the sacred reduces this world to a profanity. See Agamben, *Profanations*, trans. Jeff Fort (Brooklyn, NY: Zone Books, 2007), particularly the chapter entitled "In Praise of Profanation," pp. 73–92. See also Leland de la Durantaye's illuminating essay "*Homo Profanus*: Giorgio Agamben's Profane Philosophy" in *boundary* 2 35, 3 (Fall 2008): 27–62.

52. "It [the magnanimity of Billy and Vere] is given no power to prevent the now settled outcome of the action," Berthoff observes. "Yet its radiance is beyond catastrophe. It is such as can survive those decisive accidents of individual existence — age, health, station, luck, particular experience — which Melville consistently presented the lives of his characters as being determined by. Now the narrative has come to its defining climax. Here the tone is set for what remains to be told, and not at the pitch of tragedy — the tone of exalted acceptance and muted patient joy which will be heard in the account of Billy in irons like a 'slumbering child,' in Billy's 'God bless Captain Vere!' in Vere's dying with Billy's name on his lips (not remorse, Melville specifies), and finally, and with what sure art, in the gravely acquiescent music of the closing ballad" (EM, p. 194).

53. "Who cannot see that this [liberal humanist] ethics [proclaiming the "rights of man"] which rests on the misery of the world hides, behind its victim-Man, the good-Man, the white-Man? Since the barbarity of the situation is considered only in terms of 'human rights' — whereas in fact we are always dealing with a political situation, one that calls for a political thought-practice, one that is peopled by its own authentic actors — it is perceived from the heights of our apparent civil peace, as the uncivilized that demands of the civilized a civilizing intervention. Every intervention in the name of a civilization *requires* an initial contempt for the situation as a whole, including its victims. And this is why the reign of 'ethics' coincides, after decades of courageous critiques of colonialism and imperialism, with today's sordid self-satisfaction in the 'West', with the insistent argument according to which the misery of the Third World is the result of its own incompetence, its own inanity — in short, of its *subhumanity*" (E, pp. 12–13).

54. HS, pp. 183–184; my emphasis. Agamben's understanding of bare life is extremely complex, but for my purposes here, this definition from *Homo Sacer* should suffice.

55. That Melville was aware of the devastating irony of this "decisive" sentence is borne witness to by his repeated use of the same irony in *Moby-Dick*, when, in a the soliloquy addressed to "ye great gods"(chapter 37) after the crew has taken the oath of allegiance to his "fiery pursuit," Captain Ahab says: "Come, Ahab's compliments, come and see if ye can swerve me. Swerve me? Ye cannot swerve me, else ye swerve yourselves! Man has ye there. Swerve me? The path to my fixed purpose is laid with iron rails, whereon my soul is grooved to run. Over unsounded gorges, through the rifled hearts of mountains, under torrents' beds,

unerringly I rush! *Naught's an obstacle, naught's an angle to the iron way!"* (M-D, p. 168; my emphasis). This unintended prophecy comes devastatingly true during the culminating three days of Ahab's fiery pursuit, when the repeated spectral "nothings" of the lookout's answer to Ahab's repeated question, "What d'ye see?" materializes as Moby Dick, the nothingness of being that he has objectified and made "practically assailable." For an amplified reading of this climactic moment of *Moby-Dick*, see *EA*, pp. 140–145.

56. As opposed to the "Spirit" (as in the Hegelian sense of the principle of presence), the revenant is the unnamable absence that, as it were, the principle of presence will have nothing to do with, but precisely in putting it that way acknowledges its haunting "reality." Whereas in the old metaphysical dispensation, which privileges the eye, we look (or visit) the temporal phenomena of being, in the new dispensation the latter look at or "visit" us. See Jacques Derrida, *Specters of Marx: The State of the Debt, the Work of Mourning, and the New Internationalism* (New York: Routledge, 1994), pp. 6–9.

Chapter 2. Criticism of Billy Budd, Sailor: *A Counterhistory*

1. Harrison Hayford and Merton Sealts Jr., "Editors' Introduction," in BB, pp. 243–39.

2. CE, pp. 1–21.

3. RBB, pp. 51–95.

4. See esp. Sacvan Bercovitch, *The American Jeremiad* (Madison: University of Wisconsin Press, 1978); id., *The Rites of Assent: Transformations in the Symbolic Construction of America* (New York: Routledge, 1993); Richard Drinnon, *Facing West: The Metaphysics of Indian-Hating and Empire Building* (Minneapolis: University of Minnesota Press, 1980); Edgar Dryden, *Melville's Thematics of Form: The Great Art of Telling the Truth* (Baltimore: Johns Hopkins University Press, 1968); C. L. R. James, *Mariners, Renegades, and Castaways: The Story of Herman Melville and the World We Live In (1953)*, ed. Donald E. Pease (Hanover, NH: University Press of New England, 2001); Donald E. Pease, *The New American Exceptionalism* (Minneapolis: University of Minnesota Press, 2010); David Reynolds, *Beneath the American Renaissance: The Subversive Imagination in the Age of Emerson and Melville* (Cambridge, MA: Harvard University Press, 1988); Michael Paul Rogin, *Subversive Genealogies: The Politics and Art of Herman Melville* (Berkeley: University of California Press, 1985); John Carlos Rowe, *At Emerson's Tomb: The Politics of Classic American Literature* (New York: Columbia University Press, 1997); EA and HMAC; It should not be forgotten, as it has been by most of the commentators on *Billy Budd*, that, as in the latter, Melville repre-

sents the worlds of two of these texts, *Moby-Dick* and *The Confidence-Man*, as ships of state.

5. George Washington Peck, "Review of Herman Melville's *Pierre; or, The Ambiguities*," *American Whig Review*, November 1852, repr. in *Herman Melville: The Contemporary Reviews*, ed. Brian Higgins and Hershel Parker (New York: Cambridge University Press, 1995), p. 443.

6. In invoking the term "onto-political" in referring to Melville's critique of "American exceptionalism," I am pointing to the crucial distinction between a traditional (Enlightenment) disciplinary understanding of the "political" (as a compartmentalized discourse and practice that is more or less independent of ontology (the representation of being), or culture, or economics, or gender, or race relations, etc.) and Melville's proleptic — and abiding — awareness of the indissoluble continuity of these sites on the continuum of being. For an extended discussion of this matter, see EA, pp. 204–225.

7. For extended analyses of the history of the reception of Melville in America, in which he returns as a specter to speak back to those who silenced him, see William V. Spanos, "A Genealogical History of the Reception of *Moby-Dick*, 1850–1945," in EA, pp. 12–22, and "Melville's Specter: An Introduction," in HMAC, pp. 1–17.

8. These early British critics of *Billy Budd* refer to Melville's work as a "tragedy," but without clearly defining the term. I, however, interpret this Aristotelian term from a poststructuralist or de-structive perspective: a work of verbal (and temporal) art that deliberately generates pity and terror (a contradictory motion towards and away from the protagonist), only to bring this anxiety (the contradictory and destabilizing motion of the soul in the world) *in the end of the temporal process* into harmony (*catharsis*). Tragedy in this sense is a naturalized supernaturalism — a secular theology — whose purpose is, as Berthold Brecht perceived long ago, to pacify all manner of social and political (worldly) resistance. See *EA,* pp. 47–61.

9. M. H. Abrams, *Natural Supernaturalism: Tradition and Revolution in Romantic Literature* (New York: Norton, 1971). See also Edward W. Said's brief but telling contrapuntal reading of Abrams's influential representation of humanism, in *Orientalism* (New York: Vintage Books, 1978), p. 114. In chapter 4, I show that this eulogized humanist "naturalized supernaturalist" imagination is complicit with the "political theology" on which, according to the German National Socialist political theorist Carl Schmitt, the normalization of the sovereign state of exception depends. See Carl Schmitt, *Political Theology: Four Chapters on the Concept of Sovereignty*, trans. George Schwab (Chicago: University of Chicago Press, 2005).

10. HMS, p. 33.

11. See Spanos, "The Confidence-Man: Cavilers and Con Men," in HMAC, pp. 167–213.

12. John Freeman, *Herman Melville* (London: Macmillan, 1926), pp. 135–136.

13. This was the first scholarly essay on Melville to be published in the United States.

14. E, pp. 4–17.

15. WI, p. 37. Misquoted by Weaver, Melville's phrase has since been emended to read "innocence and infamy, spiritual depravity and fair repute."

16. Robert Milder, a more recent humanist Melvillean scholar, observes that, like "Shakespeare in *The Winter's Tale* or Milton in *Samson Agonistes*, Melville, it appeared, had surmounted his anger and reconciled himself to . . . what? Much of the confusion, wrangling, and downright ill will of *Billy Budd* criticism stems from the failure of early readers to specify what Melville's testament was an acceptance *of*. To Raymond Weaver, for example, *Billy Budd* was an effort to 'justify the ways of God to man,' yet Weaver's neat Miltonic formulation was almost directly contradicted by his appeal to the celebration of human greatness that marks high tragedy" (CE, p. 3). Milder's point is technically valid perhaps (though in distinguishing between Christian and humanist understanding of being, he does not take into account the degree to which the later, post-Renaissance Europe had accommodated classical tragedy to a certain major strain of Christianity), but it should not obscure, as it has obscured, the reality that both the Christian understanding of the human condition and that of high humanism (the tragic view) assume that the dynamics of earthy conflict — ontological and sociopolitical — end in elevating quiescence or acceptance as the supreme ethical value. This was forcefully argued (and represented in his anti-tragic theater) by Berthold Brecht a half century ago, and is being argued in different but related ways at the present moment by Alain Badiou, Giorgio Agamben, and Slavoj Žižek.

17. AR, pp. 500–501.

18. In concluding that Melville comes in the end to accept necessity in *Billy Budd*, Matthiessen is echoing Lewis Mumford's *Herman Melville: A Study of His Life and Vision* (1929; rev. ed., New York: Harcourt, Brace & World, 1963): "These are the fundamental ambiguities of life: so long as evil exists, the agents that intercept it will also be evil, whilst we accept the world's conditions. . . . Rascality may be punished; but beauty and innocence will suffer in the process far more. . . . Melville had been harried by these paradoxes in *Pierre*. At last he was reconciled. He accepted the situation as a tragic necessity; and to meet that tragedy bravely was to find peace, the ultimate peace of resignation, even in an incongruous world" (pp. 356–357).

19. HM, p. 296.

20. Warner Berthoff, "'Certain Phenomenal Men': The Example of *Billy Budd*," *ELH* 26 (1960): 334–51; repr. in EM.

21. Milton R. Stern, *The Fine Hammered Steel of Herman Melville* (Urbana: University of Illinois Press, 1968), pp. 206–239; Richard Harter Fogle, "*Billy Budd*: The Order of the Fall," *Nineteenth-Century Fiction* 15, 3 (September 1960): 189–205.

22. I derive the term "problematic" from Louis Althusser. For an extended account of the oversight of the sighting of the problematic, see Spanos, "'Benito Cereno' and 'Bartleby, the Scrivener': Reflections on the American Calling," in HMAC, pp. 105–166.

23. Berthoff quotes Pearson, "*Billy Budd*: 'The King's Yarn,'" *American Quarterly* 3 (Summer 1951): 99–114: "'What Melville was doing was to try to give in as universalized a way as possible . . . another redaction of the myth which had concerned Milton . . . in the trilogy of his three major works,'" and adds, "the Christian myth, that is, of the fall from innocence and the promise of redemption" (EM, p. 186).

24. It is at this point that Berthoff's perspective distinguishes itself somewhat from Matthiessen's. Whereas the latter emphasizes Billy, the common sailor, as the exemplar of magnanimity to identify it with a nonelite democracy, Berthoff emphasizes Lord Nelson, the uncommon man, to identify magnanimity with a humanist elitism.

25. See Martin Heidegger, "Letter on Humanism," in *Basic Writings*, ed. David Farrell Krell (San Francisco: Harper Collins, 1993), pp. 224–225; *Parmenides*, trans. André Schuwer and Richard Rojcewicz (Bloomington: Indiana University Press, 1992), pp. 39–45; Martin Bernal, *Black Athena: The Afroasiatic Roots of Classical Civilization* (New Brunswick, NJ: Rutgers University Press, 1987); William V. Spanos, "Culture and Colonization: The Imperial Imperatives of the Centered Circle," in *America's Shadow: An Anatomy of Empire* (Minneapolis: University of Minnesota Press, 2000), pp. 64–125.

26. At a crucial point in his essay, where he defines magnanimity, Berthoff returns to Milton to acknowledge his presence in Melville's text, but now as a humanist: "The Milton who matters here . . . is not the Christian poet of paradise lost and regained but the prideful humanist whose dedication to the idea of magnanimity is proverbial in English letters" (EM, p. 195).

27. C-M, p. 66. For an amplified reading of this, to Melville, fundamental comportment in the face of the contingencies of being, see Spanos, "Cavilers and Con Men: *The Confidence-Man: His Masquerade*," in HMAC, pp. 168–172.

28. Phil Withim, "*Billy Budd*: Testament of Resistance," *Modern Language Quarterly* 20 (June 1959): 115–127. See also Leonard Casper, "The Case Against

Captain Vere," *Perspective* 5 (Summer 1952): 146–152, repr. in *Melville's* Billy Budd *and the Critics*, ed. William T. Stafford, 2nd ed. (Belmont, CA.: Wadworth, 1968), pp. 212–215; and Karl E. Zink, "Herman Melville and the Forms — Irony and Social Criticism in 'Billy Budd,' " *Accent* 12 (Summer 1952): 131–139.

29. Edgar Dryden, "Epilogue," in *Melville's Thematics of Form: The Great Art of Telling the Truth* (Baltimore: Johns Hopkins University Press, 1968), pp. 199–216; Joyce Sparer Adler, "*Billy Budd* and Melville's Philosophy of War and Peace," in *War in Melville's Imagination* (New York: New York University Press, 1981), pp. 160–185; originally published in *PMLA* 91 (1976): 266–78; Brooks Thomas, "*Billy Budd* and the Judgment of Silence," in CE, pp. 199–211; originally published in *Bucknell Review* 27 (1983): 51–78; Sharon Cameron, " 'Lines of Stone': The Unpersonified Impersonal in Melville's *Billy Budd*," in id., *Impersonality: Seven Essays* (Chicago: University of Chicago Press, 2007), pp. 180–204; Nancy Ruttenburg, "Melville's Anxiety of Innocence: The Handsome Sailor," in *Democratic Personality: Popular Voice and the Trial of American Authorship* (Stanford, CA: Stanford University Press, 1998), pp. 344–378; Eve Kosofsky Sedgwick, "Some Binarisms (I): *Billy Budd:* After the Homosexual," in *Epistemology of the Closet* (Berkeley: University of California Press), pp. 91–130; Gregory Jay, "Douglass, Melville, and the Lynching of Billy Budd," in *Frederick Douglass and Herman Melville: Essays in Relation ed.* Robert S. Levine and Samuel Otter (Chapel Hill: University of North Carolina Press, 2008), pp. 369–395.

30. Robert Milder, "Introduction: The Development of *Billy Budd* Criticism," in CE, p. 7. The second emphasis is mine. As Milder's later remarks about *Billy Budd* in the chapter entitled "Alms for Oblivions" in his *Exile Royalties: Melville and the Life We Imagine* (Oxford: Oxford University Press, 2006), pp. 338–347, testify, this prestigious Melville scholar's position on Melville's late phase did not change after the emergence of New Americanist readings of the novella. This late discussion of Melville's novella is a revised and amplified version of "Melville's Late Poetry and *Billy Budd*: From Nostalgia to Transcendence," in CE, pp. 212–223; originally published in *Philological Quarterly* 66 (Fall 1987): 493–507. See also Milder, "Herman Melville, 1819–1991: A Brief Biography," in *A Historical Guide to Herman Melville*, ed. Giles Gunn (Oxford: Oxford University Press, 2005), pp. 50–53.

31. For a more or less similar version of this form of the testament of acceptance position contemporary with Milder's, see Bruce L. Grenberg, "*Clarel* and *Billy Budd*: No Other Worlds but This," in id., *Some Other World to Find: Quest and Negation in the Works of Herman Melville* (Urbana: University of Illinois Press, 1989), 190–212.

32. RBB, p. 87. The two exceptions Parker names are Milton R. Stern (*Billy Budd, Sailor* [Indianapolis: Bobbs-Merrill, 1975]), and Thomas Scorza (*In the*

Time Before Steamships [DeKalb: Northern Illinois University Press, 1979]), pp. 87–88). These critics, as far as I can tell, are the only ones who have overtly rejected Hayford and Sealts's decision about the text of *Billy Budd*, preferring, as Parker puts it, "the form of a text which is first published . . . as the 'received text' " at the expense of the "authentic" text, the text that, according to the scholarship of Hayford and Sealts, the author intended (RBB, pp. 89–90).

33. RBB, pp. 92–93. Parker's humanist commentary on the New Historicism should give pause to those recent critics who, in the name of a new humanism, are turning against poststructuralist theory on the grounds that its "antihumanism" denies agency.

34. "Let's put the situation bluntly: . . . People who write about almost any aspect of *Billy Budd* without working through the Genetic Text are pretty much wasting their time," Parker says (RBB, p. 100).

35. RBB, p. 109; my emphasis. This laborious effort can be seen in Parker's return in the last section ("Textual Problems and Interpretations") of his book, to the question of the "Preface," which he dismisses at the beginning. There, after stating that "I want to avoid creating the impression that [the 'Preface'] is crucially important in the interpretation of *Billy Budd*," he goes on to undertake a convoluted reading of it to prove that it does not function as a (traditional) preface because of its "irresoluteness": "Except for the fact that the first sentence specifies that the year of the narrative is 1797, one could suspect from the content of the two paragraphs that a major focus of the following narrative would be ultimate general reforms paradoxically initiated by revolution in France and mutiny on British ships and coming to fruition much later, far into the nineteenth century. The section seems to set up the reader to expect a story about a real mutiny grounded in serious naval abuses, a mutiny put down by execution. . . . But the fact is that Melville himself did not see such possibilities in the two paragraphs. The very inconclusiveness, the evenhandedness, is what made the section inappropriate at the spot where Melville drafted the words to fit. Because he had been led into irresolution which distracted from his progress in the story, he removed the passage" (RBB, p. 168). In putting it this way, Parker not only precludes reading the "Preface" as deliberately other than a traditional preface, but, in the process, also backs into the ideological view that the late Melville was indeed a political reactionary, precisely the view he articulates in the passage quoted in my text.

36. For an amplified reading of Melville's critique of what Nietzsche (and Foucault) called "monumental history" in *Israel Potter*, see Spanos, "Herman Melville's *Israel Potter*: Reflections on a Damaged Life," in HMAC, pp. 59–67.

37. For readings of *Billy Budd* fundamentally similar to Parker's, see Wendell Glick, "Expediency and Absolute Morality in *Billy Budd*," *PMLA* 60, 8 (March 1953): 103–110, repr. in William T. Stafford, *Melville's* Billy Budd *and the Critics*,

2nd ed. (Belmont, CA: Wadsworth, 1968), pp. 165–172; and, esp., Christopher Sten, "Vere's Use of the 'Forms' and Ends in *Billy* Budd," *American Literature* 47 (March 1975): 37–51, repr. as "The Dilemma of Nature and Culture: *Billy Budd* as Problem Novel," in *The Weaver-God: Melville and the Poetics of the Novel* (Kent, OH: Kent State University Press, 1996). Like Parker and so many of the critics who adhere in one form or another to the acceptance school, these critics' "Old Americanist" (exceptionalist) problematic blinds them to the possibility that the eighteenth-century Britain of Melville's novella, far from being the savior of (Christian) "civilization" against the barbaric "atheism" of Napoleonic France, as they all too glibly assume, is, like its enemy, a tyrannical and imperial nation ruthlessly committed to establishing its hegemony over the world. This blindness is especially evident in Sten's essay, in which he represents Vere's execution of Billy Budd, however tragic, as absolutely justified: "Billy, like Christ, is sacrificed not by a 'martinet' but by a benevolent despot who uses inhuman means to effect ends that are at once tragic and potentially redeeming, even 'divine': the death of a blameless man and 'the peace of the world and the true welfare of mankind'" (p. 306). Nowhere in the criticism that expresses sympathy with Vere or Vere's problem is there to be found any question about the nation he is serving and civilization he is defending.

38. YI, pp. 1–20.

39. YI, pp. 12–13. Ironically one of the essays in the collection, Larry Reynold's "*Billy Budd* and American Labor Unrest: The Case for Striking Back," is written from a manifestly politically conservative perspective.

40. William V. Spanos, "The Indifference of *Differance*: Retrieving Heidegger's Destruction," in *Heidegger and Criticism: Retrieving the Cultural Politics of Destruction* (Minneapolis: University of Minnesota Press, 1993), pp. 81–131; an earlier version of this essay was published as "Retrieving Heidegger's Destruction: A Response to Barbara Johnson," in *Society for Critical Exchange Reports* (Fall 1980).

41. Edward W. Said, "Reflections on American 'Left' Literary Criticism," in *The World, the Text, and the Critic* (Cambridge, MA: Harvard University Press, 1983), pp. 158–177.

42. As Nancy Ruttenburg puts it, echoing Barbara Johnson: "Form and chaos battle continually for domination, mirrored in the tale's political context of brutal repression and anarchic revolution. The text survives in fragile equilibrium, suspended over the deadly space — which reveals how very proximate the text's antitheses are. . . . Melville *unequivocally* is not choosing sides: not between acceptance and resistance, conservatism and liberalism, or God and the devil" (Ruttenburg, "Melville's Anxiety of Innocence," p. 371; my emphasis). In a note signaling the critical community to which she belongs, Ruttenburg adds: "The enduring 'accep-

tance' and 'resistance' schools of *Billy Budd* criticism were initiated by E. L. Grant Watson's 'Melville's Testament of Acceptance' and Philip Within's '*Billy Budd*: Testament of Resistance.' For a cogent critique of this either/or approach to the text, see Johnson, 'Melville's Fist'. Eve Sedgwick, in 'Some Binarisms (I),' also points out that the novel is 'about the placement and replacement of the barest threshold' and thus 'continues to mobilize desires that could go either way' (94)" (ibid., p. 496). In a related vein, Sharon Cameron writes: "My interest lies in examining this transcendence or excess, for what constitutes the compelling power and the sublimity of *Billy Budd* arises from the moments when characters seem weirdly permeable to each other, and when what explains character — distinctions which are then effaced — also seems to explain everything else [the politics of the particular kind of war in which the *Bellipotent* is engaged, I assume]. But if the erosions of distinction constitute *Billy Budd*'s power, the story's coherence rather depends on the maintenance of the distinctions which are then effaced. Thus what is so haunting in *Billy Budd* is these contradictory imperatives" (Cameron, " 'Lines of Stone,' " p. 183). Cameron's overdetermination of binaries — and their effacement — as such blinds her, like Johnson, Sedgwick, and Ruttenburg, to the global historical context in which the terrible story of Billy Budd is embedded and thus to the actual imbalances of political power, that is, to her equalization of the power relations, ordained by the state of exception, that exist on board the *Bellipotent*, Like the others in this theoretically informed group, Cameron inadvertently, however more complexly, affiliates her reading with that of the traditionalists who adhere to the thesis that *Billy Budd* was the late Melville's "testament of acceptance."

43. MF, p. 87.

44. Brook Thomas, "*Billy Budd* and the Judgment of Silence," *Bucknell Review* 27 (1983): 51–78, repr. in CE, p. 210.

45. Paul Brodtkorb Jr., "The Definitive *Billy Budd*: 'But Aren't It All a Sham?' " *PMLA* 82 (1967): 602–612, repr. in CE: "I would argue that the story escapes advocating either conservative or liberal moral choices, eludes liberal or conservative critical rhetoric, and retreats onto a twilit ground where few important human actions are rationally choosable" (CE, p. 125). Brodtkorb's conclusion about the late Melville's state of mind is more complex — more "existential" — than that of most of the critics who adhere to the testament of acceptance thesis: "[W]hat the story silently records is Melville's last and dogged making up of his mind (as he once prematurely told Hawthorne that he had 'pretty much' done) to be annihilated. If this is the story's inmost 'inside narrative,' it explains why one's overall impression of *Billy Budd* is of something like patience, directed at passion. The serenity of Melville's 'acceptance,' it seems to me, is real enough as *serenity*; though it is not like the serenity of Nirvana or Christian resignation, but more like that of an infinite and in the end gentle despair accepted by a man about to leave

the *merely* human world of time" (CE, pp. 125–126; my emphasis). But in the end, as the reduction of the world of time to an afterthought, as the glaring adverb especially suggests, Brodtkorb's existential conclusion remains affiliated with that of the critics from whom he sought to distance himself.

46. Ironically, these essays on *Billy Budd* introduce motifs concerning power relations on board the *Bellipotent* in the process of arriving at undecidability that, if followed through, would, I suggest, call into question their ultimately quiescent political conclusion. This is evident in some degree in Eve Kosofsky Sedgwick's brilliant essay "Some Binarisms (I)," which, in reading *Billy Budd* as Melville's deconstruction of the prevailing binary opposition between homosexual and heterosexual (Claggart and Vere) as a symbolic deconstruction of the relay of binarisms informing political authority on board the *Bellipotent* (Vere), could have been interpreted as a devastating critique of the martial law (state of exception) if it were not sidetracked by the equalizing logic of undecidability. This possibility, however, is especially true of Nancy Ruttenburg's essay, in which the theme of repressed mutiny (inaugurated at the Nore) haunts every aspect of life on board the *Bellipotent*, including Billy's symbolic assault on Claggart. Referring to Vere's announcement of his decision to execute Billy, she writes. "To the extent that the assembled sailors wholeheartedly reject Vere's narration of Billy's crime and Claggart's victimization as a falsification of the fundamental moral difference between the two men, they ironically complete that dynamic by which the lie of mutiny establishes the truth of mutiny. Although this last pent-up release of feeling is not permitted to expend itself in a full-scale uprising, its short-lived manifestation is sufficient to establish it as part of a familiar pattern. The sailors' reaction to Vere's announcement, itself marked by the suppressed word, conforms to that pattern of recoil and blow — failed articulation and inevitable displacement by violence — by which the vocal current can be traced. Receiving its energy from the continued confinement of the word, the vocal current sweeps through the text, implicating all hands" (Ruttenburg, "Melville's Anxiety of Innocence," pp. 360–361). In the process of invoking the specter of mutiny, however, Ruttenburg, like Sedgwick, unaccountably in my mind, abandons this telling insight into the inexorably violent logic of power relations under the state of exception, which could be extended into the three "appendices" to the story, in favor of pursuing the theme of undecidability.

47. Lawrence Thompson, *Melville's Quarrel with God* (Princeton, NJ: Princeton University Press, 1952), pp. 379–38; Casper, "The Case Against Captain Vere"; Edgar Dryden, *Melville's Thematics of Form: The Great Art of Telling the Truth* (Baltimore: Johns Hopkins University Press, 1968), pp. 209–216.

48. Joseph Schiffman, "Melville's Final Stage: A Re-examination of *Billy Budd* Criticism," *American Literature* 22 (1950): 128–136; and Phil Withims "*Billy*

Budd: Testament of Resistance," *Modern Language Quarterly* 20 (June 1959): 115–127.

49. See Spanos, "American Studies in the 'Age of the World Picture': Thinking the Question of Language," in *The Future of American Studies,* ed. Donald E. Pease and Robyn Wiegman (Durham, NC: Duke University Press, 2002), pp. 387–418. Pease's work is a notable exception to this generalization. See especially his *The New American Exceptionalism* (Minneapolis: University of Minnesota Press, 2009). Of the few New Americanists who have written about *Billy Budd,* only Jonathan Arac, as far as I know, has interpreted the story according to the imperatives of the state of exception that constitutes the fundamental condition of life on board the *Bellipotent*. But according to Arac, Melville is evoking an American past, the Civil War, not the American future, the imperial Spanish-American global conflict: "For the United States . . . the experience of the Civil War gave a powerful new shape to national narrative. By virtue of the war and of Lincoln's death, understood as martyrdom, the state itself (in the sense of the sovereign power, not in the sense of the united 'states') became sanctified, taking on the prestige that had previously been reserved for the 'Union' and the People." This new American reverence for earthly power made possible Melville's final work of prose fiction 'Billy Budd'" (Arac, *The Emergence of American Literary Narrative, 1820–1860* [Cambridge, MA: Harvard University Press, 2006], p. 234). According to Arac, however, Melville, apparently fearful of the volatility of the "people," sides with this new "sanctified," post–Civil War "sovereign power," albeit one informed by "conscience" or "principle," which is epitomized by Captain Vere and his decisionism: "the 'jugglery of circumstances' means that Billy's righteousness counts as mutiny. In explaining the case to the drumhead court-martial he has summoned, Vere emphasizes the need to 'strive against scruples that may tend to enervate decision.' At whatever pain, he avoids Hamletism. . . . Vere shows that power may have conscience, and even moral beauty. Feeling still the 'primeval' in 'our formalized humanity,' he takes Billy Budd to his bosom like Abraham when he is about to sacrifice Isaac" (ibid., p. 236). In thus identifying Melville with Captain Vere, Arac betrays his inaugural insight and thus takes his place among those critics who opt for a basically conservative late Melville. Arac's reading of *Billy Budd* enables us to consider the state of exception in the light of the centralization of the American democratic state, but it also obscures the negative implications of this post–Civil War turn to "sovereign power."

50. See n. 42 above.

51. Alain Brossat, "L'inarticulable," *Lignes* 8, *Vainqueurs/Vaincus: Un monde en guerre* (May 2002): 58–59.

52. I am referring especially to the following synecdochical passage: "The white whale swam before him as the monomaniac incarnation of all those mali-

cious agencies which some deep men feel eating in them, til they are left living on with half a heart and half a lung. That intangible malignity which has been from the beginning; to whose dominion even the modern Christians ascribe one-half of the worlds; which the ancient Ophites of the east reverenced in their statue devil; — Ahab did not fall down and worship it like them; but deliriously transferring its idea to the abhorred white whale, he pitted himself, all mutilated, against it. All that most maddens and torments; all that stirs up the lees of things; all truth with malice in it; all that cracks the sinews and cakes the brain; all the subtle demonisms of life and thought; all evil, to crazy Ahab, were visibly personified, and made practically assailable in Moby Dick. He piled upon the whale's white hump the sum of all the general rage and hate felt by his race from Adam down; and then, as if his chest had been a mortar, he burst his hot heart's shell upon it" (M-D, p. 184). See also Melville's similar characterization in *The Confidence-Man* of the "Indian-hater par excellence" (C-M, pp. 149–150).

Chapter 3. Billy Budd: *A Symptomatic Reading*

1. See Louis Althusser, "From *Capital* to Marx's Philosophy," in Louis Althusser and Étienne Balibar, *Reading* Capital, trans. Ben Brewster (London: Verso, 1968), pp. 25–28. See also William V. Spanos "Althusser's Problematic: Vision and the Vietnam War," in AE, 35–56; published earlier as "Althusser's Problematic in the Context of the Vietnam War: Toward a Spectral Politics," in *Rethinking Marxism*, 10 (Fall 1999), 1–21.

2. See IA, pp. 201–207; Larry J. Reynolds, "*Billy Budd* and American Labor Unrest: The Case for Striking Back," in *New Essays on* Billy Budd, ed. Donald Yannella (New York: Cambridge University Press, 2003), pp. 21–48; and Andrew Delbanco, *Melville: His World and Work* (New York: Knopf, 2005), pp. 297–322. Unlike Trachtenberg and Delbanco, Reynolds approvingly identifies the Melville of *Billy Budd* as a political conservative who implicitly equates the Haymarket Riots with the civilization-destroying radicalism of the French Revolution.

3. Charles Olson, "Projective Verse," in id., *Selected Writings*, ed. Robert Creeley (New York: New Direction, 1966), p. 23.

4. EA, pp. 77–87.

5. According to poststructuralist thinking, all inquiry, including the "disinterested inquiry" of science (or humanism), begins with presuppositions ("fore-structures"). The difference between scientific (or humanist) and poststructuralist inquiry is that the former is blind to its presuppositions, whereas the latter acknowledges them but puts these abstractions at risk in the face of temporal/existential worldly experience. See Martin Heidegger's discussion of the "hermeneutic circle" in *Being and Time*, trans. John Macquarrie and Edward Robinson (New

York: Harper & Row, 1962), pp. 358–364. See also William V. Spanos, *Heidegger and Criticism: Retrieving the Cultural Politics of Destruction* (Minneapolis: Minnesota University Press, 1993), pp. 55–60.

6. Hayford and Sealts all too easily equate the deletion of something previously written as an absolute rejection of the thought it contained. From a merely psychological perspective, revision is a lot more complicated than that. To delete a statement from a text does not necessarily mean to delete it from the mind that has thought it.

7. The matter of this "discarded" preface is, as I have noted, more or less repeated in chapter 3 of the Hayford and Sealts edition (BB).

8. Herman Melville, *Billy Budd and Other Tales* (New York: New America Library 1961); this text is based on the one edited by Frederick Barron Freeman and corrected by Elizabeth Treeman (Cambridge, MA: Harvard University Press, 1956).

9. See, e.g., Richard Harter Fogle, "*Billy Budd*: Order of the Fall," *Nineteenth-Century Fiction* 13, 3 (December 1960): 189–205; Milton R. Stern, "The Politics of Melville's Poetry," from the Introduction to *Billy Budd, Sailor (An Inside Narrative)* (Indianapolis: Bobbs-Merrill, 1975), xiv–xxxiv, reprinted in CE, pp. 143–156; Larry J. Reynolds. "Bill Budd and American Labor Unrest: The Case for Striking Back," pp. 21–48; Despite their assertion of neutrality, Harrison Hayford and Merton Sealts, "Editors' Introduction," in BB, pp. 1–39, and RBB, pp. 108–113, clearly belong to this group.

10. E, p. 69. See Alain Badiou, *L'être et l'événement* (Paris: Seuil, 1988), trans. Oliver Feltham as *Being and Event* (London: Continuum), 2005), for his full treatment of "the event."

11. Melville also refers to the British dramatist and songwriter Charles Dibdin (1745–1814) in *Typee*, chap. 29, *Redburn,* chap. 30, and *White-Jacket*, chaps. 23 and 90 (BB, p. 145). Hayford and Sealts note that Jay Leyda, in "aptly remarking [in *The Portable Melville* (New York: Viking, 1952)] that when an examination is made of 'the British poets who attracted Melville, the modest songs of Charles Dibdin will get their due,' suggests that 'Dibdin's "Poor Tom Bowling, the darling of our crew,"' may have waked the old memory that produced Melville's last book." Following Leyda, Hayford and Sealts interpret Melville's reference to Dibdin in *White-Jacket* as a straightforward encomium to the poet and his patriotic songs put into the mouths of the sailors: "What Melville himself wrote of Dibden in Ch. 90 of *White-Jacket* bears upon the present context [i.e., Leyda's conclusions]. After pointing out that navies, both to work ships under sail and to man their batteries, must enlist not only 'volunteer landsmen and ordinary seamen of good habits' but also 'a multitude of persons, who, if they did not find a home in the navy, would probably fall on the parish, or linger out their days in a prison,'" Melville observes that among these are

the men into whose mouths Didbin puts his patriotic verses, full of sea-chivalry and romance. . . . I do not unite with a high critical authority in considering Didbin's ditties as "slang songs," for most of them breathe the very poetry of the ocean. But it is remarkable that those songs—which would lead one to think that man-of-war's-men are the most carefree, contented, virtuous, and patriot of mankind—were composed at a time when the English navy was principally manned by felons and paupers. . . . Still more these songs are pervaded by a true Mohammedan sensualism; a reckless acquiescence in fate, and an implicit, un-questioning, dog-like devotion to whoever may be lord and master. Dibdin was a man of genius; *but no wonder Dibdin was a government pensioner at £200 per annum.* (BB, p. 146; my emphasis)

What is remarkable about Hayford and Sealts's reading of the lines from *White-Jacket* is its annulment of Melville's tellingly ironic qualification of Dibdin's stature in the last sentence of the page they quote, one that also, tacitly annuls the analo-gous, even more ironic, qualification in the passage I have quoted in my text.

12. This has been interpreted by some critics as autobiographical: Melville's apologia for the Vere-like role he played in the life of his son, Malcolm, who committed suicide. See, e.g., Laurie Roberston-Lorant, *Melville: A Biography* (Amherst: University of Massachusetts Press, 1996), pp. 595–597.

13. See Spanos, "Cavilers and Con Men: The Confidence-Man: His Masquer-ade," in HMAC, pp.173–178, 190–193, 214–217.

14. Herman Melville, "Cock-A-Doodle-Do," in id., *Piazza Tales and Other Prose Pieces, 1839–1860*, ed. Harrison Hayford, Alma A. MacDougall, and G. Thomas Tanselle (Evanston, IL: Northwestern University Library; Chicago: New-berry Library, 1860), p. 282.

15. As I have shown elsewhere, this disclosure is at the heart of Melville's *Pierre* and, more emphatically, of *Israel Potter*. See Spanos, "Pierre's Extraordi-nary Emergency: Melville and the 'Voice of Silence'" and "Herman Melville's *Israel Potter*: Reflections on a Damaged Life," in HMAC, pp. 31–34 and 57–103, respectively.

16. Edward W. Said, *Orientalism* (New York: Vintage Books, 1979), pp. 92–93: "One would no more think of using *Amadis of Gaul* [as Don Quixote does] to understand sixteenth-century (or present-day) Spain than one would use the Bible to understand, say, the House of Commons. But clearly people have tried and do try to use texts in so simple-minded a way, for otherwise *Candide* and *Don Quixote* would not still have the appeal for readers that they do today. It seems a common human failing to prefer the schematic authority of a text to the disorientations of direct encounter with the human." For Said's similar commentary on Flaubert's satire of *idées reçues* in *Bouvard et Pécuchet*, see *Orientalism*, pp. 113–116.

17. For exceptions, see Eve Kosofsky Sedgwick, "Some Binarisms (I)," in *Epistemology of the Closet*, rev. ed. (Berkeley: University of California Press, 2008), pp. 91–130; Nancy Ruttenburg, "Melville's Anxiety of Innocence: The Handsome Sailor," in *Democratic Personality: Popular Voice and the Trial of American Authorship* (Stanford, CA: Stanford University Press, 2008), pp. 344–378; and Sharon Cameron, "'Lines of Stone': The Unpersonified Impersonal in Melville's *Billy Budd*," in id., *Impersonality: Seven Essays* (Chicago: University of Chicago Press, 2007), pp. 180–204. As I have suggested in chapter 2, despite their welcome de-allegorization of Claggart (and Billy) by way of their interrogation of the apparent binaries of the story, none of these recent critics take their directive for this undertaking from the global historical context.

18. See my discussion of Melville's parodic critique of monumental history in *Israel Potter* in HMAC, pp. 57–67.

19. John Brenkman, "The Melvillian Moment" (forthcoming).

20. Hannah Arendt makes precisely this still to be fully thought point about the politics endemic to the state of exception in her powerful critique of the French Third Republic's handling of the Dreyfus Affair by way of her synecdochal account of the radical anti-Semite Jules Guérin: "The most modern figure on the side of the Anti-Dreyfusards was probably Jules Guérin. Ruined in business, he had begun his political career as a police stool pigeon, and acquired that flair for discipline and organization which invariably marks the underworld. This he was later able to divert into political channels, becoming the founder and head of the Ligue Antisémite. In him high society found its first criminal hero. In its adulation of Guérin bourgeois society showed clearly that in its code of morals and ethics it had broken for good with it own standard" (Arendt, *The Origins of Totalitarianism* [New York: Harvest Books, 1976], 1: 111). More immediately, chronologically and geographically, I think, for example, of the relationship between Senator Joseph McCarthy and the U.S. government under President Dwight Eisenhower, and, even most recently and tellingly, between Dick Cheney and the U.S. government under President George W. Bush. See Barton Gellman, *Angler: The Cheney Vice Presidency* (New York: Penguin Books, 2009).

21. See my "Althusserian" reading of "Benito Cereno" in HMAC, pp. 105–122.

22. Althusser, "From *Capital* to Marx's Philosophy," p. 24. Althusser is here distinguishing between the "oversight" of capitalist vision (its "problematic") and Marx's "informed gaze," which, precisely because it is aware of the blindness of super-vision, can *see* what the latter unwittingly is blind to.

23. Brook Thomas, "*Billy Budd* and the Judgment of Silence," *Bucknell Review* 27 (1983): 51–78. See Chapter 2 above for further commentary on this issue.

24. Herman Melville, *White-Jacket*, pp. 302–303; my emphasis. In their

"Notes & Commentary," the editors of the definitive edition of *Billy Budd* note this striking parallel, even saying that the sentence referring to Peter the Barbarian "is nearer than any other in *Billy Budd* to indicating disapproval of Vere's course of action" (BB, p. 177). Indeed, they go on to point to other, similar passages in Melville's writing, most notably in *Redburn*, *Moby-Dick*, and "I and My Chimney." But they do not pursue its implications.

25. M-D, p. 184:

The White Whale swam before him as the monomaniacal incarnation of all those malicious agencies which some deep men feel eating in them, till they are left living on with half a heart and half a lung. That intangible malignity which has been from the beginning; to which dominion even the modern Christians ascribe one-half of the worlds; which the ancient Ophites of the east reverenced in their statue devil:— Ahab did not fall down and worship it like them; but deliriously transferring its idea to the abhorred white whale, he pitted himself, all mutilated, against it. All that most maddens and torments; all that stirs up the lees of things; all truth with malice in it; all that cracks the sinews and cakes the brain; all the subtle demonisms of life and thought; all evil, to crazy Ahab, were visibly personified, and made practically assailable in Moby Dick. He piled upon the whale's white hump the sum of all the general rage and hate felt by his whole race from Adam down; and then, as if his chest had been a mortar, he burst his hot heart's shell upon it.

C-M, pp. 149–150:

The Indian-hater *par excellence* the judge defined to be one "who, having with his mother's milk drank in small love for red men, in youth or early manhood, ere the sensibilities becomes osseous, receives at their hand some signal outrage, or, which in effect is much the same, some of his kin have, or some friend. Now, nature all around him by her solitudes wooing or bidding him muse upon the matter, he accordingly does so, till the thought develops such attraction, that much as straggling vapors troop from all sides to a storm-cloud, so straggling thoughts of other outrages troop to the nucleus thought, assimilate with it, and swell it. At last, taking council with the elements, he comes to his resolution. An intenser Hannibal, he makes a vow, the hate of which is a vortex from whose suction scarce the remotest chip of the guilty race may reasonably feel secure. Next, he declares himself and settles his temporal affairs. With the solemnity of a Spaniard turned monk, he take leave of his kin; or rather, these leave-takings have something of the still more impressive finality of death-bed adieus. Last, he commits himself to the forest primeval; there, so long as life shall be his, to act upon a calm, cloistered scheme of strategical, implacable, and lonesome vengeance. Ever on the noiseless trail; cool, collected, patient; less seen than felt; snuffing, smelling — a Leatherstocking Nemesis."

26. "[T]he center . . . closes off the play which it opens up and makes possible. As center, it is the point at which the substitution of contents, elements, or terms is no longer possible. At the center, the permutation or transformation of elements . . . is forbidden. At least this permutation has always remained *interdicted*. . . . Thus it has always been thought that the center, which is by definition unique, constituted that very thing within a structure which while governing the structure, escapes structurality. This is why classical thought concerning structure could say that the center is, paradoxically, *within* the structure and *outside it*. The center is at the center of the totality, and yet, since the center does not belong to the totality (is not a part of the totality), the totality *has its center elsewhere*. The center is not the center. The concept of centered structure — although it represents coherence itself . . . is contradictorily coherent" (Jacques Derrida, "Structure, Sign, and Play in the Discourse of the Human Sciences," in *id., Writing and Difference,* ed. and trans. Alan Bass [Chicago: University of Chicago Press, 1978], p. 279).

27. HS, pp. 175–176. See also Agamben, "What Is a Camp?" in *Means Without End: Notes on Politics,* trans. Vincenzo Binetti and Cesare Casarino (Minneapolis: University of Minnesota Press, 2000), pp. 39–40. In invoking the French term *zones d'attentes,* Agamben is generalizing the spaces in airports, train stations, and ports designated by the French government (before 1992) for the detention of unwanted foreigners without allowing them access to legal recourse.

28. Herman Melville, *White-Jacket,* chap. 71. Despite the fact that Hayford and Sealts refer to this passage from *White-Jacket* in the notes and commentaries (BB, pp. 181–182), they conclude "both from their detailed study of the case and from their analysis of the novel's genesis that the hanging aboard the *Somers* should not be taken as its primary source." Some suggestion of their positive reading of the allusion to the *Somers* Affair in *Billy Budd* can be inferred from their comment, earlier in the note, on Alexander Slidell Mackenzie, the commander of the *Somers* who ordered the execution of the alleged mutineers: "Not only was Mackenzie's act vindicated by the naval court of inquiry, as Melville states, but he was also acquitted of the charge of murder (and other charges) in a subsequent court martial" (BB, p. 182). It may be true that Mackenzie's action was "vindicated" by subsequent American courts, but to read the narrator's "history recited without comment" as Melville's approval of the court's decision strikes me as willful ideological sleight of hand, given the context I have painstakingly presented.

29. ISP. For an extended analysis of Mahan's book, see chapter 1.

30. In invoking the complicity of the *theo-logos* and the *anthropo-logos,* the

supernatural and the natural, the religious and the secular, sovereignty and bare life, I am pointing to the origins of Agamben's important rendering "inoperative" (*inoperoso*) of the Sacred/profane binary in Heidegger's de-struction of meta-physics — the Being/time or Identity/difference binary that has prevailed through-out Western history.

31. For a discussion of the phenomenon of sacrifice as it pertains to "Ausch-witz" that sheds suggestive light on the problem concerning Billy's execution I am engaging, see Giorgio Agamben, *Remnants of Auschwitz: The Witness and the Archive*, trans. Daniel Heller-Roazen (New York: Zone Books, 2002), pp. 26–33.

32. I am invoking, all too simply, Arendt's distinction, developed in *The Human Condition* (Chicago: University of Chicago Press, 1958), between the maker who binds him/herself to a *telos*, that is, a vocation — a determinative means and end system that always postpones acting in the time of the now — and the political being who commits him/herself to the time of the now, which is the time of beginnings, plurality, and speech. For a succinct summary of this crucial distinc-tion, see the sections of "The Vita Activa" entitled "Labor, Work, Action" and "The Public and the Private Realms" in *The Portable Hannah Arendt*, ed. Peter Baehr (New York: Penguin Books, 2000), pp. 167–230.

33. However positively the narrator portrays the chaplain, he too, in the end, like Captain Vere, does nothing, despite his certainty of Billy's innocence, to resist the judgment of execution: "Marvel not that having been made acquainted with the young sailor's essential innocence the worthy man lifted not a finger to avert the doom of such a martyr to martial discipline. To do so would not only have been as idle as invoking the desert, but would also have been an audacious transgression of the bounds of his function, one as exactly prescribe to him by military law as that of the boatswain or any other naval officer. Bluntly put, a chaplain is the minister of the Prince of Peace serving in the host of the God of War — Mars. As such, he is as incongruous as a musket would be on the altar at Christmas. Why, then, is he there? Because he indirectly subserves the purpose attested by the cannon; because too he lends the sanction of the religion of the meek to that which practically is the abrogation of everything but brute Force" (BB, pp. 121–122).

34. The repeated references to the populace's "murmurings" is, I think, in-tended by Melville not only to recall, ironically, the "murmurings" (backsliding) of the elected Israelites — their threat to the Covenant and their divinely ordained errand into the Canaan "wilderness" — that pervade Exodus (15:22–26) and other books of the Old Testament, but also the "murmurings" of the American Puritans that threatened that covenantal people's "errand in the [New World] wilderness." I am referring to the renewing and rejuvenating cultural strategy, derived from their figural identification with the Old Testament Israelites and based on their excep-tionalist need for a perpetual frontier (or enemy), that Sacvan Bercovitch has called

"The American Jeremiad." See Bercovitch *The American Jeremiad* (Madison: University of Wisconsin Press, 1978). See also Spanos, "American Exceptionalism, the Jeremiad, and the Frontier, Before and After 9/11: From the Puritans to the Neo-Con Men," in AE, pp. 187–241.

35. John J. Gross, "Melville, Dostoevsky, and the People," *Pacific Spectator,* Spring 1956, p. 165; Lawrence Barrett, "The Differences in Melville's Poetry," *PMLA* 70 (September 1955): 606–623; Christopher Sten, "The Dilemma of Nature and Culture: *Billy Budd* as Problem Novel," in *The Weaver-God, He Weaves: Melville and the Poetics of the Novel* (Kent, OH: Kent State University Press, 1996), pp. 313–314. Despite Hayford and Sealts's claim to objectivity, they too, against those who read Captain Vere's invocation of Orpheus's lyre as ironical, adhere to the view that in *Billy Budd,* Melville identifies his *poiēsis* with a political conservative ethos. See BB, pp. 195–196. For a reading of Vere's uses of the Orpheus myth similar to mine, see Edgar Dryden, "Epilogue," in *Melville's Thematics of Form: The Great Art of Telling the Truth* (Baltimore: Johns Hopkins University Press, 1968), pp. 209–216.

36. The identification of the forest dweller and savagery, whose origin is as old as classical antiquity (its binary opposition between sedentary and nomadic existence) pervades, as Meville knew, the discourse of colonial America, from the Puritans through James Fenimore Cooper (*The Last of the Mohicans, The Deerslayer)* and Francis Parkman (*The Conspiracy of Pontiac*) to Frederick Jackson Turner ("The Significance of the Frontier in American History"). See Gilles Deleuze and Félix Guattari, "Treatise on Nomadology: The War Machine," in *A Thousand Plateaus: Capitalism and Schizophrenia,* trans. Brian Massumi (Minneapolis: University of Minnesota Press, 1987), pp. 351–423. See also Richard Waswo, *The Founding Legend of Western Civilization: From Virgil to Vietnam* (Hanover, NH: Wesleyan University Press 1997); and William V. Spanos, *America's Shadow: An Anatomy of Empire* (Minneapolis: University of Minnesota Press, 2000).

37. EA, pp. 85–87, 112–113, 174–177.

38. Herman Melville, *Pierre, or, The Ambiguities*, ed. Harrison Hayford, Hershel Parker, and G. Thomas Tanselle (Evanston, IL: Northwestern University Press; Chicago: Newberry Library, 1971), pp. 141–142. See also M-D, pp. 166–185.

39. See, e.g., Ishmael's comment on representing the living whale in *Moby-Dick*: "[A]ny way you may look at it, you must needs conclude that the great leviathan is that one creature in the world which must remain unpainted to the last. True, one portrait may hit the mark much nearer than another, but none can hit it with any very considerable degree of exactness. So there is no earthly way of finding out precisely what the whale really looks like. And the only mode in which you can derive even a tolerable idea of his living contour, is by going a whaling

yourself, but by so doing, you run no small risk of being eternally stove and sunk by him" (M-D, p. 26).

40. See esp. Martin Heidegger, "What Is Metaphysics?" in *Basic Writings*, ed. David Farrell Krell (New York: Harper & Row, 1977), p. 98:

> The nothing—what else can it be for science but an outrage and a phantasm? If science is right, then only one thing is sure: science wishes to know nothing of the nothing. Ultimately this is the scientifically rigorous conception of the nothing. We know it, the nothing, in that we wish to know nothing about it.
>
> Science wants to know nothing of the nothing. But even so it is certain that when science tries to express its proper essence it calls upon the nothing for help. It has recourse to what it rejects. What incongruous state of affairs reveals itself here?

41. BB, p. 200. See also RBB, pp. 159–161.

42. RBB, pp. 159–161: Parker subscribes to Hayford and Sealts's conclusion that this "official" account is an anomaly but maintains that, despite its anomalous nature, it retains a viable function.

43. This conclusion is underscored by the telling fact that the four adherents of the school of undecidability to whom I have referred—Barbara Johnson, Eve Sedgwick, Nancy Ruttenburg, and Sharon Cameron—either disregard or marginalize this ironically central "appended" "official" narrative in their readings of Melville's tale.

44. In a soliloquy addressing the "gods," by whom I take Melville to mean the personified differential dynamics of being that would deconstruct the narrative that Ahab has fabricated to justify his "monomaniacal" and "unerring" "fiery pursuit" of the white whale, Ahab says, "Swerve me? Ye cannot swerve, else ye swerve yourselves! Man has ye there; Swerve me? The path of my fixed purpose is laid with iron rails, whereon my soul is grooved to run. Over unsounded gorges, through the rifled hearts of mountains, under torrents' beds, unerringly I rush! Naught's an obstacle, naught's an angle to the iron way!" (M-D, p. 168). For an extended reading of this decisive passage of *Moby-Dick*, see EA, pp. 131–150.

45. Michel Foucault, "Nietzsche, Genealogy, History," in *Language, Counter-Memory, Practice: Selected Essays and Interviews*, ed. Donald F. Bouchard, trans. id. and Sherry Simon (Ithaca, NY: Cornell University Press, 1977), pp. 160–161.

46. Jacques Derrida, *Specters of Marx: The State of the Debt, the Work of Mourning, and the New International*, trans. Peggy Kamuf (New York: Routledge, 1994), pp. 6–7, 99–103.

47. Jewel-blocks "hang from the ends of yards where studding-sails are hoisted," Hayford and Sealts note (BB, p. 201). "The name given to each of two small blocks

suspended at the extremities of the main and fore-topsail yards, through which the halyards of the studding-sails are passed" (*Oxford English Dictionary*, s.v.).

48. Arendt, *Human Condition*, 192ff.

49. This ideological contrast pervades the literature and historiography of British imperialism. I shall restrict my reference to two representative instances: Daniel Defoe's *Robinson Crusoe*, ed. Michael Shinagel (New York: Norton, 1994), and Joseph Conrad's *Heart of Darkness*, ed. Robert Kimbrough (New York: Norton, 1988). Meditating on his situation following the appearance of the cannibals on "his island," Crusoe writes:

> That this would justify the Conduct of the *Spaniards* in all their Barbarities practis'd in *America*, where they destroy'd Millions of these People, who however they were Idolators and Barbarians, and had several bloody and barbarous Rites in their Customs, such as sacrificing human Bodies to their Idols, were yet, as to the *Spaniards*, very innocent People; and that the rooting them out of the Country, is spoken of with the utmost Abhorrence and Detestation, by even the *Spaniards* themselves, at this Time; and by all other Christian Nations of *Europe*, as a meer Butchery, a bloody and unnatural Piece of Cruelty, unjustifiable either to God or Man, and such, as for which the very Name of a Spaniard is reckon'd to be frightful and terrible to all People of Humanity, or of Christian Compassion: As if the Kingdom of *Spain* were particularly Eminent for the Product of a Race of Men, who were without Principles of Tenderness, or the common Bowels of Pity to the Miserable, which is recken'd to be a mark of generous Temper in the Mind. (*Robinson Crusoe*, pp. 124–125)

Recalling the brutal Roman conquest of Britain (and the Belgian imperial project in the Congo), Marlow tells his rapt listeners:

> Mind, none of us [Englishmen] would feel exactly like this. What saves us is efficiency — the devotion to efficiency. But these chaps were not much account really. They were colonists, their administration was merely a squeeze, and nothing more, I suspect. They were conquerors, and for that you want only brute force — nothing to boast of, when you have it, since your strength is just an accident arising from the weakness of others. They grabbed what they could get for the sake of what was to be got. It was just robbery with violence, aggravated murder on a great scale, and men going at it blind — as is very proper for those who tackle a darkness. The conquest of the earth, which mostly means the taking it away from those who have a different complexion or slightly flatter noses than ourselves, is not a pretty thing when you look into it too much. What redeems it is the idea only. An idea at the back of it, no sentimental pretence but an idea; and

an unselfish belief in the idea — something you can set up, and bow down before, and offer a sacrifice to. (*Heart of Darkness*, p. 10)

As Melville well knew, this ideological contrast enabled by the exceptionalist ethos also, ironically, pervades the rhetoric of American literature and historiography.

50. In putting Melville's refusal of the American calling in this way, I am not simply invoking his lifelong quarrel with Puritanism. I am also pointing to what seems to me a productive synthesis of Louis Althusser's notion of "interpellation" (the call that produces the subjected subject) and Giorgio Agamben's sustained critique of the "ethics" of the "vocation" as this privileged notion has been formulated under the auspices of Western metaphysics, that is, as an essentialist ethics that reduces the "now" of finite existence (what I call the "occasion") to nothing more than a means to an end. It is no accident that the following passage in which Agamben rejects this "ethics of the vocation" follows a section devoted to Melville's Bartleby:

> The fact that must constitute the point of departure for any discourse on ethics is that there is no essence, no historical or spiritual vocation, no biological destiny that humans must enact or realize. This is the only reason why something like an ethics can exist, because it is clear that if humans were or had to be this or that substance, this or that destiny, no ethical experience would be possible — there would only be tasks to be done.
>
> This does not mean, however, that humans are not, and do not have to be, something, that they are simply consigned to nothingness and therefore can freely decide whether to be or not to be, to adopt or not to adopt this or that destiny (nihilism and decisionism coincide at this point). There is in effect something that humans are and have to be, but this something is not an essence nor properly a thing: It is the simple fact of one's own existence as possibility or potentiality. But precisely because of this things become complicated; precisely because of this ethics becomes effective. (Agamben, "*Ethics*," in id., *The Coming Community*, trans. Michael Hardt [Minneapolis: University of Minnesota Press, 1993], p. 41)

51. E, pp. 40–41, 46–48.

52. George Washington Peck, "Review of Herman Melville's *Pierre; or, The Ambiguities*," *American Whig Review*, (November 1852), 446–454; repr. in *Herman Melville: The Contemporary Reviews*, ed. Brian Higgins and Hershel Parker (New York: Cambridge University Press, 1995), p. 413.

53. EA, pp. 12–36. For a succinct account of the "Old Americanist field imaginary that harnessed *Moby-Dick* to the Cold War," see Donald E. Pease, "*Moby-Dick* and the Cold War," in *The American Renaissance Reconsidered: Selected*

Essays from the English Institute, 1982–1983, ed. Walter Benn Michaels and Donald Pease (Baltimore: Johns Hopkins University Press, 1985).

Chapter 4. American Exceptionalism and the State of Exception after 9/11: Melville's Proleptic Witness

1. I am referring to the passage of the Patriot Act (acronym for Uniting and Strengthening America by Providing Appropriate Tools Required to Intercept and Obstruct Terrorism, passed by the U.S. Congress by wide margins and signed into law by President George W. Bush on October 26, 2001, in the aftermath of 9/11.

2. See Donald E. Pease, "The Global Homeland: Bush's Biopolitical Settlement," *boundary 2* 30, 2 (Fall 2003): 1–18.

3. See "Report of the International Committee of The Red Cross (ICRC) on the Treatment by the Coalition Forces of Prisoners of War and Other Protected Persons by the Geneva Conventions in Iraq During Arrest, Internment and Interrogation" (February 2007), www.globalsecurity.org/military/library/report/2004/icrc_re port_iraq_feb2004.htm (accessed June 4, 2010); and the powerful analysis by Mark Danner in his review, "The Red Cross Torture Report: What It Means," *New York Review of Books* 56, 7 (April 30, 2009). See also n. 5 below.

4. This persistent feature of the Bush administration's domestic and foreign policy was called "airbrushing" by the United States during the Cold War to distinguish its "openness" to historical reality from the Soviet Union's strategic suppression of it.

5. See the eight secret memos released on March 2, 2009, by the Obama administration written by members of the Bush administration's Office of Legal Council (Justice Department), including John C. Yoo, Jay Bybee, and Robert J. Delahunty in the wake of 9/11: www.huffingtonpost.com/2009/03/02/secret-bush-memos-release_n_171221.html (accessed May 9, 2010).

6. The phrase "plenary executive powers," which appears often in the memoranda of the Office of Legal Council, is the English translation of the French legal expression *pleins pouvoirs,* which, according to Giorgio Agamben, was often used to characterize the state of exception, refers "to the expansion of powers of the government and in particular the conferral on the executive of the power to issue decrees having the force of law." Its use by members of the U.S. Department of Justice's Office of Legal Council suggests their unequivocal awareness of its connection with the state of exception. SE, p. 5.

7. Originally enacted in 1878 during the Reconstruction period, this act limits the power of the federal government to use the military for domestic law enforcement. For the Office of Legal Council's reinterpretation of this law, see John C. Yoo and Robert J. Delahunty's memorandum to Alberto Gonzales, Council to the

President, "Authority to Use Military Force to Combat Terrorist Activity Within the United States, Oct. 23, 2001."

8. The grotesque, dehumanized rationalizations that characterize the arguments in these memos — their forced reinterpretation of constitutional law to confirm their preconceived ideological end — cannot help but recall, not only the arguments in behalf of America's ill-advised intervention in Vietnam and its brutal conduct of the war in the secret memoranda of *The Pentagon Papers,* but, even more damning, the ventriloquized reasoning of Adolph Eichmann that Hannah Arendt identified as "the banality of evil." See Arendt, *Eichmann in Jerusalem: A Report on the Banality of Evil*; rev. ed. (New York: Viking, 1965). See also Spanos, "Global American: The Devastation of Language Under the Dictatorship of the Public Realm," *Symploke* 16, 1–2 (Spring–Fall 2009): 171–214.

9. See esp. Giorgio Agamben, "In Praise of Profanation," in *Profanations*, trans. Jeff Fort (New York: Zone Books, 2007), pp. 71–92.

10. HS, p. 123. See also Hannah Arendt, "The Decline of the Nation-State and the End of the Rights of Man," in *The Origins of Totalitarianism,* new ed. (San Diego: Harcourt Brace, 1979), pp. 267–302; Theodor Adorno, "Zeitalter der Konzentrations-lager," in id., *Gesammelte Schriften,* 20 vols., ed. Rolf Tiedemann et al. (Frankfurt a.M.: Suhrkamp, 1973–1986; Carl Schmitt, *The Concept of the Political,* exp. ed., trans. George Schwab (Chicago: University of Chicago Press, 2007), and *Political Theology: Four Chapters on the Concept of* Sovereignty, trans. George Schwab (Chicago: University of Chicago Press, 2005).

11. HS, p. 123. For Agamben's luminous discussion of the concentration camp as the space of the "limit situation" — the threshold between the human and the inhuman (bare life), as in the case of those whom the Jewish survivors of Auschwitz called *Muselmänner* (Muslims); see Giorgio Agamben, *Remnants of Auschwitz: The Witness and the Archive*, trans. Daniel Heller-Roazen (New York: Zone Books, 1999), pp. 47–52.

12. For a significant dissenting view, see John Brenkman, *The Cultural Contradictions of Democracy: Political Thought Since September 11* (Princeton, NJ: Princeton University Press, 2007), pp. 55–71.

13. SE, p. 13. It is, after all, not the totalitarian state as such that has precipitated the urgency of the question of the state of exception, since these states are by definition states in which the exception is the rule. The contemporary urgency of this question has been precipitated, rather, by the paradoxical spectacle of a modern democratic state in which the state of exception becomes increasingly the rule: "It is," Agamben writes, "important not to forget that the modern state of exception is a creation of the democratic-revolutionary tradition and not the absolutist one" (SE, p. 5).

14. SE, p. 11.

15. Donald E. Pease, *The New American Exceptionalism* (Minneapolis: University of Minnesota Press, 2009).

16. This, of course, is basically the thesis of the now extremely influential Weimar and National Socialist political theorist Carl Schmitt in *Concept of the Political*, and of Agamben's meditation on the modern state of exception: "A world in which the possibility of war is utterly eliminated, a completely pacified globe, would be a world without the distinction of friend and enemy and hence a world without politics. It is conceivable that such a world might contain many very interesting antitheses and contrasts, competitions and intrigues of every kind, but there would not be a meaningful antithesis whereby men could be required to sacrifice life, authorized to shed blood, and kill other human beings. For the definition of the political, it is here even irrelevant whether such a world without politics is desirable as an ideal situation. The phenomenon of the political can be understood only in the context of the ever present possibility of the friend-and-enemy grouping, regardless of the aspects which this possibility implies for morality, aesthetics, and economics" (Schmitt, *Concept of the Political*, p. 35). Though Schmitt does not underscore it, his analysis of the concept of the political involves the following important equation: friend vs. enemy = politics = national renewal.

17. BB, p. 63.

18. Alexis de Tocqueville, *Democracy in America*, vol. 1, trans. Henry Reeve, rev. Francis Bowen (New York: Vintage Books, 1990), pp. 70–97.

19. See William V. Spanos, "Herman Melville's *Israel Potter*: Reflections on a Damaged Life" in HMAC, pp. 57–67. On the American jeremiad see Sacvan Bercovitch, *American Jeremiad* (Madison: University of Wisconsin Press, 1979), and William V. Spanos, "American Exceptionalism, the Jeremiad, and the Frontier, Before and After 9/11: From the Puritans to the Neo-Con Men," in AE, pp. 191–198.

20. This secularization of America's divine election is reflected in Tocqueville's *Democracy in America*, vol. 1: "The gradual development of the principle of equality [in America] is, therefore, a providential fact. It has all the characteristics of such a fact: it is universal, it is lasting, it constantly eludes all human interference, and all events as well as all men contribute to its progress" (p. 6).

21. This term derives from M. H. Abrams, *Natural Supernaturalism: Tradition and Revolution in Romantic Literature* (New York: Norton, 1971) via Edward Said's critical use of it to indict the "secularism" of nineteenth-century Orientalism in *Orientalism* (New York: Vintage Books, 1979), pp. 114–115. My use of Abrams's phrase in the context of American cultural history is intended to remind those modern theorists of the state of exception, like Agamben, who derive their insistent identification of modern secular politics with the sacred from Carl Schmitt's equation of the modern concept of sovereignty with a secular "theology" in *Political Theology*, that this

secularization of the sacred is especially crucial in the formation of the American democratic polity. See also n. 33 below.

22. See http://stateoftheunionaddress.org/2002-george-w-bush (accessed May 7, 2010); paragraphing added.

23. See also Samuel P. Huntington, *The Clash of Civilizations and the Remaking of World Order* (New York: Simon & Schuster, 1996), which expands his influential essay "The Clash of Civilizations," *Foreign Affairs,* Summer 1993.

24. For an amplified analysis of Huntington's *Who Are We?* as an American jeremiad, see Spanos, "American Exceptionalism, the Jeremiad, and the Frontier, Before and After 9/11," in AE, pp. 219–236. Though this chapter places Huntington in the long and persistent jeremiadic tradition inaugurated by the Puritans, it does not explicitly relate it to the state of exception.

25. In a chapter in *Who Are We?* entitled "The Deconstruction of America," Huntington writes: "The deconstructionists promised programs to enhance the status and influence of subnational, racial, ethnic, and cultural groups. They encouraged immigrants to maintain their birth country cultures, granted them legal privileges denied to native born Americans, and denounced the idea of Americanization. They pushed the rewriting of history syllabi and text books so as to refer to the 'peoples' of the United States in place of the single people of the Constitution. They urged supplementing or substituting for national history the history of subnational groups. They downgraded the centrality of English in American life and pushed bilingual education and linguistic diversity. They advocated legal recognition of group rights and racial preferences over the individual rights central to the American Creed. They justified their actions by theories of multiculturalism and the idea that diversity rather than unity or community should be America's overriding value. The combined effect of these efforts was to promote the deconstruction of the American identity that had been gradually created over three centuries and the ascendance of subnational identities" (*WAW,* pp. 228–229).

26. WAW, p. 64. In appropriating Sacvan Bercovitch's brilliant analysis of the American jeremiad, Huntington fails to indicate that the latter's intention was fundamentally a critical one.

27. It is no accident that in his speech of September 11, 2006, to Congress commemorating the fifth anniversary of the attacks on the World Trade Center and the Pentagon, President Bush said "The war against the enemy is more than a military conflict. It is the ideological struggle of the 21st century, and the calling of our generation" (George W. Bush, "Address to the Nation on the Five-Year Anniversary of 9/11," www.presidentialrhetoric.com/speeches/09.11.06.html (accessed May 24, 2010).

28. HMAC, pp. 197–198.

29. By "monumental history," I mean the traditional historiography that Fou-

cault, via Nietzsche, criticizes from his genealogical perspective. See Michel Foucault, "Nietzsche, Genealogy, History," in *Language, Counter-Memory, Practice: Selected Essays and Interviews*, ed. Donald F. Bouchard, trans. id. and Sherry Simon (Ithaca, N.Y.: Cornell University Press, 1977), pp. 139–164. And see also pp. 132–133 above.

30. WAW, p. 263; my emphasis. Charles Krauthammer is a highly visible, vocal, and influential neoconservative media pundit.

31. HS, pp. 183–184; my emphasis.

32. For a philological critique of this hegemonic understanding of the American calling, one that has its point of departure in constellating Bartleby's refusal to be called ("I prefer not to") into Louis Althusser's concept of interpellation, see Spanos " 'Benito Cereno' and 'Bartleby, the Scrivener': Reflections on the American Calling," in HMAC, esp. pp. 140–145.

33. The two disciplines that have determined the conclusions of the great majority of the commentaries, past and present, concerning the question of the state of exception thus far have been jurisprudence and political science. As I have suggested, it is thus the indifference to or lack of knowledge of the complex yet continuous cultural history of the United States, particularly of the origins and development of the American exceptionalist national identity, that has contributed to this failure to perceive the distinction to which I have pointed by way of my reading of *Billy Budd*.

34. Schmitt, *Concept of the Political*, p. 79. See also "The Age of Neutralization and Depoliticization," in *Concept of the Political*, pp. 89–96; my emphasis.

35. "All significant concepts of the modern theory of the state are secularized theological concepts not only because of their historical development—in which they were transferred from theology to the theory of the state, whereby, for example, the omnipotent God became the omnipotent lawgiver—but also because of their systematic structure, the recognition of which is necessary for a sociological consideration of these concepts. The exception in jurisprudence is analogous to the miracle in theology. Only by being aware of this analogy can we appreciate the manner in which the philosophical ideas of the state developed in the last centuries," Schmitt writes (*Political Theology*, p. 36). Schmitt, of course, subscribes to this conservative secular or "political" theology, in which Identity constitutes the condition for the possibility of difference (Us versus them). In this, he is a significant precursor of the neoconservative intellectual deputies of the Bush administration such as Samuel Huntington, Charles Krauthammer, Dick Cheney, John Yoo, Jay Bybee, and Robert Delahunty, to name only those few to whom I have referred.

36. As Tracy B. Strong puts it in her introduction to Schmitt, *Concept of the Political*, in answer to the question of "how a man who wrote with some eloquence about the dangers of universalism could have written what he wrote in support of

Nazi policies," Schmitt "thought (or persuaded himself for some period of time) that the opponents of the regime were, in fact, enemies, who, in fact, posed a threat to the German identity. If the last is true . . . then what needs attention in Schmitt's theory is not the attack on universalism but the overly simplistic notion of friend. There is a way in which Schmitt allowed his notion of enemy to generate his idea of friend" (p. xxiv). In other words, the problem with Schmitt's understanding of the friend–enemy opposition is that he unquestioningly accepts the validity of the idea of the nation as a self-identical whole grounded in nativity: a "people" as opposed to the "multitude," in Michael Hardt and Antonio Negri's terms (*Empire* [Cambridge, MA: Harvard University Press, 2000], pp. xxiii–xiv).

37. As I suggest in chapter 3, Melville's portrait of Captain Vere is intended to remind his American readers of his portraits of Captain Ahab in *Moby-Dick* and of the "Indian-hater par excellence" in *The Confidence-Man*.

38. In an *Auseinandersetzung*, the end of dialogue is neither the reconciliation of opposites nor victory in a war to the end. The antagonists belong together in strife and exist to achieve worldly presencing, not presence: "The *polemos* [in Heraclitus's Fragment 53, to which Heidegger is referring] is a conflict that prevailed *prior to everything divine and human, not a war* in the human sense. The conflict, as Heraclitus thought it, first caused the realm of being to separate into opposites; it first gave rise to position and order and rank. In such a separation cleavages, intervals, distances, and joints opened. In the conflict — Aus-einander-setzung, setting apart — a world comes into being. Conflict does not split, much less destroy unity. It constitutes unity, it is *a binding-together*, *logos*. *Polemos* and *logos* are the same" (Martin Heidegger, *An Introduction to Metaphysics*, trans. Ralph Manheim [New Haven, CT: Yale University Press, 1987], p. 62; my emphasis). See also "The Origin of the Work of Art," in Martin Heidegger, *Basic Writings*, ed. David Farrell Krell, rev. ed. (San Francisco: HarperSanFrancisco, 1993), pp. 174–176, 179–182, 188–190.

39. Edward W. Said, *Culture and Imperialism* (New York: Knopf, 1993), p. 332.

40. "In this conception, such-and-such being is reclaimed from its having this or that property, which identifies it as belonging to this or that set, to this or that class (the reds, the French, the Muslims) — and it is reclaimed not for another class nor for the simple generic absence of any belonging, but for its being-*such,* for belonging itself. Thus being-*such,* which remains constantly hidden in the condition of belonging . . . and which is in no way a real predicate, comes to light itself. The singularity exposed as such is what ever you *want,* that is, lovable" (Giorgio Agamben, *The Coming Community,* trans. Michael Hardt [Minneapolis: University of Minnesota Press, 1993], pp. 1–2).

41. See SE. Analyzing Walter Benjamin's notion in "Critique of Violence"

(1921) of the "pure violence" of the "real" state of exception (as opposed to the violence of the "mythico-juridical" state of exception), Agamben writes:

> Benjamin's thesis is that while mythico-juridical violence is always a means to an end, pure violence is never simply a means — whether legitimate or illegitimate — to an end (whether just or unjust). The critique of violence does not evaluate violence in relation to the ends that it pursues as a means, but seeks its criterion "in a distinction within the sphere of means themselves, without regard for the ends they serve."
>
> Here appears the topic . . . of violence as "pure medium," that is, as the figure of a paradoxical "mediality without ends" — a means that, though remaining such, is considered independently of the ends that it pursues. (SE, pp. 61–62)

See also Agamben, *Means without End: Notes on Politics*, trans. Vincenzo Binetti and Cesare Casarino (Minneapolis: University of Minnesota Press, 2000). As in the case of Said, and a propos of Melville's refusal to be answerable to the American "calling," I suggest, Agamben's "means without end" implies a radically profane world of "now time" and a playful ethics of finitude as opposed to a metaphysical or teleological time, which, in positing a distant end, privileges the notion of unerring destiny and imposes a "vocation" or a "calling" on humanity. For an illuminating discussion of "Agamben's repeated claims that mankind has no historical *task*, *calling*, or *vocation*," see Leland de la Durantaye, "Homo profanus: Giorgio Agamben's Profane Philosophy," *boundary* 2 35, 3 (Fall 2008): 58–62.

bare life, 22, 31, 33, 87, 115, 137, 146; and Billy Budd, 34–35, 118–121

Barrett, Laurence, 125; "The Differences in Melville's Poetry," 173n42, 193n35

Benjamin, Walter, 101, 144, 146, 202–203n41

Bercovitch, Sacvan: the American jeremiad and, 154–156, 192–193n34; *The American Jeremiad*, 171n31; *Rites of Assent*, 176n4. *See also* American jeremiad

Bernal, Marin, 179n25

Berthoff, Warner, 34, 45, 69; on *Billy Budd*, 50–56, 119

Billy Budd: allusions to America in, 76–79, 116–117, 136–139; American modernity and, 2–3; appendices of, 33–34; Billy Budd in, 34–35, 118–121, 137–139; "Billy in the Darbies" in, 133–136; John Brenkman on, 101–102; Alain Brossat on, 100–102; as cautionary tale, 11–24, 116, 136, 149–150, 159–160; Claggart in, 87–101; the coming community and, 160–163; critical histories of, 37–38; Dansker in, 95–97; deconstructive readings of, 65–69; drumhead court in, 102–115; exceptionalism (American) and, 70–74; the frontier and, 15–24, 118; global visibility of, 36; HMS *Bellipotent* in, 90–102; "inside story" of, 125, 131, 159; the late style and, 32–33; narrator of, 75–79, 105–108; Horatio Nelson in, 24–31, 85–87; official account of events in, 129–132; Orphic measure in, 125–127; the police state and, 90–102; "Preface" and, 5–10, 10–13, 80–85, 165n1, 169n21, 181n35; "ragged edges" of, 69–70, 127–136; as specter, 39, 55–56, 140; spectrality in, 121–125, 128–136; symptomatic reading of, 73–74, 75–79, 136–137; as "testament of acceptance," 31–32, 39–45; as "testament of refusal," 139–140, 196n50; as "testament of resistance," 57, 70–71; Vere in, 88–90; as worldly text, 32–33, 114–115, 131

Bin Laden, Osama, 157

biopolitics, and bare life, 115, 119–121, 144, 150

Bowen, Mewwrlin, *The Long Encounter: Self and Experience in the Writing of Herman Melville*, 173n42

Brecht, Berthold, on tragedy, 177n8, 178n16

Brenkman, John: *The Cultural Contradictions of Democracy*, 198n12; "The Melville Moment," 101–102

British exceptionalism, 84, 95, 138, 147–149

Brodtkorb, Paul, 45; "The Definitive *Billy Budd*: 'But Aren't It All a Sham?'" 183–184n45

Brossat, Alain, 72–73; "L'inarticulable," 100–102, 114

Burke, Edmund, *Reflections on the Revolution in France*, 4–5

Bush, George W., 3, 72, 94; the American calling and, 151, 200n27; the normalization of state of exception and, 141–143, 150–160; State of the Union speech (January 29, 2002), 150–153; the "war on terror" and, 100, 139–143, 145, 170n27

Bybee, Jay, and Carl Schmitt, 201n35; "the war on terror" and, 143

Cameron, Sharon, 58, 65, 69, 72, 105, 183n42, 189n17, 193n43; "'Lines of Stone': The Unpersonified Impersonal in Melville's *Billy Budd*," 189n17

Carlyle, Thomas, 45

Casper, Leonard, 70; "The Case Against Captain Vere," 179–180n28, 184n47

Cervantes, Miguel de, *Don Quixote*, 88, 188n16

Cesaire, Aime, *Cahier d'un retour au pays natal*, 173n41

Chase, Richard, 166n8

Cheney, Richard B. (Dick): as Claggart type, 189n20; Schmitt, Carl and, 201n35; the "war on terror" and, 39, 143

Cloots, Anarcharsis, 172–173n41

Conrad, Joseph, *Heart of Darkness*, 195–196n49

Cooper, James Fenimore, 193n36

Creeley, Robert, 78

Kasson, John, 14; *Civilizing the Machine*, 170–171n28

Krauthammer, Charles, 157, 201n35

Lazo, Rodrigo, "The Ends of Enchantment: Douglass, Melville, and Expansionism in the Americas," 171n32

Lewis, R. W. B., 166n8

Mahan, Alfred Thayer, 171n36; American empire-building and, 19–24, 136; the frontier and, 16–17, 23, 118, 149; *The Influence of Sea Power upon History, 1660–1783*, 16–24, 171–172n36; Horatio Nelson and, 19–21, 31

Manifest Destiny, 149

Marx, Karl, 11

Marx, Leo, 14; *The Machine in the Garden*, 170n28

Matthiessen, F. O.: the American jeremiad and, 47; *American Renaissance*, 45, 166n8; on *Billy Budd*, 45–48, 52, 56; and the Cold War, 48

McCarthy, Joseph, 71, 94, 189n20

Melville, Herman: "Bartleby, the Scrivener," 2, 37, 41, 50, 54, 57, 70, 136, 139, 151, 196; *Battle Pieces and Aspects of the War*, 165n2; "Benito Cereno," 1–2, 37, 41, 50, 54, 70, 71, 102, 125, 127, 136; *Clarel*, 62; "Cock-A-Doodle-Do," 28–29, 86–87, 174n45; Cold War representation of, 45, 48; *The Confidence-Man*, 2, 28, 36, 37, 41, 50, 54, 55, 70, 73–74, 110, 139, 146, 149, 172n41, 186n52, 190–191n25; "The Encantadas, or Enchanted Isles," 171n32; errancy and, 126, 127–136, 167–168n5; forty-year silence of, 2, 39, 40, 45, 55–56, 137, 140, 165n2; *Israel Potter*, 2, 37, 41, 50, 70, 136, 146, 181n36; the late style and, 32–33, 35, 139–140; *Moby-Dick*, 2, 32, 37, 45, 50, 54, 70, 73, 79, 95, 110, 132, 136, 139, 146, 149, 172n41, 175–176n55, 190n25 (quote), 193–194n29 (quote); *Pierre*, 31, 37, 39, 41, 50, 54, 62, 70, 126, 146, 148–149; *Redburn*, 187n11; Carl

Schmitt and, 161–163; the state of exception and, 1–3, 73–74, 141–146, 147–150; *Typee*, 187n11; *White-Jacket*, 26–27, 71, 73, 75, 107–108, 117, 173–174n44, 187n11. See also *Billy Budd*

Melville revival (American), 45–56, 140

Melville revival (English), 7, 10, 33–34, 38–45

Milder, Robert, 58–59, 63, 178n16, 180n30; *Critical Essays on Melville's Billy Budd, Sailor*, 36; *Exiled Royalties: Melville and the Life We Imagine*, 173n42, 180n30

Milton, John, 39, 42, 50–51, 53, 179n23

monumental history, 29–30, 62, 86–87, 135, 148–149, 156, 181n36, 200–201n28

multitude, 27, 43, 113–115, 121–125, 133–136, 202n36

Mumford, Lewis, 45; *Herman Melville*, 178n18

Murry, John Middleton, 10, 39, 168n19; on *Billy Budd*, 40–41, 56

Nancy, Jean-Luc, 72

narrative, and closure, 69–70, 78–79, 125–136

Negri, Antonio, 202n36

Nelson, Admiral Horatio, 19, 51, 61, 83–87, 173n44

New Americanists, 32, 37, 38–39, 69, 71–72, 185n49

New Critics, 8–9, 63–65, 68

Nietzsche, Friedrich, 4; and genealogical history, 29–30, 86–87, 132–133, 161, 181n36

Noone, John B., Jr., "*Billy Budd*: Two Concepts of Nature," 173n42

Obama, Barack, 143

occasion, etymology of, 78–79

Old Americanists, 35, 71–72, 182n37, 196–197n53. *See also* New Americanists

Olson, Charles, 78; "Projective Verse," 186n3

Orpheus's lyre, 125–127, 128, 131, 158, 193n35

Paine, Thomas, 4–5, 166n9; *The Rights of Man*, 167n10
Parker, Hershel: on Hayford and Sealts, 59–63, 79, 165n5, 167n12, 169n21, 181n33; *Reading* Billy Budd, 6, 9, 36–37; on the "Preface," 181n35
Parkman, Francis, *The Conspiracy of Pontiac*, 193n36
Pearson, Norman Holmes, 51, 179n23
Pease, Donald E.: American exceptionalism and, 146; *The Futures of American Studies* (ed. with Robyn Wiegman), 185n49; "Global Homeland: Bush's Biopolitical Settlement," 197n2; "*Moby-Dick* and the Cold War," 166n8, 196n53; *The New American Exceptionalism*, 185n49
Peck, George Washington, 39, 166n7, 177n5
people (vs.) people, 26, 28, 73–74, 113–115, 121–125, 133–136, 147. *See also* multitude
Posse Comitatus Act of 1878, 143, 170n27, 197–198n7
poststructuralism, as anti-metaphysical, 64–65
Puritans (American), and American exceptionalism, 70, 138–139, 145, 148–150, 154–157

Ranciere, Jacques, 72
"Report of the International Committee of The Red Cross on the Treatment by Coalition Forces of Prisoners of War and Other Protected Persons by the Geneva Conventions in Iraq During Arrest, Internment and Interrogation," 197n3
revenant, 35, 39, 133. *See also* spectrality
Reynolds, David, *Beneath the Americdan Rennaissance*, 176n4
Reynolds, Larry J., "Billy Budd and American Labor Unrest," 169n21, 182n39, 186n2, 187n9
Richards, I. A., 9; *Principles of Literary Criticism*, 168n17
Robertson-Lorant, Laurie, *Melville: A Biography*, 188n12
Rogin, Michael Paul, *Subversive Genealogies*, 176n4

Rousseau, Jean-Jacques, 68
Rove, Karl, 143
Rowe, John Carlos, *At Emerson's Tomb*, 176n4
Rumsfeld, Donald, and the "war on terror," 143
Ruttenberg, Nancy, 58, 65, 69, 72, 105, 182–183n42, 184n46, 189n17, 194n43; "Melville's Anxiety of Innocence: The Handsome Sailor," 180n29

Said, Edward W.: the contrapuntal polis and, 163, 173n41; *From Oslo to Iraq and the Road Map*, 168n18 (quoted); late style and, 1, 32, 139; *Orientalism*, 177n9, 188n16; "Reflections on American 'Left' Literary Criticism," 182n41; textual attitude, 88–89, 188n16; and worldliness and, 31, 40, 64–65
Schiffman, Joseph, 70; "Melville's Final Stage: A Re-examination of *Billy Budd* Criticism," 184n48
Schmitt, Carl, 144, 145, 146; the friend/enemy opposition and, 157, 161–162, 199n16, 202n36; political theology and, 159, 177n9, 199–200n21, 201n35 (quoted); *Political Theology*, 177n9, 199n20
Scorza, Thomas, *In the Time Before Steamships*, 181n32
Sedgwick, Eve Kosovsky, 58, 65, 69, 72, 105, 183n42, 184n46, 194n43; "Some Binarisms (I): *Billy Budd*: After the Homosexual," 180n29, 183n42, 189n17
September 11, 2001, 71, 100–102, 114–115, 139, 141–143
Smith, Henry Nash, 14; *The Virgin Land*, 170n28
Somers Affair, 18, 31, 48, 77–78, 108, 116–18, 137, 171n35, 191n28
Spanos, Adam V., "Strategy and Event: The Politics of Anticolonialism," 169n24
Spanos, William V.: *American Exceptionalism in the Age of Globalization*, 155–156; "American Studies in the Age of the World Picture: Thinking the

Spanos, William V. (*cont.*)
  Question of Language," 185n49;
  America's Shadow, 179n25, 193n36;
  The Errant Art of Moby Dick, 2, 140,
  168n15; "Global American: The Devastation of Language Under the Dictatorship of the Public Realm," 198n8;
  *Heidegger and Criticism: Retrieving
  the Cultural Politics of Destruction*,
  187n5; *Herman Melville and the
  American Calling*, 2, 140; "The Indifference of *Differance*: Retrieving Heidegger's Destruction," 182n40
spectrality, 39, 55–56, 121–125, 128–36
state of exception, 1–3, 7, 9–10, 32, 73–
  74, 87, 95–97, 100–102, 108–115,
  136–127, 189n20; American exceptionalism and, 141–163, 146–150; the
  "people" under, 121–125; *See also*
  American exceptionalism
Sten, Christopher, 125–26; "Vere's Use
  of the 'Forms' and Ends in *Billy
  Budd*," 182n37, 193n35
Sterne, Milton R., 50; *The Fine Hammered Steel of Herman Melville*,
  169n21, 173n42, 179n21, 180n32;
  "the Politics of Melville's Poetry,"
  187n9
Strong, Tracy, on Carl Schmitt, 201–
  202n36

Thomas, Brook, 58, 70; on *Billy Budd*,
  68–70; "*Billy Budd* and the Judgment
  of Silence," 180n29
Thompson, Lawrence, 70; *Melville's
  Quarrel with God*, 184n47
Tocqueville, Alexis de, 148, 149; *Democracy in America*, 199n18 (quoted)

Tomlinson, H. M., 10
Trachtenberg, Alan, 169–170n27; *The
  Incorporation of America*, 12–16,
  186n2
Trilling, Lionel, 166n8
Turner, Frederick Jackson, 14; the fron-
  tier and, 15–16, 149; *The Frontier in
  American History*, 170n28, 193n36

United States, as national security state,
  70

Voltaire, 41, 50, 86; *Candide*, 88,
  188n16

Waswo, Richard, *The Founding Legend
  of Western Civilization*, 193n36
Watson, E. L. Grant, 10, 39, 69, 183n42;
  on *Billy Budd*, 42–43, 56
Weaver Raymond, 5, 39; on *Billy Budd*,
  43–45, 56, 178n16
Webster, Daniel, and Bunker Hill Monument orations, 149
Wiegman, Robyn, 185n49
Withims, Phil, 70; "*Billy Budd*: Testament of Resistance," 179n28, 183n42,
  184–185n48

Yannella, Donald, *New Essays on* Billy
  Budd, 63–64
Yeats, William Butler, 75, 94
Yoo, John, and Carl Schmitt, 201n35; the
  "war on terror" and, 143, 170n27,
  197–198n7

Zink, Karl E., "Herman Melville and the
  Forms—Irony and Social Criticism in
  'Billy Budd,'" 180n28